COLLINS
BUSINESS
ENGLISH
DICTIONARY

COLLINS
BUSINESS
ENGLISH
DICTIONARY

P. J. Flynn and M. J. Wallace

COLLINS E•L•T   London & Glasgow

Collins Educational
8 Grafton Street
London W1X 3LA

10 9 8 7 6

First published 1984, reprinted 1986, 1988, 1989, 1990

Computer typeset in Photon Baskerville
by SB Datagraphics. Printed and bound in Hungary
by Interpress

ISBN: 0 00 370220 0

Contents

Introduction

In this dictionary you will find clearly explained the meanings of over 4000 words and phrases commonly used in a wide variety of business situations. They include terms used in management, marketing, accountancy, and commerce generally. They also include some computer terms that are now widely used.

The dictionary concentrates on business terms in common use in the UK, but occasionally US terms have been explained (e.g. **Dow Jones Index**), where this has been thought useful.

ALPHABETICAL LISTING
Items have been listed in strict alphabetical order, except for certain phrases, which are entered under the most significant word: for example, **on record** is listed under **record**.

CLEAR DEFINITIONS
The editors have had, between them, more than thirty years' experience of teaching Business Studies and English Language Studies to non-native speakers of English and they have written the dictionary particularly with the needs of the non-native speaker in mind. Great care has therefore been taken to make sure that the explanations of meanings are clear and easy-to-follow.

The editors have as far as possible confined themselves to a defining vocabulary of 2000 words. As a rule, words which have been used in the explanations outside this vocabulary level are printed **like this**, showing that they are defined in the dictionary. In order to avoid confusion, where words printed in this way come immediately after the headword, they are separated from the headword by a colon (:), like this:

> **new issue**: **shares** offered to the public for the first time.

EXAMPLES
To make the meanings even clearer, very many words and phrases have been given example sentences to show how they are used, for example:

> **market demand** the total sales of a **product** in a period (usually a year). *The market demand for our brand of soup is 12,000,000 cans this year.*

Where there is more than one way of referring to something, both expressions are listed and the reader is referred from one to the other, for example:

fixed expense *see* **fixed charge**.

In addition, where it has been thought that they might be of use, words which are related in meaning to the word being defined are also given, for example:

macroeconomics the study of the whole **economy** of a country i.e. a country's production, demand, prices, **imports**, **exports** etc. and their effects on each other. *See also* **microeconomics**.

PARTS OF SPEECH
Parts of speech (e.g. *noun, verb, adjective*) have not been given, except where the same word is defined as more than one part of speech, e.g: **export** *verb* and **export** *noun.*

USAGE LABELS
Labels such as *formal* and *informal* have been used to give help with the level of usage, e.g. **dole** (*informal*), **emolument** (*formal*), **Murphy's Law** (*informal and humorous*).

FIELD LABELS
Where it has seemed helpful, field labels have been used to show which area of business (or related area) the definition refers to, e.g. **attachment** (*law*), **lay days** (*shipping*).

INTERNATIONAL ORGANISATIONS
The main international organisations relevant to commerce and business generally are listed, normally with the following information: function of the organisation, when it was formed, details of membership, where its headquarters is situated, and its official language(s).

APPENDICES
Some key terms (e.g. **profit and loss account**, **master budget**) are illustrated in the appendices with actual detailed examples. The appendices also include a list of the world's currencies, and a list of examining bodies in the UK which award recognised business qualifications.

Acknowledgments

We should like to thank our editors: Gordon Jarvie for initiating the project and supervising the early stages, and Annette Capel and Sarah Thorpe for seeing it to completion with much-appreciated patience and understanding.

We owe a special debt of gratitude to Iseabail Macleod for bringing to the manuscript her expertise as a skilled and experienced lexicographer.

Special thanks are also due to the staff of the Management Department, and other departments, of Napier College who gave generously of their time in double-checking meanings in various specialised areas. In particular, grateful thanks are due to Lynn Parkinson for her unstinting help in this respect.

We are grateful to Kathleen McGeorge for typing preliminary drafts, and to Marjorie Scott for typing the final version.

Finally, thanks to our wives, Nancy and Eileen, for their loving support during the writing of this book.

PJF
MJW

A

A1 (1) best quality. *Your goods must be in A1 condition.* (2) tested and found in excellent condition according to **Lloyd's Register of Shipping**.

ABC *see* **Audit Bureau of Circulation**.

above-the-line advertising expenditure money paid for advertising, using any of the following: cinema, magazines, newspapers, posters, radio, television.

absenteeism failure of workers to go to work, often without good reason.

absentee landlord one who owns property but rarely visits it and who appoints an agent to collect the rent.

absolute address the exact position of a piece of information in the **memory** of a **computer**.

absolute monopoly the complete control by one company or organisation of the production of a **product** or the supply of a **service** for which there are no others offered. *British Rail have an absolute monopoly of inter-city rail service.*

absorption the taking over of a small company by a larger one; during this **process** the small company may lose its original name. *See also* **takeover**, **merger**.

absorption costing a method of deciding how much it costs to produce something. The total costs are divided by the number of units produced so that each unit carries the same share of all the costs.

abstract short form of a report or **document**. *An abstract of the report has been prepared so that you don't have to read the whole thing.*

accelerator a **theory** that the amounts of money which a company spends on new factories or machinery depends on the amount that people spend in the shops. Thus if people spend more money this extra spending will cause an increase in the amount that companies will spend on new factories or machines or materials for making goods. This in turn will make more jobs and more spending.

acceptable quality level the greatest amount of faulty units that will be allowed by a **production manager**.

acceptance a written promise to pay the amount shown on a **bill of exchange**. The person accepting the conditions on the bill of exchange (the **acceptor**) will do so by signing across the face of the bill.

access a way in which something can be reached or entered.

access time the amount of time between asking for and getting information from a **computer**.

accident insurance: insurance covering loss as a result of injury or death from an accident.

accommodate to lend money over the period of time taken to arrange a formal loan.

accommodation money lent over a short period of time until the borrower can find other **funds**. *We are urgently looking for an accommodation from the bank to cover our expenses for the next few days.*

accommodation bill a type of **bill of exchange**; the person who signs it has received no goods or services in exchange but is only helping someone by means of the bill to raise money.

accommodation party a party who accepts or signs an **accommodation bill**.

account (1) a record or statement of money received and paid out. See also **account balance, current account**. (2) an arrangement for keeping money in a bank etc. (3) a regular customer of a company. *This firm brought £1,000 of our goods last week – it's becoming one of our best accounts.*

on account as an advance payment for money that is owed. *Can you give me £6 on account now and the rest next week.*

accountancy the profession of an **accountant**; the management of the **financial** affairs of a company. *See also* **accounting**.

accountant a person who is qualified to record and report on the movement of money into and out of a company and also to prepare a company's **annual accounts**.

account balance (1) the amount that is overpaid or is owing for goods or **services**. (2) the difference between the totals of all the **debit** entries and all the **credit** entries in an **account**.

account executive a person, especially in an **advertising agency**, who is responsible for all matters relating to one or more customers (**accounts**) of a company, and who tries to improve business relations between the accounts and the company. *See also* **account** (meaning 3).

accounting the activity of recording and reporting on the movement of money or goods into and out of a company. *See also* **accountancy**.

accounting machine a machine for preparing **invoices, payrolls** and other **accounting** records.

accounting period (1) the normal time between the date of one **balance sheet** of a company and the date of the next. (2) the period of time, e.g. a week or a month, at the end of which a company regularly examines its financial position.

account payable the amount of money owed by a buyer to a seller for goods or **services** received.

account payee only words written across the face of a cheque. They mean that the amount shown on the cheque will be paid only into the **bank account** of the person who is to receive the money.

account receivable the amount of money owed to a company by a customer (or **debtor**).

account stated the **account** between two people or organisations who have been trading with each other showing a balance which they have agreed upon.

accredited agent an agent who has **documents** from a company which prove that he has power to act on behalf of that company.

accrued charges expenses which have occured and which are due to be paid at a date in the future. For example, if a company pays for electricity at the end of every three months then the cost of the first month's electricity is an accrued charge.

accrued interest the **interest** which is due but not yet paid. For example if a bank pays interest on savings only at the end of the year then the interest due on the first six months' savings is accrued interest.

acid test *see* **liquidity ratio**.

acknowledgement a notice to the sender of goods or money informing him that they have been received.

acquisition the act of one company buying over another.

acquisitive society a society in which people always want to buy the very latest things on the market, sometimes used to describe the people of the rich places of the world.

across-the-board applying to everyone, to all cases: *an across-the-board wage increase* i.e. the same amount of increase is given to each worker in the factory.

action (*law*) a civil case in a court of law.

action limit (**quality control**) the line on a chart which shows when action must be taken to reject or improve a **product**.

active partner one who shares in the ownership of a company and takes an active part in the running of the business. *See also* **sleeping partner**.

activity chart a chart which shows each part of the work to be done and also the time for each part of the work to be finished.

activity sampling recording of the work that is being done by a worker or a machine at certain times so that total work done over the whole period can be **estimated**.

act of bankruptcy any action by which a **debtor** becomes liable to be judged by the court as unable to pay his debts (i.e. be judged **bankrupt**), e.g. the act of leaving the country to avoid paying bills, the informing of **creditors** that he cannot pay his debts.

act of God something unexpected which happens without human help, e.g. a flood which destroys a factory or a storm that sinks a ship.

ad. (*informal*) short for **advertisement**.

added value *see* **value added**.

address the position of information in the **memory** of a **computer**.

addressing machine an office machine for putting addresses on envelopes or letters, using metal plates each of which has a separate address on it.

adjourn (*formal*) to end (a meeting) for a stated time.

adjournment (*formal*) the act of **adjourning**. *The Chairman called for an adjournment until Tuesday.*

adjudication the decision of a court of law between two **parties**, e.g. between a company and a **trade union**.

adjuster (**insurance**) a person who **assesses** losses for an **insurance company**.

adjusting entry something written into a company's accounts, done so that the accounts will show the correct financial position at a certain date. For example, if an error is found then an adjusting entry would be made instead of the error itself being changed.

administration (*or, informal* **admin.**) (1) the controlling or managing of something, especially a public or private organisation. (2) paperwork in a company such as form-filling or letter-writing.

administrative expenses money that a company pays which is separate from the costs of actually producing the goods in the factory, e.g. the salaries of office staff or the cost of telephone and postage.

administrator (1) a person who controls or directs the affairs of a company. (2) a person who is appointed by a court to take charge of the possessions of someone who has died without leaving a will.

ad valorem (*Latin*) according to value, usually used of a tax or duty put on certain goods by a country. The tax will vary according to the value of the goods.

advance (1) a loan or **overdraft** from a bank. (2) a loan by a company to a worker until his wages are paid. (3) a payment by a company of part of the cost of goods or **services** which it has still to receive.

advance factory (*UK*) a factory built in certain areas of the country before it is really needed in the hope that businessmen will rent or buy it and so attract work in that area.

adverse trade balance (or **adverse balance of trade**) a situation when the value of a country's **exported** goods is less than the value of its **imported** goods. *See also* **balance of trade**.

advertise to make (something, usually goods or **services**) known to companies or the general public, e.g. by means of newspapers, magazines, psoters, **point-of-sale**, cinema, television or radio.

advertisement (1) a notice of something which is being **advertised**. (2) the act of **advertising**.

advertisement manager the person in charge of the selling of **advertising** on behalf of a company owning one of the following: newspapers, magazines, cinemas, television stations, radio stations or poster sites. *Compare with* **advertising manager**.

advertising the planning or **publishing** of facts or opinions to arouse people's interest and persuade them, e.g. to buy something.

advertising agency a company which provides the **services** of designing and making **advertisements**, placing them in suitable **advertising media**, and carrying out research.

advertising manager a person in charge of planning and overseeing a company's advertising. *Compare with* **advertisement manager**.

advertising media the means by which a company informs people of its goods or services, e.g. newspapers, magazines, posters, cinemas, television and radio.

advertising rates the basic charges made by the owners of the **advertising media** for the use of their **services**. *See also* **advertisement manager**.

advertising strategy the overall plan of how, where, when and at what cost a company's **advertising** will be carried out.

advertising theme the subject matter which is repeated in all of a company's **advertising**, e.g. the goodness of the product (*Guinness is good for you*) or the low prices.

advice note a printed sheet sent by a supplier to a customer containing details (e.g. quantity, weight) of goods ordered but not yet delivered.

advocate (*in Scotland*) a **barrister**.

affiliated company a company that is owned by another company, but usually managed separately.

affluence the state of being affluent.

affluent having plenty of money and/or possessions: *the affluent society*, i.e. people in rich countries who have plenty of money to spend.

after-sales service service provided by a seller to a buyer after the sale has been made, e.g. advice, repairs or **servicing** of goods. *Our garage gives free after-sales service.*

agency (1) the business, or office of an agent. (2) a business or organisation which gives a certain **service**.

agenda a list of what is to be discussed at a meeting.

agent a person who represents another person, company etc., with that person's or company's approval, often with a written **contract** stating this.

agent's commission the sum of money paid to an **agent** for selling something for someone else, usually an agreed percentage of the selling price.

agreed procedure the steps which should be taken in an agreed order, to help in the smooth running of a business, e.g. for the settling of any dispute between a company and its workers.

agreement (1) a **contract**, usually written, between one person or company and another. (2) the act or fact of agreeing.

AIDA the first letters of 'Attention, Interest, Desire, Action'. These are the **responses** of a buyer that some salesmen are trained to get so that a sale can be made.

aided recall (**market research**) a method used to help a person remember a **product** or an advertisement by reminding the person of something connected with the product or advertisement. For example when used to test how good an advertisement has been the person might be shown part of the advertisement to see if he can remember the rest of it.

air cargo (*or* **air freight**) goods which are sent by air.

air terminal a place in a town where one can get transport to and from an airport. *See also* **terminal**.

air waybill (*or* **air consignment note**) a **document** prepared by the carrier of the goods (or his **agent**) stating the nature of the goods, the name of the sender and the charges for carrying the goods. The conditions of the **contract** of carriage are usually included.

ALGOL (*stands for* algorithmetic language) a **computer language** used mainly for **programming** scientific problems.

all found of payment, with all the necessary things (e.g. food) added on. *His army pay was thirty pounds a week all found.*

all-in-rate (*or* **all-in-price**) a rate or price that includes all the extras which are in addition to the basic rate or price. For example an **all-in-price** of a **product** to a buyer would include delivery charge, duty, tax, etc.

allocation a part that is given; a share of something. For example, a buyer may want ten cases of some **product** which is in short supply but his allocation may only be five.

allocation of overheads the charging of a part of a cost or overhead to a particular department of a company, e.g. a part of the total rent to each department of a large store.

allotment the number of **shares** which have been given to people who have applied to buy a new issue of shares.

allowance (1) a sum of money given regularly, e.g. an allowance of £50 per week to a salesman for travelling expenses. (2) money taken off the cost or price of somthing, usually for a special reason. For example, a shop may make an allowance of £10 off the price of a new television set because the buyer has pointed out a slight mark on it. (3) the allowed difference of size in the manufacture of a **product**. For example, a company may decide to make steel bars 250 millimetres long with an allowance of 1 millimetre either way. In this case bars of 251 and 249 millimetres would be acceptable. (4) the amount of a person's **income** on which **income tax** is not charged.

allowed time the time agreed between a company and a worker for certain activities, e.g. meals, or cleaning his/her machine.

amalgamate to join together (two or more companies or groups). *In 1976 the trade unions for engineering workers and foundry workers joined to form the Amalgamated Union of Engineering and Foundry Workers.*

amalgamation the act of **amalgamating**.

amortization the recovery of money, in parts, over a period of time, e.g. when payment is made by **instalment**, or, if a company buys a machine which it thinks will last five years it may decide to recover this money by charging its **profit and loss account** with one-fifth of the machine's value each year, for five years. *See also* **depreciation**.

analog computer a **computer** in which the **data** are represented by measurements (lengths, angles, voltages) rather than by numbers, used especially in science and industry. *See also* **digital computer**.

analyse to make an **analysis** of.

analysis the breaking down of something into parts so that a closer study can be made. *Total sales this year were above last year's total but an analysis has shown that sales to most European countries were less this year.*

annual *adjective* yearly; appearing or happening once a year: *annual report.*

annual *noun* a book or magazine produced once a year, with the same title but different information for each year.

annual abstract of statistics a book produced each year by the UK government giving details of all the main features of the **economy**.

Annual General Meeting a company meeting which takes place once a year to which all its **shareholders** are invited, as requested by law. At this meeting the year's **profit and loss account** and **balance sheet** are discussed, and directors of the company are appointed.

annual report a report sent each year by a company to the members of the company, and to certain other persons. It usually contains the **profit and loss account**, **balance sheet** and details of the company's activities during the previous twelve months.

annuity a fixed sum of money which is paid yearly to a person for a number of years. Annuities can be bought from an **assurance company**. For example, a person could arrange with an assurance company to pay the company now an agreed sum of money in return for a yearly income, or annuity, of (say) £1,000 from his sixty-fifth birthday until his death.

anticipated profit a profit which is yet to be earned, e.g. the profit a company will earn on goods that are made but not yet sold.

anti-dumping duty a tax on certain **imported** goods to prevent them being sold at prices lower than the home-produced goods.

anti-trust legislation *(US)* laws to encourage competition, usually price competition, by preventing **mergers** or **amalgamations** which could result in higher prices.

applicant a person who puts in an **application** for something.

application (1) a request for something, e.g. a job, a place in a college etc. *Applications must be in by Friday.* (2) a way in which something can be put to use. *The new invention has several applications in industry.* (3) (**computers**) a type of problem to which **data-processing** methods can be applied. (4) hard work: *to succeed by sheer application.*

application form a **document** which is filled in and signed by a person who is applying for something, e.g. a job, a passport, a driving licence.

application package (**computers**) a **program** which has been designed to do a special job, e.g. list all the sales figures, or keep up to date all the wages to be paid.

applied economics the part of **economics** which has to do with the study of practical problems, e.g. the study of the selling price and demand for UK oil.

apply (1) to use for a certain purpose. *They applied all their resources to the building up of new business.* (2) **apply for** to make a (formal) request for (something), usually in writing: *to apply for a job.* (3) to put onto. *Apply the glue with a knife.* (4) to be effective or fitting. *These rules do not apply here.*

appraisal interview a discussion to judge the value of a person using the **appraisal method**.

appraisal method a method of judging the ability of a person to do his work. This method requires the manager and the worker to agree on a certain plan of work, to train the worker to do that work and then after an agreed time to review what has been achieved by the worker. *See also* **appraisal interview**.

appreciate to increase in value. *Because the company has been making large profits the market value of its shares has appreciated.*

appreciation an increase in the value of something. *The appreciation in value of my house is due to the high demand for houses in this area.*

apprentice a young person who works for a company for an agreed number of years to learn a trade.

apprenticeship (the time of) being an **apprentice**. *I want to be an engineer but it requires a five year apprenticeship.*

appropriation the practice of setting aside a sum of money for a special purpose. *The company's advertising appropriation this year will be £100,000.*

appropriation account the part of the **profit and loss account** which shows how the **net profit** is divided between tax, **dividends** and **reserves**.

approval: on approval a method of selling goods by which they are sent, at the buyer's request, for examination. If he does not like them he will send them back within an agreed time. If he likes them (i.e. if they meet with his **approval**) he will keep them and pay within an agreed time.

aptitude test a type of examination used to judge if a person will be able to do a certain type of job.

arbitration the method used to settle a **dispute** between the people involved (e.g. **a trade union** and a company) by which they agree that the dispute will be decided by an independent person (the **arbitrator**).

arbitration clause a condition in a **contract** which states that if there is a **dispute** between the **parties** to the contract the matter will be settled by a fair and independent person (the **arbitrator**).

arbitrator a person chosen by the **parties** in a **dispute** to settle any

matter on which they cannot agree. The arbitrator is chosen in the belief that he/she will be fair and will suggest a method of agreement based on common sense rather than law.

archive (1) a place in which records of various kinds are stored for reference. (2) (**computers**) the place in which information is stored and to which the computer has not got direct **access**.

area sample a method of **sampling** whereby a number of towns, or districts are first randomly selected (i.e. chosen by chance) and then within those chosen a **random sample** is taken. *See also* **stratified sampling, cluster sampling**.

arithmetic mean the result when all the quantities in a set of quantities are added together and the total is divided by the number of quantities in the set. For example, the arithmetic mean of 3, 1, 6, 2 and 8 is found by dividing the total (20) by the number of quantities (5) which is 4. Often shortened to **mean** or **average**.

array (1) a series of numbers arranged in a specified order, e.g. from the highest to the lowest. (2) a set of numbers arranged in rows and columns.

arrears money that is due but not yet paid.

articles of association the rules and conditions covering the relationship between a company, its **shareholders** and its directors.

artwork the original drawings or pictures for something, e.g. an **advertisement**.

'A' shares (*or* **non-voting shares**) shares in a company which have the same rights as **ordinary shares** but do not allow the owner to vote at a meeting of **shareholders** of the company.

assembly line a method of manufacture by which a **product** passes along a line of workers or machines in a factory. At each stage along the line work is done on the product until it is completed.

assess to judge the quality or worth of (a person or thing).

assessment a judgement, e.g. of the ability of a person to do a certain task. *The company makes an assessment of the progress of all trainee managers every three months.*

assessor (1) a person who decides the amount of tax to be paid by someone. (2) person who decides the value of damage done to property for **insurance** purposes.

asset something that is owned by a person or a company, such as money, a building, a car. *See also* **fixed assets** *and* **current assets**.

asset stripping the act of taking over a company then selling off the **assets** to make a profit.

assign (1) to **transfer** to others (the rights to money or property). This can be done legally by a deed of assignment. (2) to set aside for someone's use: *An office will be assigned you for the time you are working here.*

assignee the person to whom something has been **assigned**.

assignment (1) the **transfer** to another of rights to money or property. (2) a signed agreement about a transfer of rights to money or property. (3) a task that has been given to a person. *He is working abroad on a special assignment.*

assignor a person who **assigns**.

associated company a company which is partly owned by another company (i.e. between 20% and 49% of its **shares** are owned by another company).

associate director a person who acts as a director of a company with the company's approval, but who has not been formally appointed as a director.

associated states non-member states of the **EEC** which have special trade agreements with the EEC.

Association of Scientific, Technical, and Managerial Staffs (*or* **ASTMS**) a UK **trade union** for professional and clerical workers.

assurance *see* **insurance**.

assurance company *see* **insurance company**.

assured a person who enters into an **assurance** contract.

ASTMS *see* **Association of Scientific, Technical, and Managerial Staffs**.

A.T.M. (*or* **Automatic Telling Machine**) a **computerised cash dispenser**, used mainly in banks.

attachment (*law*) the stopping of the sale, or disposal, of a **debtor's** money or goods (which are in the hands of a third **party**) until the settlement of a **claim** against the debtor.

attitude survey (1) (**market research**) a method of finding out what people think of a **product**, by question-and-answer or by group discussion. (2) a method used to find out what workers think of their work, or work place or company, with a view to improving these.

attorney (1) a person who is appointed to act on behalf of someone else, especially in legal matters, or under the **power-of-attorney**. (2) (*US*) a lawyer.

Attorney General the chief legal officer of the government in some countries.

auction *noun* a method of selling goods in which the goods are sold to the highest bidder. These sales usually take place in auction rooms where buyers can see the goods to be auctioned.

auction *verb* to sell goods in this way.

auctioneer a person who sells goods at an **auction**. He is an agent of the owner of the goods offered for sale, and is paid a **commission** on the sale of the goods to the highest bidder.

audience (1) a group of people reading, listening, watching any of the **media**, but especially television, cinema or radio. (2) a group of people listening to or watching a performance such as a play, speech or film.

audience research the finding out of facts about what kind of people watch certain television programmes, read certain newspapers etc; such information is useful e.g. in deciding where to advertise.

audio-visual aids teaching aids which can be both seen and heard such as films, television or slides with spoken explanations.

audit *noun* an examination of a company's **books of account** to make sure they are a fair and true record of a company's trading.

audit *verb* to examine (**books of account**) in this way.

Audit Bureau of Circulation (ABC) (*UK*) an organisation which provides proof of the actual sales of newspapers and magazines.

auditor a person appointed by a company to examine the **books of account**. He/she has to state if the accounts are a fair and true record and the resulting report becomes part of the company's **annual report**.

authorised capital the amount of **capital** up to which a company may issue **shares**. A company's authorised capital will be stated in its **memorandum and articles of association** and is usually also shown in the company's **balance sheet**. *See also* **nominal capital**.

authority the power to do something or to get others to do something. *Do you have authority to sign this cheque? The manager has the authority to employ or dismiss workers.* (2) an organisation which has certain powers, especially from the government: *a local authority*.

automatic data processing any form of **processing** of information (data) by a machine.

Automatic Telling Machine *see* **A.T.M.**

automatic vending the sale of goods, such as cigarettes, from a machine where one pays by putting money into the machine. *There is an automatic vending machine on each floor.*

automation the use of machines that need little or no human control to do work which used to be done by people.

autonomous work groups a group of workers who decide their own output of work, when and how the work will be done and who will do it. Sometimes also they carry out their own trading. In a company with autonomous work groups, the management are advisors only and do not make decisions for the group.

average (1) *see* **arithmetic mean**. (2) (**marine insurance**) sharing of the loss of a ship's **cargo** amongst several **insurers**.

average cost the cost resulting from dividing the total **costs** (**fixed costs** plus **variable costs**) by the number of units produced.

average fixed cost the cost resulting from dividing the total **fixed costs** by the number of units produced.

average variable cost the cost resulting from dividing the total **variable costs** by the number of units produced.

award a decision reached by an **arbitrator** when a **dispute** between two **parties** has been sent to him for settlement.

B

back cover (advertising) the outside of the back page of a magazine which carries an advertisement.

backdate to put a date on (an agreement or **document**) which is earlier than the date on which it was drawn up. For example, on 30 June a **trade union** may reach an agreement with a company for a wage increase which is backdated to 1 June.

back duty tax which should have been paid in the past and which is payable now.

backer a person or organisation that supports a business idea with money.

backlog (1) an amount of work which has gathered over some time and which still has to be done, e.g. when one has been on holiday, or away from work through illness. (2) an amount of goods which still have to be sold.

back pay wages which are due for work done but which were not paid at the proper time.

back-to-back credit: credit given to a foreign buyer by a UK bank or **finance** house which is acting as a contact between a foreign seller and the foreign buyer. The seller gives the papers covering the sale to the UK bank (or finance house) which then issues them in its own name to the buyer, the seller's name being kept secret.

back-up something ready to be used in place of another should it fail, e.g. a back-up power supply to be used if electricity should fail.

back-up storage (**computers**) tape or disk copies of information for use if the computer's original tapes or disks should be lost or damaged.

backward integration taking over by a company of another company which supplies it with **raw materials** or parts for manufacture, e.g. if a company which sells canned foods takes over the company which supplies the cans.

bad debt money which is unlikely to be paid, and which is treated as a loss. *The company finally went bankrupt because it had so many bad debts.*

bad faith (in) a dishonest state of mind: (with) an intention to cheat. *You don't have to follow a contract if you can prove it was signed in bad faith.*

bailee a person who has possession of the goods of another for a certain purpose with the agreement of that other, e.g. a shoe repairer, a garage, a dry-cleaner.

bailor a person who gives his goods or property to a **bailee**.

balance *noun* (1) the difference between the total **credit** entries and the total **debit** entries in an **account**. (2) what is left over; the remainder.

balance *verb* to make the total **credit** entries equal the total **debit** entries of (an **account**).

balance brought forward (*or* **balance b/fwd**) the net **balance** on an **account** brought forward from the previous **accounting period**.

balance carried forward (*or* **balance c/fwd**) the net **balance** on an **account** brought forward to the next **accounting period**.

balance in hand money which can be used for payments.

balance of payments a country's **balance sheet** of total payments to other countries and the total received from them of goods and **services**. *See also* **balance of trade**, **invisible assets**.

balance of trade the difference between a country's **exports** and **imports** of goods. The balance of trade is said to be favourable when the value of exported goods is more than the value of imported goods.

balance sheet a statement showing the value of a company's **assets** and its **liabilities** at a certain date.

balance-sheet ratios methods of using figures from a balance sheet to show how well or badly a company or its management are doing. Often figures from the **profit and loss**

account are also used to give either a **ratio** or percentage measurement. *See also* **current ratio, debtors to sales ratio, liquidity ratio, return on capital employed**, and appendix 2.

balanced budget a plan in which the expected **income** matches the expected payments.

balancing item an entry of an amount of money in the **balance of payments** account to correct any errors made in the account during a particular period.

ballast heavy material which a ship carries to keep it steady at sea.

banded pack a form of **sales promotion** in which two or more **products** are bound together, usually with tape with the details of the reduced-price offer.

bank a company with which money is placed to be kept securely and where it can earn **interest**, and where loans and other **financial** business are carried out.

bank account an **account** (meaning 2) with a bank. *See also* **current account, deposit account**.

bank-book a book in which a record of the money one puts into and takes out of a bank is kept, a **passbook**.

bank charge an amount charged by a bank for its **services**.

bank cheque *see* **bank draft**.

bank deposit any money paid into a **current account** or a **deposit account** in a bank.

bank draft (*or* **bank cheque** *or* **banker's draft**) a cheque drawn by a bank promising to pay a stated sum on demand at a named office of the bank.

banker's order instructions to a bank to pay a stated sum of money to a person or organisation at certain dates.

Bank for International Settlements (*or* **BIS** *or* **BIZ**) an international bank established by agreement with the Swiss government in 1930 in order to encourage the co-operation of the central banks of twenty-nine countries. It also acts as an **agent** in the settlement of international **financial** matters. Membership: the central banks of twenty-five European countries plus Japan, South Africa, Turkey and the United States. Headquarters: Basel, Switzerland. Official languages: English, French, German, Italian.

bank giro a method by which payment of an **account**, or other payments, can be made using **giro** forms available in UK post offices and banks.

bank holiday (*UK*) any normal working day on which banks and certain public offices are closed by law.

bank hours the times when banks are open to the public to do business.

bank loan any loan of money by a bank for a certain period at any agree **interest rate**.

banknote a **document** from a bank which promises to pay the bearer on demand and which is used as money.

bank overdraft the amount of cash which a bank allows a customer to draw out of his **account** and which is more than the amount that he or she has actually paid in. It is therefore a loan from the bank, and **interest** is charged on it.

bank reserves the money held by a bank to meet demands by customers.

bankrupt *adjective, noun* (a person who has been) legally judged to be unable to pay his/her debts.

bankrupt *verb* to make (a person) **bankrupt**.

bankruptcy the state of being **bankrupt**.

bank statement a list, sent by a bank to a customer showing the amount of money paid into and taken out of the customer's **account** with the bank, and the **balance** remaining.

bar chart information given in the form of broad lines or **columns** drawn on paper, e.g. showing a company's sales for each month of the year. The difference in the height of the columns shows the difference between sales each month.

bargain *verb* to talk about an agreement or **contract** with the aim of changing or improving some part of it. *The union bargained for hours with the management over the amount of the wage increase.*

bargain *noun* (1) an agreement. *They finally struck a bargain on the price.* (2) something that is being sold for less than its real value. *They are selling it for £10 off the usual price – it's a bargain.*

barratry any unlawful act done by a captain or crew of a ship to harm the owner's rights, e.g. sinking the ship or stealing the ship.

barrister a lawyer who has the right to speak and argue in the higher courts of law in England.

barter *verb* to exchange goods for other goods by way of payment, instead of using money. *The two countries bartered wheat in exchange for oil.*

barter *noun* this system of exchange: *to trade by barter.*

base rate the lowest rate of **interest** which **clearing banks** offer to **depositors** of money. The rate of interest charged to borrowers will vary from $\frac{1}{2}\%$ to 5% above that for **deposits**, depending on the kind of loan. The clearing bank base rate changes from time to time depending on economic conditions.

BASIC (*stands for* Beginner's All-purpose Symbolic Introduction

Code) a **computer language** which uses ordinary English words.

basic rate (1) (*also* **basic wage**) the lowest possible wage that can be paid for a job, not counting **overtime**. (2) the lowest rate of **income tax** which applies when **allowances** have been taken off **income**.

batch an amount of materials or parts of a **product** which is ordered or produced at one time. *We will need to make a batch of 25-millimetre screws for today's orders.*

batch processing (**computers**) groups of records which are **processed** by the computer, one group at a time, e.g. if a company first enters all its **invoices** on the computer, followed by information on say **stocks**, then wages.

batch production manufacture of the same article in groups rather than singly, e.g. the manufacture of metal screws of the same size, or the manufacture of shoes of the same size. *See also* **batch, mass production**.

bear (**stock market**) a person who sells **shares** in the belief that their price is about to fall. He or she may then buy them back more cheaply. *See also* **bull, bear market**.

bearer a person who is in possession of a **document**, e.g. of a **bill of exchange** which is 'payable to bearer' i.e. payable to the holder of the bill.

bearer bonds: documents of ownership to **stocks, shares, debentures** etc. Ownership can be **transferred** by simply handing the bonds over to someone else, as bearer bonds are made out to 'bearer' and not to a named person.

bearish (**stock market**) having or expecting falling **share** prices.

bear market (**stock market**) a situation when the price of shares is falling. *See also* **bull market**.

below-the-line promotion expenditure money spent to increase sales by means other than advertising in newspapers, magazines, television, radio, cinema or posters, e.g. by offering prizes with a **product**, or giving one free with every one bought or paying for a **sponsored** event. *See also* **sales promotion**.

bench mark anything by which something else can be measured. *We should aim for a profit of £1 on every £10 of sales – that's the bench mark for success in our business.*

beneficiary a person who receives some gain, especially money or property.

benefit-in-kind a gain or advantage, other than the payment of money, e.g. the regular use of a company car given to a worker.

Benelux Economic Union a group of three countries (Belgium, Luxembourg and Netherlands) formed to develop **economic** links and to have a common **policy** also in **financial** and social matters. The present organisation was created 1958. Headquarters: Brussels. Official languages: French, Dutch.

bequest a gift of money or property left in a will. *See also* **legacy**.

b/f *see* **brought forward**.

bias *noun* a tendency to favour one point of view although there is not enough proof, or the proof is faulty.

bias *verb* to cause to have a **bias**. *The sample was biased in favour of male tastes.*

bid (1) an offer to buy something at a certain price, especially at an **auction**. (2) an offer by one company to buy all the **shares** of another. *See also* **takeover bid**.

bilateral agreement an arrangement or **contract** between two sides, e.g. two companies.

bilateral trade the exchange of goods and/or **services** between two countries.

bill *noun* (1) *see* **bill of exchange**. (2) an **invoice**. (3) a statement of the amount that has to be paid for goods or **services**, especially in a restaurant or hotel (*US* **check**).
   take up a bill (*or* **retire a bill**) to pay a **bill of exchange** on or before the date on which it is due.

bill *verb* to send or give (someone) an **invoice** or statement of the amount that has to be paid.

bill-broker a person or company that buys **bills of exchange** and **promissory notes**, often at less than their **nominal value** in order to cash them or else to sell them again.

billing the total amount of business done by an **advertising agency** during a certain period.

bill of entry (*UK*) a **document** required by **Customs** and Excise showing details of goods that are to be **imported**.

bill of exchange a written order without any conditions addressed by one person to another, signed by the person giving it, requiring the person to whom it is addressed to pay immediately or at some stated time a certain amount of money to a named person, or to the bearer of the bill; often used for foreign trade.

bill of health a certificate which states whether or not the crew of a ship are known to be suffering from any disease which can be easily spread to other people. A statement that they are not suffering from such a disease is called a **clean bill of health**.

bill of lading (*or* **B/L**) (**exporting**) a **document** which states the **terms** and conditions under which goods are to be transported, giving the name and address of the customer receiving the goods and the details of the goods themselves.

bill of sale a written agreement which gives the legal ownership of goods to another person, but not the actual possession of the goods. A bill of sale is often used to raise money, the borrower taking back the legal ownership when he repays the money borrowed.

bills payable (accounting) bills of exchange held and due for payment by the holder at some time in the future.

bills receivable (accounting) bills of exchange held and due to be paid to the holder at some time in the future.

binary code: computer data or computer instructions written using the **binary system**.

binary system (computers) a number system in which there are only two base numbrs (0 and 1); thus in binary system $1 = 01$ but $2 = 10$, $3 = 11$, $4 = 100$.

bin card (*or* **bin tag**) a card kept near a container showing the amount of goods in it and sometimes showing also the amount ordered, amount sold from the container etc.

BIS *or* **BIZ** *see* **Bank for International Settlements**.

bit the smallest piece of information in a **computer**, i.e. either 1 or 0. *See also* **binary system**.

black *verb* of workers, to refuse to handle (certain goods) because they think that to handle them will be against either their own interest or the interest of some other workers. For example during a **strike**, goods normally handled by the **strikers** may be **blacked** by other workers.
   in the black having money in one's bank account. *We're in the black again at last.*

blackball to exclude (a person) from a club or society by means of a secret vote of the members.

black economy that part of the **economic** activity of a country which is carried out in secret to avoid paying tax, or because the activity is illegal.

blackleg (*or* **scab**) a person who continues to work during a **strike**, or who takes the place of someone else who is on strike.

blackleg (*or US* **scab**) *verb* to act in this way.

blacklist *noun* a list of persons or organisations who are considered to be slow payers of **bills**, or non-payers of bills, often made up by **credit agencies**.

blacklist *verb* to put the name of (a person or organisation) on such a list.

black market a **system** involving the illegal buying or selling of goods or **currencies** when their sale is **rationed** or officially controlled.

blank cheque a cheque which is fully completed except for the amount of money to be paid, which the person cashing the cheque can fill in.
   give someone a blank cheque to allow someone an unlimited amount of money to spend.

blank endorsement the act of writing one's name on the back of a **bill of exchange** etc. so that it becomes payable to the person who possesses it (the **bearer**).

blanket agreement an agreement on wages or conditions of work etc., reached between representatives of the employers and representatives of the workers. A blanket agreement applies throughout the whole industry and not just certain factories.

blanket coverage advertising which is directed at the public generally and not a specified **target audience**.

blanket policy an **insurance policy** which covers many different types of risk, e.g. a house may be insured against fire, theft and other risks under one blanket policy.

blending mixing together of different kinds or quantities of something (often tea, coffee, whisky or tobacco) in order to make it more attractive to a possible buyer.

blind test a method of finding out how popular a new **product** might be with possible customers; members of the public are asked to give their opinion of a product without being given any information about what **brand** it is.

block *noun* (1) a metal, rubber or plastic plate used for printing photographs or drawings. (2) (**computers**) a group of **characters** (letters, numbers etc.) which is treated as a unit.

block *verb* (1) to make or form into a block. (2) to prevent the use or transfer of (money or other assets), usually for a political or legal reason. *see* **blocked account**.

blocked account a **bank account** from which no cash may be withdrawn except (perhaps) under certain conditions. For example a government may block the accounts of all foreigners, either completely or by stating that the cash in the account must be spent in the country in which it has been banked.

blocked currency coins and notes used within a country which may not be taken out of the country, e.g. because the country has **balance of payments** problems.

block release a system of training by which trainees are allowed to leave their jobs for blocks of time (e.g. several weeks) with full pay so that they can go to an institute of further or higher education. *See also* **day release, sandwich course**.

block vote (*or* **card vote**) a form of voting often used in **trade union** conferences where the voting power is decided by the number of workers which each **delegation** is supposed to represent. Thus a delegation which represents three million members could outvote two delegations which represent only one million members each.

blow up to make (a photograph, or part of a photograph) much bigger.

blow-up a photograph, or part of a photograph that has been made much bigger.

blue book (*informal*) a yearly report by the UK Central Statistical Office called **National Income and Expenditure**, containing a great deal of information relating to **economic** trends in the UK.

blue-chip investment an **investment** which is thought to be very safe, often because the company involved is a very large one, has been operating for some time and is known for good management. *See also* **gilt-edged securities**.

blue-collar workers people who work with their hands in industry, especially to distinguish them from office-workers or **white-collar workers**.

blueprint (1) a special type of photographic print of a design or technical drawing in which the design or drawing appears in white on blue paper. (2) a plan or way of doing something which has been followed by others or which has been laid out in some detail.

blurb a written description of something which is intended to persuade people to buy the thing described, especially the description put on the cover of a book by a publisher.

board of directors a group of senior **executives** of a company who are responsible for directing the **policy** of the company and who have the final powers of control within the company.

body copy the main text of written matter in an advertisement, as opposed to the headlines or illustrations that go with the advertisement.

body matter small type (printed words) in an advertisement.

bold face a printing type consisting of thick black letters which makes words more easily noticed, as with the headwords of this dictionary.

bona fide (*Latin*) done in **good faith**, without trying to hide something which should be known. For example a **contract** may not be **valid** if it has not been made in good faith: *a bona fide agreement. See also* **bad faith, good faith.**

bond *noun* a legal written promise to pay a sum of money at a certain time, or under certain conditions. Governments and public companies issue bonds in return for money lent to them. *See also* **debentures, bearer bonds.**
    in bond of goods, kept in a special store called a **bonded warehouse**, until duty is paid or until the goods are cleared from bond for **exporting**.

bond *verb* to put (goods) into a **bonded warehouse**. (2) (*law*) to place (a person) under a bond.

bonded goods goods on which **duty** has to be paid and which are kept in a **bonded warehouse** until removed for sale. Such goods are said to be **in bond**, a **bond** being signed by the owners stating that the duty will be paid when the goods are removed for sale.

bonded warehouse a place where goods on which **duty** is due may be kept until the duty is paid or until the goods are cleared (examined) by **customs** for **export**.

bonding of salesmen a system by which an employer **insures** himself against dishonesty or carelessness by salesmen that he employs.

bonus an extra amount of money paid out which is above what has been agreed; thus an employee may get a Christmas bonus in addition to his usual wages, or extra pay for successful work, a **shareholder** may get a **bonus issue**, or a person who has **invested** in an **insurance policy** may get a bonus **dividend**.

bonus issue (*or* **scrip issue**) the giving out of **shares** to **shareholders** in a company in proportion to the number of shares they already have.

bonus pack a way of making a **product** more attractive to customers by giving more than the usual amount of the product but at the same price as would be charged for the usual amount.

bonus payment a method of rewarding successful workers, e.g. salesmen, by giving them a **bonus**.

book debts amounts due from **debtors** in the **books of account**.

book-keeping the recording of the **accounts** of an organisation.

books of account the records in which the **financial** affairs (**transactions**) of a business are shown. They may be in book form, on cards, on **magnetic tape** or on **magnetic disks**.

book token a **voucher** (meaning 2) which can be exchanged for a book or books in a bookshop.

book value the worth of a company's **assets** as shown in its **accounts**. The **market value** of the assets may be much higher. For example, the value of a company's buildings will be reduced in the accounts each year by a certain amount (**depreciation**).

boom *noun* a time of very fast general **economic** growth, bringing with it an increase in wages, prices, profits, employment and business opportunities. *See also* **depression, recession, slump, trade cycle**. (2) a time of fast growth and/or increased profits in a company.

boom *verb* to experience a **boom**. *The country in booming. The oil business is booming.*

boom *adjective* showing fast growth and/or increased profits: *a boom economy.*

boom market a market in which demand is greater than supply, causing an increase in prices.

bought-out parts parts of a company's **products** which are bought from other companies.

bounce (*informal*) of a cheque, to be returned by a bank to the person or company presenting it for payment because there is not enough cash in the **account** of the person who has signed it to cover the amount of the cheque.

bourse (*French*) term used in France and certain other countries for a **stock exchange**.

boycott *verb* to avoid social and/or business relations with (a person, a company or a country) in an effort to change their ways of thinking.

boycott *noun* the act of **boycotting**. *The country's business was suffering because of a trade boycott.*

brainstorming a group **technique** used to produce new ideas; the main emphasis is on the quantity of ideas produced even though some of them may seem ridiculous; at a later stage the ideas are discussed and compared until some practical suggestions appear.

branch *noun* (1) a division or section of a large business which is in a different area from the main division or section, e.g. a branch office. (2) (**computers**) a departure from the normal sequence (order) in a **program**.

branch *verb* (**computers**) to depart from the normal sequence (order) in a **program**. *See also* **branch out**.

branch manager a person in charge of a **branch** (meaning 1).

branch out to open another section of a business.

brand a class of goods from a manufacturer with a name or mark which makes them different from other goods in the same kind. *This is my favourite brand of tea. See also* **trademark**.

brand awareness the extent to which those who are interested in buying a certain kind of goods are familiar with a certain **brand** name in connection with the goods they are interested in.

branded goods goods sold under the **brand** names of their manufacturers or suppliers.

brand image a general idea of a **brand** in the minds of those who might be interested in buying a certain kind of goods.

brand leader the goods of a particular **brand** which have the largest share of the market for goods of that type.

brand share *see* **market share**.

break (*or* **commercial break**) a period of time on radio or television which is used for broadcasting advertisements.

breakage (1) the number or amount of goods that have been broken e.g. while being moved from one place to another. (2) payment to replace the value of goods that have been broken.

break even to reach the point where the amount of money that has gone out and the money that has come in are exactly **balanced** and no profit or loss is made. *See also* **break-even point**.

break-even analysis a **system** of working out the costs and the **incomes** for different levels of sales in order to find out the level of sales at which no loss (or profit) is made. Sales beyond this level should result in a profit.

break-even chart a chart which shows the **fixed costs**, the **variable costs**, the total costs and the profit or loss at various levels of sales.

break-even point a point at which the total costs of a **product** or **project break even**. Sales beyond this point should result in a profit.

breaking bulk the activity of buying goods in large quantities and selling them in smaller quantities, as done by a **wholesaler**.

break-up value (*or* **liquidating value**) what the **assets** of a company would be worth if it had to go out of business.

bribe *verb* to try to persuade (a person) to do something illegal or dishonest by offering something (e.g. a sum of money) in return.

bribe *noun* what is offered in order to **bribe** a person.

bridging loan a short-term loan of money to allow one to buy one **asset**, e.g. a new house, while awaiting the sale of another asset, e.g. the buyer's present house, to pay for it.

brief *noun* (1) a short list of the main points which must be kept in mind when a course of action is being taken. (2) a list of things which a person in a certain job may or may not do. *It is not within my brief to accept money from clients.*

brief *verb* to tell (a person) the main points about something he/she has to do.

British Standards Institution (*or* **BSI**) an independent organisation supported by the government, which lays down certain standards, e.g. for the measurements of buildings etc.

brochure a small thin book produced e.g. to advertise a **service**.

broken lot goods for sale in less than the usual quantity, or in a set that is not complete, perhaps because they have been damaged in some way.

broker an agent who buys or sells goods, **shares, services**, etc. for someone else in return for a **commission** (usually a percentage of the value of the goods etc. sold). *See also* **insurance broker, stockbroker**.

brokerage payment made to a broker by his client for buying or selling goods, **shares, services**, etc. for the **client**.

brought forward (*or* **b/f**) the total of figures at the top of a page which has been carried forward from the bottom of a previous page. *See also* **carry forward**.

budget (1) a **financial** plan of what money may be received either over a certain period of time or in connection with a certain project, and how the money will be spent. (2) a national financial plan covering a certain period (usually a year) for what the government expects to receive from taxes etc. and what the money will be spent on; in Britain this plan is usually referred to as **the Budget**.

budgetary control a method of checking on the **financial** success or failure of a business activity by making detailed **estimates** of everything to do with it over a certain period of time and comparing those with what actually happens so that the right action can be taken. *See also* **master budget**.

budget period a period of time covered by a **budget**.

buffer stock (*or* **minimum stock** *or* **reserve stock** *or* **safety stock**) the quantity of goods or materials kept in store for future use in case of difficulties in supply, or an unexpected demand for these goods.

building society an organisation which encourages people to save by paying **interest** and then lends this money at a higher rate of interest to people who want to buy their own homes. The money lent to the home-buyers is secured by means of a **mortgage** on the house that has been bought.

built-in obsolescence (*or* **planned obsolescence**) a method of increasing sales either by designing the goods sold in such a way that they will last only for a limited time and will have to be replaced, or by regularly introducing designs which will make the customer feel that his present model is out-of-date.

bulk buying the buying of goods in large quantities, usually to get them at a lower price.

bulk cargo goods carried in a ship which are all of the same kind, and not usually divided into separate containers, e.g. oil, wheat.

bull (**stock market**) a person who buys **shares** with a view to selling them at a profit before he is due to pay for them. *See also* **bear, bull market**.

bulletin (1) a newsletter or information sheet from a society, association or other group. (2) an official announcement. (3) a type of news broadcast giving only the main items of news. *See also* **bulletin board.**

bulletin board (1) (*US*) a noticeboard on which announcements, advertisements etc. can be placed. (2) a very large painted outdoor advertisement, usually placed in a prominent position, and often lit up in some way.

bullion gold or silver in the form of bars or dust, but not in the form of coins.

bullish (**stock market**) having or expecting rising **shares**.

bull market (**stock market**) a situation when the prices of **shares** are rising. *See also* **bull, bear market**.

bureau de change (*French*) a type of small bank or a section of a bank, where dealings are made in foreign currency, e.g. by cashing **travellers' cheques**.

burst *noun* (1) the broadcasting of a number of television advertisements within a short period of time. (2) (**computers**) putting a number of **records** into a **store** but with gaps of time left for the computer to be used for other purposes.

burst *verb* (**computers**) to divide (the continuous printed sheet coming

from the computer) into separate sheets.

business *noun* (1) commercial activity: *to take up business as one's career.* (2) a particular organisation involved in commercial activity; a company. *The Government is encouraging small businesses.* (3) what one does to earn a living; duty or occupation. *What line of business are you in?*

business *adjective* connected with commercial activity: *a business career.*

business agent (1) *see* **agent.** (2) (*US*) a full-time official of a **trade union** who represents a local **branch** during **negotiations** with employers and also acts as its **treasurer.**

business card a small card which can be used to introduce oneself or which can be left with a person who might want to contact one again; it usually has one's name, position in one's organisation, and the address and phone number of the organisation.

business cycle *see* **trade cycle.**

business enterprise = **business** (meaning 2).

business forecasting judging what is likely to happen in the future to a company's sales, costs and profits. Forecasts are made usually after considering the trends of things which affect the company, e.g. the **economy**, the industry that it is in and the activities of **competitors.**

business game *see* **management game.**

business indicators facts or information helpful for anyone who has to make decisions about a business activity. *In the petrol business, the number of new cars sold is a good business indicator.*

buyer (1) a person who buys goods for a business. (2) a person in charge of a department concerned with buying goods. (3) a person in charge of a department in a **department store.** (4) anyone who buys something; a customer.

buyer credit money allowed by a bank etc. to a person or company to buy goods or **services**.

buyer's market a situation in which a certain **product** is plentiful, resulting in a low price and low profit for the seller. *See also* **seller's market**.

buying behaviour (**marketing**) a way in which people behave when deciding whether or not to buy a certain **product** and the personal thoughts and feelings as well as other circumstances in the situation which will affect their behaviour.

buying motives (**marketing**) the things which make a person or company willing to buy something, e.g. price, delivery times, brand loyalty.

buzz group a small group formed to discuss and share ideas on a certain matter. *See also* **brainstorming, syndicate**.

bylaw (*also* **byelaw**) (1) (*UK*) a law which has not been passed by Parliament itself but by some organisation which has the backing of Parliament, e.g. a **local authority** or a **nationalised industry**. (2) (*US*) a regulation made by a **corporation** which states how the corporation should be organised and run. (*UK* **articles of association**).

by-line a line which comes below the title of an article in a newspaper or a magazine, giving the name of the author.

by-product something produced as a result of the manufacture of something else. For example, sawdust is a by-product of the manufcture of tables, chairs etc.

byte a group of **bits** (usually eight) which operate as one unit in a **computer**.

C

CA *see* **Chartered Accountant**.

CAA *see* **Civil Aviation Authority**.

cable *noun* (1) a thick bundle of wires usually laid underground or under the sea and used for sending messages. (2) a message sent in this way. *Send a cable to our agent in Germany.*

cable *verb* to send (a message) in this way: *to cable information overseas.*

CACM *see* **Central American Common Market**.

calculate to work out (a figure, cost etc.) by using numbers.

calculated risk a decision to do something, where a risk is known, because the rewards (either **financial** or other) make the risk worth taking. *Even a shrewd businessman will occasionally take a calculated risk.*

calculation the act or result of **calculating**.

calculator an **electronic** machine which can perform a limited number of mathematical operations. *See also* **computer**.

calendar month (1) one of the twelve divisions of the year according to the calendar. (2) a period from a date to the same date in the next month, according to the calendar. *His contract runs for two calendar months, from 10 January to 10 March.*

call (1) a demand by a company for payment of part or all of the money due on a **partly-paid share**. *See also* **called-up capital, option dealing**. (2) a visit by a salesman to one of his customers. *Our best salesman does twelve calls a day.*
  at call especially of money in a bank, without delay. For example, a company that places money in a bank at call can have it back without delay, on request.
  on call ready to go to work if called for. *There is always a doctor on call during the night.*

call analysis a study of the pattern of visits by a salesman to his customers.

call-back pay *see* **call-in pay**.

called-up capital that part of the value of the **ordinary shares**

which a company has asked its **shareholders** to pay. *see also* **call** (meaning 1).

call-frequency the number of visits that a salesman makes to his various customers in a given time. *See also* **calling cycle**.

calling card = **business card**.

calling cycle the average time between calls by a salesman on any particular customer. The *calling cycle in our salesforce is four weeks. See also* **call frequency**.

call-in pay (*or* **call-back pay**) a form of payment made to a worker who is actually called in to do a job for which he has kept himself ready on his employer's instructions.

call report a short written account of a visit by a salesman to a customer, or a **prospect**, which he will send to his manager.

campaign an organised series of actions intended to reach some result: *an advertising campaign.*

cancel (1) to make a mark on (something, e.g. a postage stamp) to prevent it being used (again). (2) to say that (something) should not be done or should not happen, even although it has already been agreed: *to cancel an order/an appointment.*

C and F (*or* **Cost and Freight**) in international trade, cost and freight. When an **exporter** quotes a C and F price, his price includes all costs up to loading the goods over the ship's rail and freight up to a named foreign port. *See also* **CIF, CIFC, FAS, FOB**.

canvass (1) to call on (people) for some purpose, e.g. to try to get their support, to find out their opinions on something or to sell them some **product**. *See also* **cold canvassing**. (2) to call on (a selected **sample** of people, or a complete group of people) in order to find out their opinions, for research purposes.

canvasser a person, especially a salesman or saleswoman, who **canvasses**. *See also* **cold canvassing**.

CAP *see* **Common Agricultural Policy**.

capacity (1) the amount that something can hold or contain: *The tank has a capacity of fifty litres.* (2) a position, e.g. in an organisation: *to act in the capacity of a manager.* (3) an ability to pay a debt when it is due. *See also* **due date**. (4) ability to perform a task or to produce something. *This machine is working at maximum capacity,* i.e. it is not able to work harder or produce more. (5) (**computers**) the number of words or **characters** that can be **stored**. (6) (**computers**) the range of numbers (within certain limits) that can be **processed** in a **register**.

capital (1) the money belonging to people or companies which is available for **investment**. *The amount of capital needed to start a business is much greater than it was ten years ago.* (2) the amount of money made available to a company by its owners, banks or **investors**. *He started his business with a capital of £10,000, only £5,000 of which was his own money; the remainder was put up by his bank.* (3) the amount of **assets** left to a business after all of its current debts have been paid. (4) *short for* **nominal capital**. *See also* **capital employed**.

capital account (1) a record of **transactions** which relate to the partners or owner of a business, showing the **capital invested** in the business and the amounts taken out of the business. (2) a section of a country's **balance of payments** statement, which records all payments not in the **current account**.

capital allowance a **system** of allowing the amount of money spent by a company on **fixed assets** (e.g. machinery, buildings, etc) to be taken off the profit before tax is charged.

capital assets the possessions of a company, such as buildings, which are used in running the business.

capital budget a **financial** plan covering a stated time, showing the expected **purchases** of **fixed assets** (e.g. buildings, machinery), the dates, and the sources of money for payment of the **assets**. It will also show the timing and **income** from the expected sale of any of the company's fixed assets during the same period.

capital charges the costs related to money used in the business, e.g. cost of **interest** on money borrowed for the **purchase** of **assets**.

capital employed (1) all the money **invested** in a business or project less the money that is currently owed. (2) **fixed assets** plus **current assets** less **current liabilities**. *See also* **net assets** and appendix 2.

capital expenditure money spent by a company to buy **fixed assets**, e.g. land, buildings, machinery, office furniture, vehicles, etc.

capital formation an increase of **fixed assets** in a company, e.g. by getting more factories, machinery, etc.

capital gain a rise in the value of a **fixed asset**, e.g. a building.

capital-gains tax a tax on gains from the sale of a **fixed asset**. Some assets are exempt from this tax, e.g. privately-owned cars and household goods.

capital goods manufactured goods that are used to produce, or help in the production of, other goods, e.g. factory buildings, machinery and tools.

capital–intensive describes an industry, e.g. oil-refining, which uses a large amount of machinery in relation to the number of workers in producing the goods. *See also* **labour-intensive**.

capital investment (1) the buying by a company of **assets** needed to carry on its business, e.g. land, buildings, machinery, etc. *See* **capital expenditure**. (2) the buying of **stocks** and **shares** to make a gain. (3) putting money into a **deposit account** to gain **interest**.

capitalise (1) to change the **reserves** of a company into **capital** by issuing free **shares** to **shareholders** (usually called a **bonus issue**). (2) to provide capital for (a business). (3) **capitalise on** to turn (something) to one's advantage. *The firm capitalised on its out-of-town location by selling to rural markets.*

capitalism an **economic system** that encourages the private ownership of industry and commerce.

capitalist *noun and adjective* (1) (a person or organisation) owning or controlling a large amount of wealth. (2) (a person or organisation) supporting **capitalism**.

capital levy a tax on the total value of a person's money and possessions, a wealth tax

capital movement the flow of money between countries, e.g. **investment** in **assets**, the sale of such assets, loans, the repayment of loans.

capital structure the way in which the **capital** of a company is made up, e.g. **shares** and long-term **loans**. *See also* **gearing**.

capital transfer tax a tax applied to the giving of **assets** as a gift, or in a will at death.

caption a short printed explanation of a photograph, drawing etc.

captive audience usually used in relation to advertising, a group of people who must watch or listen since they have no choice in the matter, e.g. a cinema audience. *The advertising spot during the TV news is quite costly – there's a large, captive audience.*

captive market buyers who must buy a certain **product** from a certain supplier because they have no choice in the matter. *Owners of Polaroid cameras are a captive market for Polaroid films.*

carbon (1) (*also* **carbon paper**) (a sheet of) specially-coated paper put between sheets of writing paper to make copies on the sheet(s) below. (2) (*also* **carbon copy**) a copy made using **carbon paper**.

card-carrying member an active member, especially of a **trade union** or political party.

card index a box or tray of cards arranged in a special order and on which is written information on some subject, e.g. a list of books in a library in alphabetical order of author.

card punch a machine that puts information onto cards in such a way that a **computer** can read and understand it, used in the preparation of **punched cards**.

card reader a **device** used to feed **punched cards** into a **computer**.

card vote a vote taken by a count of cards (e.g. membership cards of a **trade union**) held up by members at a meeting or conference. One member may hold more than one card, depending on how many people he represents. *See also* **block vote**.

career a job or profession for which one is trained and which one intends to follow. *Jim's a teacher, a very worthwhile career.*

car expenses costs related to owning and using a car, e.g. petrol, garage, rent, repairs, road tax.

cargo goods carried on an aircraft, ship or vehicle, usually in exchange for payment. *The ship carried a cargo of cotton. See also* **freight charge**.

car hire (1) the temporary use of a car in return for payment. (2) the business of car hire. *Their charges for car hire are reasonable.*

Caribbean Community and Common Market (*or* **CARICOM**) a group of 12 countries formed in 1973 for **economic** co-operation between members. Headquarters: Georgetown, Guyana. Official language: English.

CARICOM *see* **Caribbean Community and Common Market**.

carriage (1) the carrying of goods for payment; the cost of this. *The goods were £100 but carriage cost another £10.* (2) the part of a typewriter which moves the paper along.

carriage forward the cost of delivery of the goods (**carriage**) to be paid by the receiver of the goods.

carriage free when goods are delivered by the seller at no cost for delivery. *This furniture is £150, carriage free.*

carriage inwards the amount a buyer pays for delivery of goods received.

carriage outwards the amount a seller charges to cover cost of delivering goods. *Our selling price for the machine is £200 plus carriage outwards £50: total cost to you £250.*

carriage paid when a seller pays the delivery charges of goods sold to a stated place. *Carriage paid, London.*

carriage return the return of the **carriage** of a typewriter to the left-hand margin.

carrier a person or business that carries goods (or people) from one place to another for payment.

carry forward (*or* **c/f**) in **accounts**, words written at the bottom of a page of figures to show that the total has to be carried over to the top of the next page. *See also* **brought forward, balance brought forward, balance carried forward**.

carte blanche full freedom of action, usually in a certain area. *The company gave the agent carte blanche on the matter of who to call on for orders.*

cartel an informal group of companies which join together to carry out **policies** for the benefit of all members, e.g. on prices, **discounts**, **products** and markets.

case history a written record of the past history of a company.

case method teaching or training through the use of **case studies** (i.e. using records of real or fictional companies to provide the learning experience of business).

case study a description of a company, usually in printed form but sometimes on slides, tape or film which is used to train people, e.g. in how to solve business problems and make business decisions.

cash noun (1) money in coin or notes. (2) in business, cash includes cheques or other **documents** that can be quickly changed into **cash in hand**, or in the bank.

cash verb (1) to receive money from a bank or a person in exchange for (a cheque). *He went to the bank and cashed a cheque for £10.* (2) to pay money to a person in exchange for (a cheque). *He was short of money, so I cashed his cheque for £20.*

cash account an **account** which records the payment and receipt of money in a business. *See also* **cash book**.

cash and carry a method of selling goods at lower prices, where the buyer not only pays cash at the time of sale (instead of receiving **credit**) and also carries the goods away himself, instead of the seller delivering.

cash-and-carry warehouse a large store where goods are sold at low prices if paid for at once and taken away by the buyer.

cash-and-carry wholesaler a business which buys goods from the manufacturers and other suppliers (usually on **credit**) and sells these goods to **retailers** at low prices providing the retailers pay for the goods at once and take the goods away themselves. *See* **cash and carry**).

cash bonus (**life insurance**) a share of the profits earned by a life insurance company paid to the insured in cash instead of being added to the amount of the **policy**. *See also* **bonus**.

cash book a **book of account** in which is recorded the payment and receipt of money. *See also* **cash account**.

cash card a plastic card from a bank etc., specially numbered for each customer, which allows the customer to **withdraw** cash (in the form of **banknotes**) from his/her **account** at any time of the day or night. The card is fed into an **A.T.M.** and, providing certain simple instructions are followed, the required amount of cash is issued by the machine.

cash discount a **discount** allowed for prompt payment. For example, $2\frac{1}{2}\%$ 10 days printed on an **invoice** means that $2\frac{1}{2}\%$ may be taken off the amount shown on the invoice if payment is made within 10 days.

cash dispenser a machine for giving out money. *See also* **A.T.M.**

cash flow (1) a supply of cash which is needed by a company to meet its regular weekly or monthly expenses. (2) the flow of cash into a company (cash inflow) in the form of payment by customers or money from the sale of **assets**, and the flow of cash out of a company (cash outflow) in the form of payment of expenses and **purchase** of assets. *We often have a cash-flow problem.* (3) the difference of cash inflow and cash outflow of a company (or of a certain project). Sometimes called **net cash flow**. *See* **cash flow statement**.

cash-flow statement a weekly or monthly plan of the expected **cash flow** (meaning 2).

cashier (1) a person in charge of all cash **transactions** in a company, i.e. the recording of the receipts and payment of cash, cheques and **bills of exchange**. (2) in a bank, a person who receives and gives out cash to the public. (3) a person who receives cash from customers in a shop etc.

cash-in-hand in business, money held to hand in the form of coin or **banknotes**.

cash on delivery (or **COD**) a condition of sale, made by the seller of the goods, that payment must be made at the actual time they are delivered, often used where goods are ordered and delivered by post. The post office will collect the cash at the time of delivery and pass the money back to the seller.

cash price the price the seller will sell at if the buyer pays immediately.

cash reserves money set aside in case of need. *The company has ample cash reserves should we decide to expand.*

cash surrender value *see* **surrender value**.

cash with order a condition made by a seller that payment must be received along with any order for goods.

cassette (1) a container of film that can be easily placed into a camera. (2) a container of **magnetic tape** that can be easily placed into a **tape recorder**.

casting vote a vote used by the **chairman** of a meeting if the votes for and against something are equal.

casual worker a worker not employed on a regular basis but only if and when there is work for him/her.

catalogue (1) a book containing a list of goods for sale with description, price and how to order, and sometimes also illustrations of the goods. *See also* **catalogue buying**. (2) a list of names, places, goods etc. in a certain order so that any item can be easily found. *In this library the catalogue is arranged by subject.*

catalogue buying buying goods by using a company's **catalogue** to choose and order them, rather than buying them in a shop.

caveat emptor (*Latin* let the buyer beware) a legal term meaning the buyer should use his common sense when buying goods, for if he suffers loss because he does not do so, the law will not help him.

CC *see* **column centimetres**.

CCC *see* **Customs Cooperation Council**.

CCTV *see* **closed-circuit television**.

Ceefax a **viewdata system** run by the British Broadcasting Corporation.

census the counting of the whole amount of something, e.g. all of the people in a country (**population** census), the total number of cars that use a certain road (traffic census). Such information helps in the planning decision of government, **local authorities** and companies. *The UK population census includes information on age, sex, occupation, number of children, etc.*

Census of Production a yearly inquiry by the government's business **statistical** office to provide information about the country's manufacturing industries, e.g. size, location, output, etc.

Central American Common Market (or **CACM** or **MCCA**) a group of Central American countries formed in 1960 to set up a **common market** of member states and a customs union. Membership: Costa Rica, El Salvador, Guatemala, Nicaragua. Headquarters: Guatemala City. Official language: Spanish.

central bank a bank set up by a government to carry out the government's **financial** business, e.g. raising loans for the government, controlling the issue of notes, and influencing the rate of interest; in the UK, the Bank of England.

centralise to move control of (something) to the headquarters of an organisation. *All the buying is done at head office – it has all been centralised.*

central processing unit (*or* **C.P.U.**) the heart of the **computer**. It **coordinates** and controls the actions of all the other units, carries out all the arithmetic and the **processes** applied to **data**.

Central Statistical Office an organisation set up by the UK government to collect and **process statistics** on **economic** aspects of UK life.

Centre for Interfirm Comparisons (*or* **CIFC**) an independent organisation set up to carry out comparisons of management **ratios** between companies on a confidential basis.

centre spread *see* **double-page spread**.

certificate an official **document** showing proof of something, e.g. marriage (marriage certificate), birth (birth certificate), education (Higher National Certificate).

certificate of health an official **document** giving details of the condition of foodstuffs, or animals, or the produce of animals, e.g. milk, beef.

certificate of incorporation a **document** from the **Registrar of Companies** as evidence that a company has met the various requirements of the Companies Act.

certificate of insurance an official **document** from an **insurance company** as proof that an insurance **contract** exists between the company and a named **party**. It is a shortened version of the insurance contract and states the main things covered by the insurance; it may be required by law, e.g. in motor insurance.

certificate of origin a **document** stating that certain goods were produced or manufactured in a named country, used when **exporting** goods to a country which charges different **tariff** rates depending on the origin of the goods.

certificate of value a written proof given by the supplier of goods that the value of goods as stated in the **export invoice** is the true value used, e.g. where the amount of tax on the goods depends on the value of the goods.

certified accountant a member of the Association of Certified and Corporate Accountants who is thus properly qualified to **audit accounts** of **limited companies**.

c/f *see* **carry forward**.

chain of command (*or* **line of command**) formal lines of **communication** in a company through which management instructions and information are passed.

chain store a shop or store which is one of many owned by the same company, each in a different place.

chair *verb* to be in charge of (a meeting); to be the **chairman** of (a meeting).

chairman (*or* **chairperson**) (1) a person in charge of a meeting. (2) the holder of the highest **office** (meaning 3) of a company, committee etc. *He has been made chairman of the board.*

chamber of commerce an association of companies in an area which tries to help and protect the trade interests of member companies.

channel of distribution (*or* **distribution channel**) the way goods go from the producer to the user. For example, a company making chocolates may decide to reach **consumers** by way of **wholesalers** to small shops to consumers, or by way of supermarkets to consumers. Each route would be a different channel of distribution. See appendix 7.

channels of communication the ways in which information flows, e.g. within a company, between managers, between managers and workers, between directors and managers. *Compare with* **communications**.

character (**data-processing**) one of a set of symbols used to represent a letter, or a number, or a punctuation mark, etc, e.g. the letter 'a' is a character in the alphabet.

charge *verb* (1) to ask (a certain amount of money) for goods or services. *How much do you charge for delivery?* (2) to make a note of (money owed) *Please charge it to my account.* (3) (*law*) to accuse (a person) formally of having committed a certain crime. *He was charged with drunken driving.* (4) to cause (a battery etc.) to take or store electricity.

charge *noun* (1) an amount of money **charged** (meaning 1). *For a small extra charge you can have the goods delivered.* (2) (*law*) the act of **charging** (meaning 3). *He has been arrested on a drugs charge.* (3) an amount of electricity held in a battery etc. (4) control; responsibility. *Who is in charge of this department?*

charge account an arrangement between companies and customers whereby goods or **services** can be bought and payment is made later.

chargehand the leader of a group of workers (usually under the level of **foreman**).

charges forward when the buyer of goods pays only when they are delivered, or after delivery when a **bill** is sent to the buyer.

chart *see* **graph**.

charter *noun* (1) a formal **document** from the king or queen or government to a city, bank, college, company, etc. stating its purposes and rights. *The university received its charter in 1963.* (2) the basic rights or principles of an organisation. *Charter of the United Nations.* (3) the act or practice of **chartering**. *See also* **charter party.**

charter *verb* to hire (a ship, plane etc.) for a special purpose.

chartered accountant a member of the Institute of Chartered Accountants in England, Wales, Scotland or Ireland, the governing body with rules of conduct which the chartered accountant must keep to. Membership of the Institute is given after passing examinations and serving a period with a company of **accountants** who are members.

charter party (*also* **charter party contract**) a **contract** between persons hiring a ship and the shipowner.

cheap (1) low-priced, not costing much money, *There are special cheap train tickets to London for students.* (2) good value for money. *This is a good quality camera going cheap.* (3) poor quality, worth little. *All she could find were cheap souvenirs.*

cheap money money which can be borrowed at low **interest** rates. A cheap money policy is sometimes carried out by governments to encourage **investment** in new factories and so increase employment and demand for goods.

cheat *verb* (1) to take money or property unfairly or dishonestly. *He cheated the customs – he didn't declare the goods.* (2) to take an unfair advantage. *He passed the examination by cheating – he copied the answers from the man in front.*

cheat *noun* (1) a person who **cheats**. (2) something done by **cheating**.

check list a list used to help the memory. Each item is usually **checked off** with a tick (✓) as it is referred to. *The engineer referred to his check list when servicing the car. Each researcher had a check list when she carried out the survey of houseowners.*

check off to mark (things on a list) to show that they have been dealt with.

check-out an exit in a self-service or supermarket store where the value of the goods bought is recorded, totalled and payment is made.

cheque a written order to a bank to pay a certain sum to the person named on the cheque from the **account** of the person who signed the cheque. A cheque is a **bill of exchange drawn** on a banker, payable on demand and is a common way of settling debts. It can also be **endorsed** and passed to someone else to pay into his/her account. *See also* **crossed cheque**.

cheque book a book of cheques given by banks to their **current account** customers.

cheque card a card given by a bank to those who have an **account** with it. It **guarantees** payment by the bank of any cheque written by the owner of the card, up to a certain amount.

chicken feed (*informal*) a very small amount of money. *That is chicken feed compared with what people get paid in the oil business.*

chief executive the person who has overall resonsibility for the day-to-day running of a business. In the case of a **limited company** the chief executive is usually the **managing director**

chip (*or* **microchip**, *or* **silicon chip**) (**computers**) a very small piece of silicon (about 6mm square) on which has been etched hundreds, sometimes thousands, of tiny **devices** which store and use **data**.

CIF in international trade, **cost, insurance and freight**. A CIF price includes all costs up to loading the goods over the ship's rail, the cost of **marine insurance** for the goods and the cost of carrying the goods from a UK port to a named foreign port. *See also* **CIFC, FAS, FOB**.

CIFC (1) international trade, cost, insurance, freight, commission. A CIFC price includes all charges given for CIF plus commission to an agent who helped to get the order and who may be an agent of the buyer or the seller. *See also* **CIF, FAS, FOB**. (2) *see* **Centre for Interfirm Comparisons**.

circular a printed announcement, advertisement, letter, of which many copies are made and sent to people who may be interested in the contents.

circulating capital *see* **working capital**.

circulation (1) the total number of copies bought or given away free of a book, magazine, or newspaper. *Newspapers today are battling to build up circulation.* (2) a movement of something, e.g. money or news from person to person. *We hope the new manager will improve the circulation of information between departments.*

Civil Aviation Authority (*or* **CAA**) a UK **authority** set up in 1971 to develop and control civil air transport in the UK, e.g. by **promoting** the reasonable interests of users of civil air transport; by deciding which air routes should be given to which airlines; by issuing **certificates** of air-worthiness.

civil case a court case dealing with the rights of private citizens.

CKD *see* **completely knocked down**.

claim *verb* (1) (especially **insurance** and law) to ask for (something due, e.g. money). *The cargo was lost when the ship sank so the company claimed under its marine insurance policy.* (2) to say that something is true. *This customer claims he has already paid his bill.*

claim *noun* the act of **claiming**. *She put in a claim to the insurance company.*

claimant (*law*) a person who makes a **claim**.

class (1) a group having qualities of the same kind. *Our customers fall into two classes: wholesalers and retailers.* (2) one of a series of grades into which certain types of **service** (especially travel) are divided: *a second-class rail ticket; fly first class; a third-class hotel.* (3) a social group. *In the UK you're in the upper class, the middle class or the working class.* (4) a group of pupils or students.

classified (1) divided or arranged in a certain order or class. *In this library all books are classified by subject.* (2) put into a secret group. *The information on the new product for the army is classified* (i.e. the public is not allowed to know about it).

classified advertising small advertisements in a newspaper or magazine arranged in a certain order or class, e.g. advertisements under 'gardening', 'personal' or 'lost and found'.

clean bill of exchange a **bill of exchange** sent to the **importer's** bank, for **acceptance** by the importer, the other shipping **documents** having gone direct to the importer. *See also* **documentary bill of exchange**.

clean bill of health *see* **bill of health**.

clean bill of lading a receipt from the **carrier** (to the person sending the goods) when goods are going by sea, which states that 'the goods are in good order and condition'.

clearance certificate a customs **document** issued to a UK ship leaving for a foreign port which states that it has obeyed UK customs **regulations**.

clearance sale a special sale of goods at lower prices to clear a seller's **stock** of goods.

clearing bank (1) a bank that is a member of the **London Bankers' Clearing House** (2) any UK **commercial bank** or **joint-stock bank**.

clerical of the work or position of a **clerk**. *We all have to do some clerical work.*

clerk (1) a person **employed** in an office or shop to do paperwork such as keeping records, filing, typing. (2) (*US*) a shop assistant.

client a person or company that pays for the **services** of a professional person or orgaisation, e.g. a lawyer, an **insurance** agency. *I can recommend this advertising agency – our company has been a client of theirs for years.* See also **customer**.

clip (1) a short-part of a film cut from a complete film. (2) a metal fastener for holding together papers or **documents**.

clipping service an **agency** which will cut out and supply pieces of news or advertisements from the press about something in return for payment. *See* **press cuttings**.

clock card a card used by workers when **clocking-in** (or **clocking-on**).

clock in (*or* **on**) of workers of a company, to record the times at which they start and finish work. *The workers here clock in at 8.30 a.m.* See also **time card**.

close company a company controlled by five or fewer **shareholders** and in which the public has less than 35% of the **shares**.

closed-circuit television (*or* **CCTV**) a television system which sends pictures by wire to a limited number of television receivers, used in education, training and for security, e.g. for watching the public in a shop etc.

closed-shop describes an organisation which employs only those people who are members of a certain **trade union**.

closing entries entries in the **books of account** at the end of an **accounting period** to allow the **profit-and-loss account** to be made up for the period.

closing prices the prices of **shares** at the end of a day's trading on the **stock market**.

closing the sale the point of a sales **interview** at which the seller asks the buyer for an order.

cluster analysis (**market research**) a method in which a variety of information on people, **products**, etc. is sorted out into groups or clusters with each cluster having broadly the same characteristics. *See also* **cluster sampling**.

cluster sampling (**market research**) a method of **sampling** by which the people to be questioned are in areas grouped or clustered together. This lessens the time and cost of interviewing. Using this type of sampling, care must be taken that **bias** does not enter the results. *See also* **area sample, cluster analysis**.

CMEA *see* **Council for Mutual Economic Assistance.**

coaching teaching or training. *The sales manager insists on coaching his staff on selling at every sales meeting.*

coaster a ship which sails round the coast from port to port.

COBOL (*stands for* Common Business Oriented Language) a **computer language** used especially in business.

Cocoa Producers' Alliance (*or* **COPAL**) a group of countries formed in 1962 to discuss common problems of pricing, producing and marketing cocoa. Members include Brazil, Cameroon, Ecuador, Gabon, Chana, Ivory Coast, Nigeria, Trinidad and Tobago.

COD *see* **cash on delivery.**

code of practice the printed conditions under which members of certain professions agree to do their business. For example, the advertising profession publishes a code of practice advising members how to conduct the business of advertising: *The Code of Advertising Practice.*

codicil a written or printed addition to a will altering, explaining or **cancelling** the will.

coin metal currency as distinct from paper currency; a piece of this. *I can give you the £1 I owe you but it's all in coin. Can you give me a five-pence coin in the change?*

cold call a sales call on a buyer (who is not yet a customer of the salesman's company) when no invitation to call has been arranged.

cold canvassing calling on buyers (who are not customers of the salesman's company) uninvited, with the hope of selling goods to the buyers.

collate (1) to examine or compare (books, records, texts etc.) so that the differences can be noted. (2) to put together individual pages of (printed matter) in a certain order.

collateral (*also* **collateral security**) something promised as **security** for the repayment of a loan. *I asked the bank for a £5,000 loan and they asked me for the title deeds to my house as collateral.*

collective bargaining: **negotiation** between the management of a company and the representatives of the workers (usually members of a **trade union**) where wages, working hours, complaints, etc. are discussed.

collective ownership ownership and control of a company shared between all who work for it. *The workers and managers bought the firm so now it's under collective ownership.*

college (1) a school for higher education usually offering degree or **diploma** courses. (2) a part of a university.

collision clause (**marine insurance**) a clause which covers a shipowner against having to pay for damage to other ships in collisions.

collusion secret agreement between two or more people with the intention of cheating or making an unlawful gain. *The manager of the shop thought there was collusion between two of his staff because a lot of stock had gone missing.*

column (1) a line of figures arranged one below the other. *Add up this column of figures.* (2) a section of printed material running from the top of the page to the bottom. *This page is divided into two columns.*

column centimetre (*or* **CC**) a unit of measurement of advertising space in newspapers, e.g. 5 column centimetres is a space 5 centimetres deep and one column wide.

combine *noun* a group of businesses joined together for a common purpose, e.g. to control prices.

COMECON *see* **Council for Mutual Economic Assistance.**

commando selling aggressive (hard-hitting) selling into a new market, often with a new **product**, and usually with a special sales force.

commerce all the activities to do with the buying and selling of goods. *Britain depends on commerce – it has trading links with every continent.*

commercial *adjective* (1) relating to **commerce** or trade between companies or countries. *He says that taxation is ruining the commercial life of the country.* (2) having a possibility of profit. *He's thinking of going into electronics; he says it's a commercial proposition.*

commercial *noun* an advertisement on television or radio or in the cinema.

commercial agent *see* **agent.**

commercial bank a bank operating through branches, dealing with private individuals, companies and other organizations and which is in business to make a profit. Examples are Lloyds, Barclays, Midland, NatWest, Royal Bank of Scotland.

commercial break *see* **break.**

commercial credit time allowed for payment between companies, e.g. **credit** given by a manufactuer when dealing with another manufac-

turer, or when selling goods to a **wholesaler** or **retailer**.

commercial treaty an agreement between two or more countries stating the conditions of trade between them.

commission (1) a payment to an agent for his part in the sale or **purchase** of goods and **services** for a **principal**, often a percentage of the value of the goods or services. (2) a payment to an employee, e.g. a salesman, over and above his salary (often a percentage of his sales) to encourage greater effort. (3) (the giving of) a task or power. *We have been given the commission for the setting up of a new committee.* (4) a committee with special (government) power: *the Forestry Commission. See also* **commission agent, auctioneer.**

commission agent a person who buys or sells goods or **services** in return for an agreed rate of **commission** (meaning 2).

committee a group of people appointed to attend to special business. *See Jones about your complaint on conditions; he's on the works committee.*

committee of inspection a group appointed by **creditors** of a company to **supervise** a company which is in **liquidation**.

commodity something sold for profit; often used to describe things which can be graded, e.g. coffee, cotton, sugar, wheat, wool, and which are bought and sold on a **commodity exchange.**

commodity exchange a market where buying and selling is recorded on a national or international scale. London is the centre for many commodity exchanges where each day's price is decided for commodities such as wool, wheat, coffee, etc. *See also* **commodity.**

Common Agricultural Policy (*or* **CAP**) a policy agreed to by all members of the **European Economic Community** to protect the

European farming industry. Under this policy the EEC fixes minimum prices for various farm **products**. **Imports** from non-members of the EEC must not fall below these prices. When EEC producers have **surplus stocks** for sale then the EEC will buy these stocks at slightly below the minimum price. The policy also encourages greater efficiency among EEC farmers by making cash grants out of the EEC **budget**.

common carrier a person or business offering to transport goods for payment. Within his own area and conditions, he has to carry goods when requested, without undue delay and at a reasonable price, and he must have a government **licence** for this type of business.

common law unwritten law based on custom and court decisions rather than laws passed by Parliament.

common market a union of several countries for **economic** purposes. *See* **European Economic Community**.

common ownership the ownership of something, e.g. land or a business, jointly shared by all, e.g. a cooperative society is a business in common ownership.

common stock (*US*) = **ordinary shares**.

(The) Commonwealth an association of countries which were in the past part of the British Empire, its main purpose being to encourage trade and friendly relations among members. Membership: 41 countries. The Commonwealth Centre is at Marlborough House, London, and the working language at Commonwealth meetings is English.

communicate (1) to make (information, news, ideas, attitudes) known to a person or group. (2) to share or exchange information etc.

communication (1) an act of making information, news, ideas, attitudes known to a person or group.

(2) a piece of information, or something containing such, e.g. a letter. *You will receive a communication from us next week.* (3) *plural* means of making **contact** with a person, group or region: telephones, telegraphs, railways, roads, airports. *After the bombing there were no communications left between the towns.*

communications mix the variety of methods which a company uses to send information to its customers, e.g. advertisements in the cinema and on television, radio, in magazines and newspapers, calls by salesmen.

communications satellite a man-made **device** above the earth which receives and sends to earth radio and television signals.

community transit form a special **document** required by the **EEC** customs for the movement of goods between member countries.

company a group of people who come together for the purposes of producing goods or offering a **service** and whose **regulation** is governed by one of the Companies Acts. A company so organised is a separate body under the law. *See* **private company, public company, joint-stock company**.

company agreement an agreement between a single company and a **trade union** in the company.

company bargaining talks between the managers of a company and **trade union** officials with the hope of reaching agreement on wages, hours of work, or conditions etc. within the company. *Compare with* **collective bargaining**.

company director a person who is a member of the **board of directors** of a company.

company man a man who is totally in agreement with all that his company is doing, and all that his company plans to do.

company promoter a person who organises the forming of a new company.

company reserves *see* **general reserves**.

company secretary the person responsible for the preparation of final **accounts**, for administering the board's affairs, and for making sure that the company's legal **obligations** are met.

company shares *see* **shares**.

company store (*US*) a shop owned and managed by the company which sells goods to company workers.

company union a **trade union** which operates within one single company.

comparison test comparing, e.g. the price, taste, design etc (or 'value for money') of competing **products**.

compatibility (1) the ability of different persons or things to agree, work, or act together. (2) the ability of **software** or **hardware** to be used with more than one type of **computer**.

compensate to give **compensation** for something.

compensating error (**bookkeeping**) an error which happens to **cancel** the effect of another error. *By mistake we overpaid £2 to Smith but then we also underpaid £2 to Jones, and because of that compensating error our cash balance is correct.*

compensation suitable payment for some loss or injury. *He suffered an accident at work and the company paid him £10,000 compensation.*

compensation for loss of office a sum of money given to a director on his leaving the company before his **contract** with the company ends, e.g. when the company is **taken over** by another company which does not need his services.

competent (1) having ability or skill to do the work required. (2) having the legal capacity. *This court is competent to deal with the case.*

competition (1) (the act of) trying to do or get something better than one's rivals. *There was fierce competition for the new contract.* (2) companies selling the same or similar **products** or **services**. *The competition are taking our customers, and our sales are down.* (3) a contest of skill or knowledge. *This company is running a competition – complete a slogan and you might win a new house.*

competitive advantage (*or* **competitive edge**) some benefit possessed by a **product** or some ability possessed by a company that makes it better in the market. *We have a great competitive advantage in our sales force – they are all highly-trained men.*

competitive claims benefits offered to buyers by the various companies selling similar **products**.

competitive edge *see* **competitive advantage**.

competitive price a price for a **product** or **service** which is low when compared to other similar products or services.

competitor a rival, in business usually offering similar **products** or **services** to buyers. *Our main competitor is Jones & Co. They've been in the same business as ours for many years.*

compilation time (1) the time taken to **compile** a **computer program**. (2) the actual time at which a computer program is compiled.

compile (1) to put facts etc. together in order to make up (e.g. a report, a dictionary). (2) to create (a **computer program**) by means of a **compiler** (meaning 2).

compiler (1) a person who **compiles**, e.g. a dictionary. (2) a **computer program** that changes instructions given in a **high-level**

language into a **binary code** (1's and 0's) which the computer can understand and act upon.

complementary goods goods which have a sales level linked to the sales of other goods because they are used together, e.g. bread and butter, cameras and films, engines and oil.

completely knocked down (or **CKD**) (**exporting**) goods delivered in parts, to be put together by the buyer. This method reduces the cost of **freight** and is sometimes used by companies supplying goods such as furniture or cars.

compliments slip a small piece of paper with a company's name and address, often put in with something being sent, when no letter is needed.

component any part of a complete **product**. *The screws and the fuse are components of an electric plug.*

composite demand the total purchase of a **product** which is used by a number of different industries, e.g. composite demand for steel will include the steel bought by the car, shipping and building industries.

composite motion a **motion** put forward at a meeting which contains a number of separate motions on the same topic.

compound interest: **interest** due on the original sum of money plus any interest already earned. For example if a bank offers 10% interest on money **deposited** with it then £100 will in one year earn £10 interest. If the £100 and the £10 interest is left in the bank for a further year the compound interest on £110 will be £11.

comprehensive insurance an **insurance** giving cover for many risks in one **policy**, e.g. a comprehensive car insurance will cover all known possible losses from accidents which happen while the car is in the owner's possession, or while it is being driven by someone else with the owner's permission.

compulsory purchase the buying of something by a government or **local authority**, using the power of the law. *Once the decision is made to build a new airport, there will be a compulsory purchase order on all these buildings.*

computer a calculating machine which can carry out complicated operations at very high speeds by **electronic** means.

computerise to cause (a machine, system etc.) to be operated by **computer**; to produce (information by computer).

computer language a **system** of words and symbols by which information can be put into a **computer**.

computer peripheral a part of a **computer system** which is not part of the **central processing unit**, e.g. a **visual display unit**, **line printer**.

con *see* **confidence trick**.

concept an idea especially one connected with a certain thing, e.g. a **product** or **service**. *The product concept for this perfume is youthfulness and romance – advertising must stress these two things. The marketing concept is really a way of thinking about business, stressing the importance of the customer.*

concession (1) something given up in a **negotiation**. *As a concession to your point about the price – we will reduce our price by £1.* (2) the right given by the owner of **premises** to another company allowing that company to trade on the premises. *Smith's has given us the concession to sell our jewellery in their department store in exchange for rent and a share of our profits from our sales.*

concessionaire a person operating a business or trade in **premises** owned by another. *See* **concession** (meaning 2).

conciliation the bringing together of the **parties** in a **dispute**, e.g. workers and management to try to reach a settlement between them. *See also* **arbitration**.

conditional having a condition attached. *The lease is conditional on the building being used as a dwelling house only.*

conditional sale agreement a **contract** for the sale of goods where it is agreed that the price may be paid in parts (or **instalments**) over an agreed period of time and where the ownership of the goods remains with the seller until the conditions of the contract are met.

conditions of sale arrangements for the sale of his goods which a seller prints on his price lists and **invoices**, and which he expects buyers to keep to when ordering, e.g. payment in one month after receipt of goods.

conference a meeting or series of meetings for discussion and exchange of ideas. *The managers are in conference. She is going to a three-day conference on microcomputers.*

confidence trick (*also, informal* **con**) a piece of business in which a person is cheated, usually by someone pretending to be something different from what he/she actually is. *See also* **con-man**.

confidential (to be) kept secret, not (to be) told to others. *Please keep this mater confidential.*

confirm to say that (something) has actually happened or will definitely happen. *We are pleased to confirm your order of 19 May.*

confirmation the act of **confirming**; something which confirms. *Could you please give me confirmation of my flights by Friday?*

confirmed irrevocable letter of credit a **letter of credit** which cannot be changed in any way without the agreement of the **exporter** and **importer**. It is supported, or **guaranteed**, by two banks, one in the exporter's country and one in the importer's country. *See* **letter of credit**.

confirming house a business that acts for a foreign buyer, **confirming** orders placed in the UK, paying for these orders and overseeing the sending of the goods to the foreign buyer who pays a **fee** to the confirming house for these **services**.

confiscate to take possession legally of (goods) against the owner's will.

confiscation the act of **confiscating**. *The goods entered the country illegally and so they were confiscated by the customs authority.*

conglomerate a large group of companies which produce a variety of **products**.

con man (*informal*) a person who plays **confidence tricks**.

consensus of opinion commonly-held views within a group. *At the meeting the consensus of opinion was that the firm should go ahead with the new model.*

consideration (1) the act or process of thinking carefully about something. *Don't do that without due consideration.* (2) something of value passing between the **parties** to a **contract**. For example, the price paid for the goods, or delivery of the goods, may be seen as legal signs that a **contract** is in being. Other requirements for a contract are offer and acceptance. (3) any kind of payment. *He will help you for a small consideration.*

consign to send (goods) to someone. *We have received your order and have consigned your goods by ship.*

consignee a person to whom goods have been sent.

consignment (1) a quantity of goods which are being delivered. *Who is this consignment of cartons for?* (2) goods sent to an **agent** for sale where ownership remains with the sender until a sale takes place. *We have sent our agent some goods on consignment. See* **goods on consignment**.

consignment note (*or* **advice note**) a printed paper describing goods which are being delivered from one **party** to another.

consignor a sender of goods.

consolidated united; combined into one.

consolidated balance sheet a drawing together into one **balance sheet** of the balance sheets of other companies within a group. *The Ajax group of companies have just published their consolidated balance sheet.*

consortium a group of companies cooperating for a specific purpose. *A consortium is trying to get the contract not only to build the hospital but to supply all the equipment as well.*

constructive dismissal a legal term for the situation where a worker decides to leave his employment because of the unfair actions of his employers; he can still **claim** that it was the fault of the employer that he had to leave. *Compare with* **unfair dismissal**.

consul a person appointed by a government, living in a foreign country, whose duties include improving the business relations between that country and his own.

consular fees charges made by a **consulate** for signing **export documents** and **invoices**.

consular invoice a special form which an **exporter** must get from a **consulate** to prove the value and origin of the goods to be exported to the **consul's** country.

consulate the office of a **consul**.

consult to discuss something with (someone else, usually an expert in some area). *We must consult a lawyer on this point.*

consultant an expert in some part of medicine or business who gives his professional advice to a person or company. *They've called in a marketing consultant hoping his advice will improve their business.*

consultation a meeting to try to get advice, or to discuss a problem, so that a decision can be made.

consultative management a style of management where managers seek the advice of those workers who may be affected by a decision, before the decision is taken.

consumer the actual user of a **product** or **service**. *Compare with* **customer**. For example, the consumer of baby-food is the baby but the customer for baby-food is the buyer.

consumer advertising advertising directed at members of the public.

consumer behaviour habits of people with regard to how and why they buy certain **products**, or shop in certain stores, or prefer certain newspapers or magazines. Suppliers of goods and **services** try to understand the buying habits of their **target markets** so that **products** and **services** can be improved to suit the market's needs.

consumer credit loans by **retailers** or **finance** houses to customers to allow them to buy goods. The loans are paid back over a period of time. Such **credit** may be **hire-purchase**, **charge account**, or **interest-free loan**.

consumer durables: **products** used by the public for a relatively long life, e.g. refrigerator, television, car.

consumer goods goods bought by the general public (as opposed to those bought by companies), e.g. food, furniture, electrical equipment, cars.

consumerism trying to protect the interests of the general public in their dealings with companies, especially in the purchase of goods and **services**.

consumer loyalty active support by customers, shown by their regular buying of a **service** or their regular use of a shop etc. *Even though there are several new shops near Benn's Store, it is still doing well – it has tremendous customer loyalty.*

consumer market all the people who buy to satisfy their own needs or those of their families. *Compare with* **industrial market**.

consumer panel (marketing) a group of people who report on their use of a **product** or **service**, usually over a period of time. They are chosen so as to represent the market for the product or service.

consumer sovereignty the power of the ordinary person as a buyer of goods in a free market; the choice of the ordinary buyer, e.g. the housewife, decides which **products** will survive and which will die out.

consumption the act of buying or using up goods or **services**. *The consumption of men's shoes is higher than that of women's shoes.*

contact *verb* to get in touch with. *You can contact her at her office.*

contact *noun* the act of **contacting**; the person one **contacts** or may **contact**. *Try to put me in contact with them. We have a contact in Paris.*

container something in which goods are held, especially a large case of standard size (the largest is 8 ft (2.4 m) × 8 ft (2.4 m) × 40 ft (12.2 m)) built to carry a large number of packages by lorry, rail, ship or air. Containers are packed at the sender's **premises** or at central **depots**.

containerization the changing over to packing goods into **containers** away from docks (instead of into small packing cases and then onto ships). Containers can go by road, rail, air or in specially-built **container ships**.

container ship a ship specially built to carry **containers**.

continent one of the large areas into which the land of the world is divided.

the Continent (*informal*) the continent of Europe except for the British Isles.

contingency something which may or may not happen. *We have a contingency fund of £5,000 to meet unexpected costs.*

contingency planning planning for events which may happen and which could disturb the main plan. *We plan to sell the new line to the shops in June and start the advertising in July but we have contingency plans if the new line is not ready by June.*

continuous production *see* **flow-line production**.

continuous research research which is regular and part of a company's normal flow of information. *With regard to sales we believe in continuous research – every month we get reports from our research agency on the rate of sale of our product to consumers.*

contraband goods which are illegally brought into or taken out of the country.

contract an agreement, which must be legally followed and obeyed, between persons or companies to do something, e.g. an offer of goods at a certain price which is accepted by a buyer.

contract of affreightment a **contract** made with a ship-owner for the carriage of goods by sea.

contract of employment a **contract** between a worker and a company on the wages, hours, etc. of the employment. In the UK a company must give everyone who works full-time for it such a contract of employment.

contract of service a **contract** between a company and its director, or senior manager (or a **consultant**), usually stating the conditions of employment and the conditions under which the employment can end.

contract in to sign a **contract** to take part in something, e.g. to join a **trade union.**

contractor (1) a person or company that enters into an agreement. (2) a company that agrees to supply materials or **labour** for building jobs.

contract out to sign a **contract** not to take part in something, e.g. not to join a state **pension scheme.**

contribute (1) to give a certain amount, especially along with others. *We all contributed to her retirement present.* (2) to write articles for a newspaper or magazine. *She contributes to the Economist.*

contributed capital money paid to a company for its issue of **shares.**

contribution (1) something **contributed.** *My contribution towards Smith's going-away gift was £1.* (2) the difference between all the **variable costs** of a **product** and its selling price.

contribution analysis a method of checking on the costs of each **product** or **service** so that the **variable costs** are shown. When taken off the sales, these costs will show the **contribution** of each product or service towards the **fixed costs.** *See also* **break-even** and appendix 3.

contribution pricing fixing a selling price for a **product** or **service** so that all **variable costs** are covered and some **contribution** helps to cover the **fixed costs.** *See* **break-even** and appendix 3.

contributory pension a worker's **pension,** the cost of which is shared by the worker and his company.

control *verb* to measure, check or keep on course; to have power over. *We have a plan of sales for each month and we place the actual sales achieved against the plan. We note the difference then decide what to do – that way we control the plan. This office is controlled from headquarters.*

control *noun* (1) the act of **controlling**; the power to **control.** *We are introducing new controls to prevent waste.* (2) *see* **control group.**

control account an **account** which checks a group of other accounts. This is done by entering in the control account the total of the **debits** and **credits** of the different accounts in the group. The **balance** of the control account should match the balance of the group of accounts.

control group a group which is the same in every way as a group which is being tested. For example, Group A, a test group (say, of housewives), may be tested to see whether they buy an existing **product** under a new label. Group B, the same in number, age, shopping habits, etc., would be offered the same product with the old label. Group B in this case is the control group, and the results of the test in Group A would be measured against the results in Group B.

controllable factors (marketing) things over which a company had some freedom of decision. For example, a company decides which **product** to make, at what selling price, through which customers, using what level of advertising. These controllable factors should be compared to the **uncontrollable** ones, e.g. the **economy,** the **competition,** new machines and methods.

controlled economy an **economy** with a very high level of government direction over what is produced, when, and at what price. Examples are UK during World War II and present-day Russia. *See also* **control** (*verb*) and **planned economy.**

controlling interest a person or group which has a majority of **voting shares** in a company. *See also* **control** (*verb*).

control unit (computers) that part of the **central processing unit** which directs the order and timing of a computer's operations.

convene to call people together for (a meeting).

convenience foods food **products** which are wholly or partly prepared or cooked when they are offered for sale.

convenience goods low-priced goods, bought regularly, which **consumers** want to buy with little effort and which are on sale in a large number of shops, e.g. canned soups, crisps, newspapers.

convenor or **convener** a member of a **trade union** who arranges union meetings usually at his place of work and who is also in charge of such meetings. *See also* **chairman.**

convertible loan stock (1) loan **stock** which is issued by a company and which carries the right to change it to **ordinary shares** or **preference shares** at some date stated on the **stock certificate.** (2) **stock** issued by the government which the holder can change into new stock (or exchange for cash).

conveyancing the legal process of **transferring** ownership of property.

cook the books (*informal*) to enter figures, or change figures, in **books of account,** dishonestly (usually for gain).

cooling-off period a period of time in which both **parties** to a **dispute** agree to take no action. This gives both time to re-consider the position. *The threatened strike has been postponed. Both sides have agreed to a cooling-off period of four weeks.*

cooperate to work together.

cooperation the act of **cooperating.**

cooperative *adjective* working together; willing to act in this way. *You will find the staff most cooperative.*

cooperative *noun* a business which is jointly owned and run by the people who work in it.

cooperative advertising the sharing of advertising costs and effort by a manufacturer and a dealer.

cooperative marketing: cooperation between a group of producers, **wholesalers** and **retailers** to produce, price and **promote** certain **products.**

cooperative society a business owned by its members who **elect** a board to run the business and who share its profits.

Cooperative Wholesale Society (*or* **CWS**) a business, jointly owned by **cooperative societies,** which buys goods on their behalf from national manufacturers. It also owns factories where it produces certain **products** (e.g. bread, coffee) also on behalf of the co-operative societies.

coordinate to organise (something) in such a way that the different parts happen together or in the right order. *A properly coordinated plan is much more likely to succeed.*

co-ownership shared ownership and often control of a business between its employees.

COPAL *see* **Cocoa Producers' Alliance.**

co-partnership a **profit-sharing** scheme in which workers have **shares** in the business in which they work.

copy (1) the words printed in an advertisement. (2) words ready to be printed as a news item in a newspaper or magazine. *We need more copy for the sports page.*

copy date the date by which material to be printed should reach the publisher to ensure it is in time for publication.

copyright the legal right to ownership by a writer of his own written work. Under the Copyright laws the work of a writer is protected from being freely copied by others unless the writer's permission is given. (This protection in law extends to the original work of artists, filmmakers, musicians, etc.).

copy test (**marketing**) a test of the **copy** (meaning 1) of an advertisement to discover the interest, understanding, appreciation, etc. of the advertisement by the reader.

copy typist a person whose job is to type the handwritten, typewritten or printed work of others.

copywriter a person who writes **copy** (meaning 1) for advertisements.

corner the market to own enough of the manufacture of a **product** or **raw material** to have control over the selling price. *They tried to corner the market in silver so that they could increase the price.*

corporate advertising advertising aimed at making a company better known and better respected.

corporate identity (*or* **corporate image**) the picture in the public's mind of a company, usually coming from the style of the company's contact with the public, e.g. by letters, company reports, advertising, **sales promotion**, delivery vehicles.

corporate objectives the long-term aims of a company, as planned by its directors (or the owner), e.g. aiming for a certain profit; aiming for a certain return on **capital employed.**

corporate planning planning by a company to set up realistic aims (or **corporate objectives**) for the future of a company.

corporate strategy high-level decisions within a company which will help to reach the long-term aims (or

corporate objectives), e.g. to **products**, prices, markets, **market share**, costs of production.

corporation an association of persons which, in law, is a separate legal body. Therefore a corporation can act on its own as if it were apart from its members.

corporation tax a tax on company profits.

correlation a measure of the relationship between two variables (e.g. the sale of umbrellas and amount of rainfall), sometimes used to help in forecasting sales. *We have discovered a strong correlation between our monthly sales of sun-tan oil and the monthly hours of sunshine.*

cost *noun* a sum of money used to pay for labour, materials, rent, salaries, etc. to provide a **product** or **service.** *See also* **expense.**

cost *verb* (1) to be sold for (a certain sum). *How much will that cost?* (2) to work out in advance how much (something) will cost.

cost accountant a person who measures, **analyses** and reports on a company's costs in any part of its activities.

cost allocation the charging of costs to certain **products**, or departments. *We allocate the advertising costs to the products on the basis of sales; so if a product has 50% of the total sales we charge it with 50% of the advertising costs.*

cost and freight *see* **C and F.**

cost-benefit analysis finding out the expected costs and the expected benefits of taking on a project so that a decision can be made to go ahead with it or not. *We did a cost-benefit analysis on opening another factory and as a result decided against it.*

cost centre a person, group, department, or piece of equipment, the cost of which is known and so can be used for **cost-control** purposes.

cost control the act of comparing actual costs with the planned (or expected) costs so that action will be taken to correct any difference in the two.

cost effectiveness of a method etc., giving value for money, often in comparison with something else, e.g. spending money on advertising in newspapers instead of on television. *We decided to switch to television advertising. We found newspaper advertising wasn't cost effective.*

costing the act or **process** of **costing** (meaning 2).

cost, insurance and freight *see* **CIF.**

cost, insurance, freight and commission *see* **CIFC.**

cost of goods sold *see* **cost of sales.**

cost of living the amount of money spent by a person or a family to keep up a certain standard of living.

cost-of-living index a measure of the **cost of living** using an **index of retail prices**, often expressed as a percentage. *The cost of living has gone up ten per cent this year.*

cost of sales (*or* **cost of goods sold**) the cost of materials, production wages, production overheads of goods sold.

cost per inquiry (advertising) a measure of the average cost of receiving an inquiry as a result of an advertising **campaign.**

cost per thousand the cost of reaching one thousand of the **target market** when advertising (in a newspaper, magazine, or on TV or radio). *We plan to use TV. The cost per thousand is much lower for us than if we use radio.*

cost-plus a method of pricing whereby all costs are added to a profit figure to reach the selling price, often used in **contracts** for **products** that take a long time to complete (e.g. ships, aircraft, roads).

cost-push inflation (*also* **wage-push inflation**) (**economics**) a **theory** that **inflation** is caused by workers demanding higher wages (without increasing **output**) followed by companies putting up prices (without an increase in demand following). *See* **demand-pull inflation.**

cost variance the difference between the planned or expected cost of something and the actual cost.

cost-volume-profit analysis a method used to examine the relationships between the cost of a **product** or **service**, the amount sold at a certain price and the profit that results.

council a group of persons appointed or **elected** to make rules or manage affairs on behalf of another body, e.g. a church, a town, a government. *The town council will decide the site for the new factories.*

Council for Mutual Economic Assistance (*or* **CMEA,** *or* **CO-MECON**) an organization formed in 1949 to encourage trade and friendly relations among its members. Membership: Albania, Bulgaria, Cuba, Czechoslovakia, German Democratic Republic, Hungary, Mongolia, Poland, Romania, Union of Soviet Socialist Republics, Vietnam. Headquarters: Moscow.

Council of Europe a group of European countries formed in London in 1949 to promote increased unity in Europe and to **cooperate** in the **economic**, social, cultural, scientific, legal and administrative areas. Membership: Austria, Belgium, Cyprus, Denmark, France, Federal Republic of Germany, Greece, Iceland, Ireland, Italy, Liechtenstein, Malta, Netherlands, Norway, Portugal, Spain, Sweden, Switzerland, Turkey, United Kingdom. Headquarters: Strasbourg, France. Official languages: English, French.

counsel *noun* a legal adviser, in England, a **barrister**, in Scotland, an **advocate.**

counsel *verb* (formal) to give advice to. *He counselled him to study the contract well.*

counterfeit *noun, adjective* illegal imitation : *counterfeit money.*

counterfoil the part of a ticket, cheque, etc. which is kept when the main part is taken off. *Keep the counterfoil as evidence of payment.*

countermand to order that (something already ordered) should not be carried out.

countersign to add a second signature to (a **document**) when this is needed for some purpose. *All cheques must be countersigned by a director.*

counter trading a form of barter, usually between countries.

countervailing duty a tax on certain goods coming into a country because another country has put on a similar tax.

coupon (1) a piece of paper given to a customer by the manufacturer of a **product** or **service** which can be used, e.g. to lessen the price. *A 'three pence off coupon for Ajax soap powder was delivered to all houses in the area.* (2) part of an advertisement, e.g. in a newspaper or magazine, inviting the reader to fill in his name and address and send it to the advertiser for more details of the product or service, or to place an order for the product or service.

coupon pack a **product** which contains a **coupon.**

cover *noun* (1) something which covers, a wrapping. *We are sending you the samples under separate cover.* (2) the outer pages of a magazine etc. (3) the **ratio** of the **dividends** of a company to its profits. (4) **security** for a loan. *What cover do you have for the loan?* (5) **insurance** against a risk. *Do you have cover in the event of a fire?*

cover charge a charge made by a restaurant etc. which is in addition to the food and drink.

covering letter a letter sent with a package etc. to explain its contents.

cover note a printed notice from an **insurance company** stating that an insurance exists and giving brief details of it.

cover page front or back pages of a magazine, where higher rates are usually charged for advertisements.

cover price the selling price of a magazine or newspaper.

C.P.U. *see* **central processing unit.**

craft union a union of workers whose job requires **manual** skills and special knowledge of the trade (or craft), usually needing a lengthy training period to be served (an **apprenticeship**) before one is fully skilled in the craft.

crate a wooden box in which goods are packed for delivery.

creative department part of an **advertising agency** where the creation of ideas and their design on paper is carried out.

credit *noun* (1) time given, or time taken, to pay for goods which have been bought. *The price for this desk is £50. We can deliver to your address now and allow you four weeks credit.* (2) an entry into an account which records money received. (*See also* **debit** *and* **letter of credit**.)
 on credit a method of paying for goods later than the time they are received. *You can have these books on credit and pay next month.*

credit *verb* (1) to believe. *I wouldn't credit him with such skill.* (2) to mark (an account) to show that money has been paid. *We have credited your account with five pounds.*

credit account a customer's account in a shop, e.g. a **department store.** This allows the customer to buy goods and pay later, as the value of the goods will be charged to the customer's credit account.

credit agency a company which for a **fee** will find out and report on the **financial** strength or weakness of a person or a company, often employed by companies before delivering goods on **credit** to new customers.

credit balance the amount of money overpaid by a customer in an **account**. When the amount of money paid (**credited**) to an account is greater than the amount owed (**debited**) the difference will be a credit balance. *See also* **debit balance**.

credit card a card from a bank, or **financial** company, or a store usually showing the signature and account number of the holder and allowing him/her to buy goods or **services** without paying at the time of sale. The amount is charged to his/her account and paid later.

credit control methods used by a company (which gives **credit**) to control the amount of credit, the time given to pay, how money is collected and its checks on new customers. *See* **credit agency.**

credit limit the point at which a company will refuse further **credit** to a customer. *I can't buy any more from Smith's department store. I've reached my credit limit.*

credit note a notice sent to a customer showing the amount of money owing to a customer because of goods being returned, or because of some error on the company's part, e.g. sending the wrong order, overcharging. *See also* **credit balance.**

creditor a person or company to whom something is owed as a result of a purchase of goods or **services** on **credit**. *He went out of business because he didn't have enough money to pay his creditors.*

credit rating the amount of **credit** that should be allowed to a customer. Some companies use a **credit agency** to help them decide the credit rating of a new customer.

credit squeeze a government decision to control the amount of loans from banks and the amount of **retail** sales on **credit.**

credit transfer *see* giro.

criterion (*plural* **criteria**) a standard against which something can be measured. *The sales manager has worked out various criteria by which the success of the sales campaign can be measured.*

crossed cheque a cheque with two lines drawn over the face of it, within which are written '& Co.' (and company). This means that the cheque can only be paid through a bank.

cubic measurement measurements of something by multiplying its length by its height by its breadth.

cum (*Latin, meaning* with) For example, stock sold **cum rights** means the buyer has rights to new issue of **stock. Shares** bought **cum dividend** means the buyer has the right to any dividend that may be about to be paid.

cumulative preference share a **preference share** which carries the right to a yearly **dividend** so that in any year when a dividend cannot be paid, it will be added to the following year's dividend and paid then.

currency coin and banknotes in use in a country for settling debts.

currency note a paper that is used as currency in a country.

currency rate the rate at which foreign currency is exchanged. *The dollar stands at 1·5 to the pound.*

currency speculator a person or company that tries to make profits from changes in **exchange rates** by selling one currency for another.

current account an account at a bank where a person or company puts money which can be **withdrawn** at any time, often done by cheque. Normally no interest is paid by the bank on money in a current account.

current assets things owned by a company which are regularly used in the business and regularly replaced (as opposed to **fixed assets**). In a manufacturing firm current assets include: **raw material, work-in-progress, finished goods, debtors, cash.** *See* appendix 2.

current liabilities a debt that must be paid by a company in the near future, usually within 12 months. In a manufacturing company these would include **creditors, bank overdraft, tax, dividends** due. *See* appendix 2.

current ratio a way of measuring a company's current debts (its **current liabilities**) in relation to what it currently owns (its **current assets**). For example, if current assets total £10,000 and current liabilities total £5,000, then the current ratio is 2:1.

current yield a measurement of the **dividend** received from a **share** in relation to the price paid for it. For example, price of share £200, dividend £20, current yield ($\frac{20}{200} \times \frac{100}{1}$ = 10%)

curriculum vitae (*or* **CV**) a brief written account of a person's past history often used to support an **application** for a job. The CV will include such things as date of birth, education, work experience etc.

custom-built made to the special design of a person or company. *For this we need a special type of drilling machine – one that's custom-built for the job.*

customer a person or company that actually buys something. *Compare with* **consumer.** A **wholesaler** of canned beans is a customer of the firm that makes the beans. The **retailer** is a customer of the wholesaler. The housewife who buys the canned beans is a customer of the retailer (and she may also be the **consumer**).

customer profile a description of the typical buyer of a **product** or **service**, usually drawn up after examining a **sample** of buyers. *The customer profile for our product is male, aged between 25 and 40, with an income of around £15,000 a year, married, and educated at university.*

customs an organisation under government control which collects taxes and duties, especially on goods coming into a country.

Customs Cooperation Council (*or* **CCC**) an organisation formed in 1952 to agree on common customs methods and to aid international trade. Membership: 87 countries. Headquarters: Brussels. Official languages: English, French.

customs duty duty or tax on goods entering or leaving a country. *See also* **excise duty.**

customs entry (*UK*) a **document** completed by an **exporter** (or **importer**) of goods, giving details of goods, weight and value. Government **statistics** of UK **imports** and **exports** are made up from this.

customs registered number a number, made up of five figures, given to an **exporter** by customs to help the export clearance of his goods. The number identifies the exporter's name and address. *See also* **clearance certificate.**

customs union a **free-trade** area in which all the countries apply the same **customs duties** (and other restrictions) on trade with countries which are outside the union. *See also* **common market.**

cut back *verb* to lower (costs) because of a fall in profit, or a fall in orders. *They're cutting back at the steel works so there's not much chance of getting a job there.*

cutback *noun* the act of **cutting back.**

cut price a price below the normal or usual price.

cut-throat competition very low prices offered by the sellers of a **product** with some sellers making their prices even lower than the others, so that little or no profit is made. *The traders in the fruit market are trying to sell off their stock of oranges before they go bad – it's real cut-throat competition as they try to get rid of them. See also* **price war**.

cutting *see* **press cutting**.

CV *see* **curriculum vitae**.

cybernetics the study of the way information moves and is controlled in business systems (e.g. a **computer**) and also in human systems (e.g. the nervous system).

D

D/A *see* **documents against acceptance**.

damages the amount of money ordered by a court to be given to a person who has suffered harm. *She sued the company for damages.*

data facts, information. *Get me all the data you can on the Smith Company.*

data base a **store** of information especially in a form which a **computer** can handle.

data-processing the handling of **data** by mechanical or **electronic** means.

date: to date until now. *He has kept a record of his sales to date.*

day book a book used to enter the daily sales and **purchases** of a company.

day release a **system** of education whereby companies allow workers one day each week away from work, without loss of pay, to attend a course of study at a college. *He is on day release to improve his chances of promotion at work.*

day shift in **shift-working**, a period of work during daylight hours, typically 8.30 a.m. to 5.30 p.m.

days of grace the number of days allowed for something, e.g. paying an **insurance premium,** after it has become due.

day-worker a worker who is regularly working during daylight hours in a company (as opposed to those working on **night shift**). *We can tell the day-workers about the new rates of pay tomorrow morning, and the nightshift workers this evening.*

dead account a customer of a company that no longer buys. *Tell our representative he can stop calling on the Ajax Company – they've closed down so they're a dead account.*

deadline a date, day or time by which something must be done. *We have to get our offer to buy into the post today if we want to meet their deadline.*

deadweight tonnage (or **d.w.t.**) the maximum weight which a ship can carry.

deal an agreement or **contract** between two or more people. *We've just signed a big deal with White Soap. We do all their advertising for twelve months.*

dealer a person who buys and sells goods either as a **wholesaler** or **retailer**. *Send out our new price list to all our dealers straight away.*

dear money money that can be borrowed only at high rates of **interest**. *See* **cheap money**.

death duty a tax on the property of a person who has died.

debenture capital company **capital** from the sale of **debentures**.

debentures: securities given for money by a company which **guarantees** the holder's rights over the company's **assets**.

debit *noun* an entry in an **account** which records money that is owed. *See also* **credit** (meaning 2).

debit *verb* to charge (an account) with the cost of goods or **services** supplied. *Did you debit the Jones account with £50 for the desk which we delivered?*

debit balance the amount of money still to be paid by an account. When the amount of money paid (**credited**) to an account is less than the amount owed (**debited**) the difference will be a debit balance. *See also* **credit balance.**

debit note a note sent to a customer showing that his **account** will be charged (**debited**) with a certain amount of money, usually sent to correct a mistake such as not charging enough for the goods when they were brought. *See also* **credit note.**

debt money, goods or services that are owed. *The amount of the Steel Company's debt is £5,000.*
in debt owing money. *They've been in debt for six months.*

debt collector a person employed to collect money that is owed to a **creditor.** *See also* **credit agency.**

debtor a person or company that owes money to another.

debtors to sales ratio a measure of the relationship between a company's **debtors** (customers who owe money) and the sales. For example if the sales are £10,000 and the debtors are £1,000 the ratio is 10:1. Sometimes the ratio is shown as a percentage: Debtors/Sales × 100 = 10%.

debug to search for and correct errors in (a **computer program**).

decentralization the **process** of moving some of the power to control a company from the head office to branches or departments of the company. *The company had grown so large that it became difficult for the directors to control it and so they introduced decentralisation.*

decision-making unit (*or* **D.M.U.**) a group of people who influence a decision to buy something. For example if a company is planning to buy an expensive machine the people who will help to decide may include the company owner (or **managing director**) the factory manager, the buyer, and the

sales manager (who will sell the **product** that the machine makes). *An important decision-making unit for the family car is made up of the husband, the wife, and the oldest child.*

decision tree a chart which shows the likely results (in branch form, hence the name) that stem from different decisions which could be taken to solve a problem.

deck cargo: cargo carried on the deck of a ship (rather than in the hold and thus more at risk in a storm).

declaration of solvency a statement made on oath by the directors of a company that it can pay all of its debts within twelve months, demanded by the Companies Acts when a company is closing down voluntarily.

deed a written agreement containing a promise by someone to do something (or not to do something) which is signed, may have a **seal** on it, a legal **contract.**

deed of covenant a written agreement to pay a fixed sum of money to a person or an organisation (usually a charity) for a stated number of years.

default *verb* (1) to fail to pay a debt when it is due. *He defaulted on the payment of the loan.* (2) to fail to appear in court when ordered to by law.

default *noun* (1) the act of **defaulting.** (2) an option in a **computer program** which the computer will choose if no other is chosen by the user.

defect a fault in a **product.** *The car had a defect in the steering.*

defendant (*law*) the person against whom a **charge** (meaning 2) has been brought. *See* **plaintiff.**

deferred put off (until a later date).

deferred annuity a type of **annuity** which begins at some time in the future.

deferred creditor a person who is owed money by a **bankrupt** but who cannot be paid until others to whom the bankrupt owes money are fully paid, e.g. the wife of a **bankrupt.**

deficit (1) the amount of something which is lacking or cannot be found. *There was a deficit of ten items in the goods which were delivered.* (2) the amount by which a person's expenses are greater than his/her **income.** *At the end of the week she had a deficit in her bank account of £20.*

deflate to bring about **deflation** in (the **economy** of a country). *The government plans to deflate the economy.*

deflation lowering of the prices of goods and **services** due to a fall in the level of work in the nation, the level of **incomes**, and the level of demand. *See also* **inflation.**

defranchise *see* **disenfranchise**.

del credere agent a special type of **agent** who gets orders for goods from a buyer and who also **guarantees** that the buyer will pay for them. The agent is usually paid a higher **commission** for this extra risk.

delegate *verb* to give (a person) the power to act on one's behalf. (2) to give (some of one's duties and powers) to a **subordinate.**

delegate *noun* a person who represents another person, or group of people at meetings. *The delegate from the trade union arose to speak. See also* **delegation.**

delegation (1) the act of **delegating.** (2) (management) the act of giving up some of one's duties and powers to a **subordinate**, perhaps because one has too much to do, or as a kind of training. (3) a group of **delegates.** *The Russian delegation arrived today.*

deliver to hand over (goods) to someone else.

delivery (1) the act of **delivering.** (2) part or all of an order on the way to a buyer or that has just arrived at a buyer's **premises.** *When the delivery arrived there were two cases short.*

delivery note a **document** which is handed over with goods as they are **delivered** to the customer, usually listing and describing the goods so that the customer can check it against what he has actually received.

demand *noun* (**economics**) the amount of a **product** or **service** wanted by people who are prepared to pay the **going price** for that product or service. *There are times when gold is in very high demand. There is no demand for red shoes this year.*

demand *verb* to **claim** as if by right. *The manager listened to the union's demands.*

demand analysis an examination of what affects the demand for a **product** or **service.**

demand curve a **graph** which shows the **estimated** demands for a **product** at different prices. *See also* **demand schedule**.

demand forecasting a method of finding out what the demand for a **product** or **service** is likely to be at different prices so that the price which might give the greatest profit can be shown.

demand-pull inflation (*or* **demand inflation**) (**economics**) a **theory** that **inflation** is caused by an increase in demand for goods which is greater than industry's ability to supply. *See also* **inflation, cost-push inflation.**

demand schedule a **table** or list of the **demand** for a **product** or **service** at various prices. *See also* **demand curve.**

demarcation dispute a disagreement between groups of workers belonging to different **trade unions** over which workers are allowed to do a certain job.

demography the study of human population, birth rates, death rates, marriage, employment, age groups etc.

demonstrate (1) to show, especially how (something) works or how (something) is done. *We can demonstrate the new machine now.* (2) to gather in large numbers in a public place to show feelings about something. *Miners have been demonstrating about pit closures for about three days.*

demonstration (1) a method of getting people to buy a **product** by showing it in action. *Our salesman will be happy to give you a demonstration of the new vacuum cleaner.* (2) a very large number of people who gather in a public place to show their feelings about something. *The workers held a big demonstration against the cut in pay.*

demote to put into a lower rank or position. *He's so poor at his new job we may have to demote him. See also* **promote** (meaning 1).

demotion the act of **demoting.**

demurrage (1) the amount of money paid when goods have to be held at a port or airport because of a delay in having the goods cleared. (2) the amount of money paid to the owner of a ship when his ship is delayed from unloading **cargo.**

denationalisation the act of **denationalising.**

denationalise to bring (a business or industry) out of public ownership and put it into private ownership. *See also* **nationalise, nationalised industry.**

denomination name for one of the grades into which certain things, especially money, are divided. *We have most denominations of banknotes.*

department a part of an organisation, usually responsible for a certain activity: *the sales department, the accounts department.*

Department of Trade and Industry (*or* **DTI**) (*UK*) a govern-ment department which gives advice and information to commercial and industrial organisations, e.g. on markets, buyers, **agents, EEC** rules, **statistics, imports, exports, tariffs.**

department store a large **retail** store with a number of departments or sections, each selling a different kind of goods, e.g. a furniture department, a men's clothing department.

deposit *noun* (1) an amount of money given to the seller of an article by the person buying it as a first payment, the buyer paying the rest of the money at a later time, either all at once or in equal amounts. *See also* **hire purchase**. (2) an amount of money left with a bank, usually to get **interest** on it, but perhaps also for safekeeping.

deposit *verb* (1) to leave in a bank (as in **deposit** meaning 1). *See also* **deposit account; depositor.** (2) to give (money) as a **deposit** (meaning 1).

deposit account a **bank account** in which money is kept with the aim of earning **interest.** *See also* **current account.**

depositor a person who puts money into a **bank account.** *See also* **deposit.**

depository a person with whom or a place where things of value are placed for safekeeping.

depot (1) a place where goods are stored, especially while waiting to be sent out. (2) a place where buses etc. are kept and **serviced.** (3) (*US*) a railway station.

depreciate to go down in value.

depreciation (1) a lowering in the value of a **fixed asset** (e.g. machinery) over a period of time. *See also* **amortisation.** (2) a lowering in the value of a currency as compared to another currency. *See also* **appreciate.**

depression a long period of low business activity resulting in high unemployment. *See also* **boom; recession; slump; trade cycle.**

depth interview (**market research**) a long conversation with a customer or **client** with the aim of getting information which might not be easy to get by other methods.

derived demand (*or* **indirect demand**) demand for goods or materials which are used in making some other **product** (which is directly needed by customers). A demand for motor cars will lead to a derived demand for the steel used to make them.

derv (*trademark: stands for* diesel-engined road vehicle) fuel used by heavy lorries etc.

design *verb* to plan how (something) is to be made: *to design a new factory.*

design *noun* (1) a plan or drawing of something that is to be made: *a design for a new car.* (2) the way something has been put together considering either what it has to do, or its appearance: *a clever design; an attractive design.* (3) the art of planning how things are to be made, especially in terms of appearance: *a student of design.*

designate appointed to a post but not yet actually in it: *the managing director designate.*

desk research finding out about something, e.g. the sales of an industry, by using information which has been already published in some form. *See also* **field research.**

despatch *see* **dispatch.**

destination the place to which a person or thing is going. *How long will the parcel take to reach its destination?*

devaluation a lowering of the value of a currency with regard to other currencies, especially when **fixed exchange rates** are in use, and the lowering is decided by the government. *See also* **revaluation.**

developing country (*or* **less developed country, under-developed country, emerging country**) a country which has begun to make some progress in using its **resources** in commerce and/or industry.

development (1) the act of using the results of research to make a **product** more attractive, useful, profitable etc. *See also* **research and development.** (2) using the **resources** of an area to make it productive. (3) an area of land which has been made productive or profitable by e.g. planting of crops or building of houses.

development area (*UK*) a part of the country which has been given special government help in order to attract business to it.

deviation a departure from what is normal, e.g. of a ship from its normal route; unless this is done for a good reason, it can make the ship's **insurance** cover **void**.

device a machine or tool which has been designed for a certain purpose.

diary method a **technique** used in **consumer** research by which a **sample** of consumers keep a record of the things they buy over a certain period of time. This shows changes in the level of sales of certain **products** and the effects of current advertising.

dictate (1) to say (something) out loud so that someone else can write it down. *She dictates all her letters.* (2) to order or force other people to do something.

dictation the act of **dictating**; what is **dictated** (meaning 1).

difference especially in banking, the difference between the amount of cash a **cashier** has at the end of a day and the amount stated in the records.

differential a difference in pay which follows different levels of experience, responsibility etc. between workers.

differential advantage something about a **product** or **service** which to a user makes it preferable to another product or service. *See also* **competitive advantage.**

digital computer a type of **computer** which can operate on **data** in number form. *See also* **analog computer.**

diploma a **certificate**, e.g. to show that one has passed the examinations of a college etc.

direct access (*or* **random access**) (**computers**) a method of storing **data** which allows it to be retrieved, from or stored at a certain **location.**

direct cost a cost directly connected with the production of a **product**, e.g. the cost of materials used or the wages paid to a worker who actually makes it.

direct expense a cost directly connected to some business activity, e.g. the wages of the people who make a **product.**

direct labour (*or* **direct wages**) (1) workers who actually make a **product.** *See* **direct cost.** (2) (*UK*) workers who are directly employed by a **local authority** on building houses and factories.

direct mail selling goods by post, i.e. by sending advertisements directly to the address of the likely buyer, inviting him/her to order by mail (by post) using an order form provided.

direct-mail shot a set of descriptions of a **product** with order forms sent to a number of different addresses at the same time. *See also* **direct mail.**

direct materials cost any payment for materials which are directly linked to the making or selling of a **product**, e.g. the cost of boxes or cartons to protect the goods.

director (1) a person chosen by the **shareholders** of a company to run the company on their behalf. (2) a person in charge of a unit or **project.**

directors' report a yearly statement from the directors of a company to their **shareholders** explaining those events which affected the year's **financial** results and giving their opinion of the company's future.

directory a book giving lists of information, often in alphabetical order: *telephone directory.*

direct selling a method of selling goods to the public without using a **retailer**, e.g. by **mail order, door-to-door selling.**

direct wages *see* **direct labour.**

disablement benefits (*UK*) money paid by the government to a person who cannot work because of injury received at work.

disc *see* **disk.**

discharge *verb* (1) to **dismiss** (a person) from employment. (2) to release (a person) from a **contract.** (3) to show formally that the conditions of a contract or agreement, **insurance policy** etc. have been met, and that one has no further claim. *He has discharged his debts.*

discharge *noun* the act of **discharging;** the evidence of this.

discharged bankrupt a person who has satisfied a court that he has done everything possible to pay his debts; this usually means that he is freed from any debts that have still not been paid. *See* **discharge** meaning 3.

discount *verb* (1) to lower the price of (something), often by a certain percentage to increase the sale. (2) to sell (a **bill of exchange**) to a third **party** (e.g. a bank) at a lower value than its **face value** in order to receive money immediately. (3) the difference between a **share**'s face value and the lower value of its selling price.

discount *noun* (1) a lowering in the price of something: *to be sold at a discount.* (2) an amount by which a price has been lowered: *a discount of 20%.*

discounted cash flow (*or* **DCF**) a method of estimating the value of money that will come from an **investment**, e.g. a new factory or machine, over the coming years. Since money loses its value over time (£1 buys less now than 3 years ago) a company will want to find out the real value (i.e. today's value) of future flows of earnings from investments. This is worked out by **calculating** at today's value the estimated income of cash over the life of the investment.

discount house (1) an organisation which buys **bills of exchange** at lower than their **face value**, in this way providing immediate cash for the owners of the bills. (2) = **discount store.**

discount rate the **interest rate** which banks charge for providing immediate cash for **bills of exchange.**

discount store (*also* **discount house**) a large **retail** shop which sells goods at lowered prices. Profit is made by cutting down the usual range of goods and the **service**, e.g. delivery to customers.

discretionary income the amount of a person's salary or wages which is left over after he/she has met all necessary expenses (e.g. rent, heating) and which can therefore be spent on whatever he/she as a **consumer** wishes to buy.

discriminate (against) to practise **discrimination** against a person, or group of people. *It is now illegal to discriminate against women in advertising of jobs.*

discrimination the act of treating some people unfairly, especially because of their sex, race, nationality, religion or political beliefs.

disenfranchise (*or* **defranchise**) (1) to take away from (a person) the right to vote. (2) to take away a **franchise**, or any other special trading privilege from.

dishonour to refuse to accept or pay (something, e.g. a properly presented cheque or **bill of exchange**). *See* **notary public.**

disinflation a lesser kind of **deflation**, in which the amount that people have to spend is reduced but unemployment is not high. *See also* **deflation, inflation.**

disk (**computers**) *see* **floppy disk, hard disk, magnetic disk.**

disk drive (**computers**) a machine which can record information onto a **floppy disk** or a **hard disk** and can play back such information.

dismiss to send (a person) away, especially from a job.

dismissal the act of **dismissing.**

dispatch (*or* **despatch**) *verb* (1) to send (goods, materials etc.) to the person who has ordered them. *I want all of today's orders dispatched by tomorrow.* (2) to do (a job or task) quickly.

dispatch (*or* **despatch**) *noun* (1) the act of sending a person or thing to a certain place. *The dispatch of these goods is urgent.* (2) an official report: *a dispatch from the Home Office.*

dispatch department (*or* **despatch department**) the department of a business which is concerned with the sending of goods to customers.

display (1) the arrangement of things to be sold so as to attract the attention of possible customers. *See also* **display advertising** (2) (**computers**) the **output** of information on a **visual display unit.**

display advertising a kind of advertising in newspapers and magazines which uses headlines, pictures, design and space to attract the reader's attention. *Compare with* **classified advertising.**

disposable of goods, designed so that they can be thrown away after use : *disposable towels.*

disposable personal income the amount of a person's wage or salary which he/she can spend after **income tax, national insurance** etc. have been taken off.

dispute a disagreement, e.g. between management and workers. *Industrial disputes often lead to strikes.*

dissolution the act of **dissolving.**

dissolve to end (a company, partnership etc.) *See also* **liquidate, wind up.**

distribute to cause (goods) to go from maker to user.

distribution (1) the actual movement of goods between companies. *See* **physical distribution.** (2) the way in which goods go from maker to user, e.g. from manufacturer to **wholesaler** to **retailer.** *See also* **channel of distribution** and Appendix 7.

distribution channel *see* **channel of distribution.**

distribution cost a cost in getting goods from the producer to the user, e.g. of sending goods by rail.

distributor a person who sells goods made by someone else, e.g. a **wholesaler** or **retailer.** *See also* **channel of distribution** and Appendix 7.

diversification the act or **process** of **diversifying.**

diversify (1) of a company, to go into new markets with new **products** or **services** (often done by taking over another company) so as to lessen the risks of only having a few products in a few markets. (2) to spread **investments,** e.g. **stocks** and **shares,** over different industries so as to lessen the risks if some investments should fail.

divestment a **process** by which a company sells its **assets** or **transfers** the ownership of part of its business to another company.

dividend (1) the amount of money paid out of profits by a company to its **shareholders,** usually a percentage of the **nominal value** of the **shares** (e.g. a **dividend** of ten percent) or as so much to the pound, dollar etc. (e.g. a dividend of 10p). (2) the amount of money paid out to the **creditors** of a **bankrupt,** expressed in the same way as (1).

dividend cover a method of expressing how much of the **net profit** of a company has been paid to the **shareholders** in the form of **dividends.** For example a dividend is 'three times covered' if one third of its net profits have been paid out in dividends.

dividend warrant a cheque which is used to pay **dividends** to **shareholders** and can be cashed at a bank, and which also contains a **tax voucher,** which shows that tax has been paid on the dividend.

dividend yield the amount paid in **dividend** as a percentage of the market price of the **share.** For example if the market price of the share is £1 a dividend of 25p would equal a dividend yield of 25%.

division a part of something which is divided up, e.g. a company which is part of a larger group of companies: *Jones & Co., a division of the Waterman Group.*

division of labour a **system** of producing goods by splitting the **process** of manufacturing into different parts and arranging for each part to be carried out by a different set of workers. *See also* **assembly line.**

dock dues the **toll** paid by ships when they enter or leave a dock, used for the upkeep of the dock.

document a piece of paper which gives proof of something and/or information about it.

document against acceptance (*or* **D/A**) describes the conditions under which the **documents** (e.g.

export invoice, bill of lading, insurance certificate etc.) which are attached to a **bill of exchange** will be given to a foreign buyer, i.e. only when he accepts the accompanying bill of exchange. He can then collect the goods. See also **bill of exchange.**

document against payment (or **D/P**) describes the conditions under which the **documents** (e.g. **export invoice, bill of lading, insurance certificate** etc.) attached to a **bill of exchange** will be given to a foreign buyer, i.e. only when he pays the bill of exchange immediately. He can then collect the goods.

documentary bill of exchange a bill of exchange to which **documents** (e.g. **export invoice, insurance certificate, bill of lading, certificate of origin**) are attached. An **exporter** will send it to a foreign customer as proof that he has sent off the goods agreed to in the **contract** of sale, or order, so that the foreign customer will **accept** the bill of exchange. See also **bill of exchange.**

documentary credit see **letter of credit, documentary.**

do-it-yourself the making or repairing of things, e.g. in the home, normally done by tradesmen; the materials needed for this: a do-it-yourself shop.

dole (informal) = **unemployment benefit**: to be on the dole.

dollar a unit of money used by the US and many other countries. See Appendix 10.

dollar area the area of the world where the US dollar is accepted as standard currency, e.g. Medway Islands, Panama Canal Zone, Puerto Rico.

door-to-door selling a method of selling goods by calling on people in their own houses. See also **canvass.**

dormant account a customer who used to buy goods regularly but no longer does so, though he might again in the future. Compare with **dead account.**

double crown a base unit of size for **posters** (20 inches by 30 inches, 508mm × 762mm).

double indemnity (US) a provision in a **life insurance policy**, which allows for twice the amount insured to be paid if the person insured dies by accident, or under other specified conditions. See also **indemnity.**

double-page spread (or **centre spread**) (advertising) a display of a single advertisement right across two pages of a newspaper or magazine.

double time wages at twice the normal rate for working at certain times (e.g. on Sundays) or under certain conditions.

Dow Jones Index (or **Dow Jones Industrial Average**) the average price of thirty of the most important company **shares** in the New York **stock market**, published daily by the Dow Jones financial news service, and intended to give an idea of how well or badly the US stock market is doing. See also **Financial Times industrial ordinary share index.**

downgrade (1) to lower the importance of or payment for (a certain post). (2) to put (a person) in a lower post than the one he/she was in. See also **demotion.**

down market of goods or **services**, at the cheaper, lower-quality end of the market: to go down market, i.e. to start providing goods or services which are cheaper and of lower quality than before.

down payment the money which is paid at the signing of a **mortgage** or **hire-purchase** agreement.

downtime (1) the time when machinery is not in use because of breakdown, routine repairs etc. (2) the time when a worker is being paid but cannot do his work for reasons that are not his fault, e.g. because a machine is being repaired.

D/P *see* **documents against payment.**

draft (1) a written order to a bank to pay a certain sum to a named person, or to the bearer of the order. (2) a **bill of exchange.** (3) a first, rough version of a letter or **document.** *This is just a first draft of the report.*

draw (1) to pull; to attract. *The new window display should draw people in from the street.* (2) to take out. *He drew £100 out of his account.* (3) to write out (a cheque etc.) (4) of money, to earn (**interest**).

drawback a repayment of **duty** which has been paid on **imported** goods when these goods are later **exported.**

drawee a person, company, bank etc. that is ordered to make a payment in a **bill of exchange**, cheque or **draft.** *See also* **drawer.**

drawer a person, company, bank etc. that draws up (i.e. writes) a **bill of exchange**, cheque or **draft** ordering someone to pay money to a third person etc. (known as the **payee**).

drill *verb* to bore into something, e.g. into the earth for oil.

drill *noun* a machine or tool for doing this.

drilling crew a group of workers who are employed to operate **drills** used for getting oil or other minerals.

drill ship a ship used in **offshore** oil operations which carries the **rig** needed for **drilling** for oil and natural gases. *See also* **off-shore oilfield; oil rig.**

drop shipment an order from a manufacturer large enough to be delivered directly to a company's branch, or shop (instead of going to a company's central store then from there to the branch).

dry goods soft goods, such as fabrics, cloths, textiles.

DTI *see* **Department of Trade and Industry.**

due date the date on which a **bill** etc. has to be paid.

dues money which has to be paid, e.g. for the use of something: *dock dues.*

dummy (1) something which is made as a copy of the real thing, e.g. to show what it will be like when finished. (2) a model of a human figure, used to show clothes. (3) a person who allows his name to be used in someone else's business deal (so that the name of the person actually doing the deal does not become known).

dump bin (*or* **dump display**) a container in a shop into which goods are piled for sale, usually in an untidy way so as to attract shoppers looking for a bargain.

dumping an unfair trade practice of sending goods that cannot be sold in the home market into overseas markets at a price much lower than the manufacturer's home market, so as to keep up production at home or else to get a price advantage over competitors in the overseas market.

duplicate *noun* something exactly like something else, a copy.

duplicate *adjective* of which there is a **duplicate**. *This is a duplicate copy of the report.*

duplicate *verb* to make a copy of.

durable goods goods which are supposed to remain in use for some time, e.g. televisions, washing machines. *See also* **consumer durables.**

Dutch auction a type of **auction** where the **auctioneer** starts at a high price and gradually works his way down until there is a **bid** for the article sold.

duty (1) a government tax on goods, especially **imported** goods. (2)

something which a person has to do as part of his/her job. *His first duty in the morning is to open all letters.*

duty-free of goods, on which no **duty** (meaning 1) has to be paid.

duty-free shop a shop, e.g. in an international airport, where goods are sold cheaply because they are free from certain kinds of **duty**.

E

E and OE *see* **errors and omissions excepted.**

early closing the closing of shops etc. at lunch-time on a certain day of the week, varying from district to district. *Early closing here is on Wednesday.*

early shift in **shift working,** the period of work during the early part of the day, e.g. 8 am–5 pm.

early warning system a technique for finding out in good time if someone is going wrong with something in a business operation. *We have an early warning system which tells us when we are getting low on fuel.*

earned income (*UK*) money which is earned because of one's direct effort in work (as contrasted with money earned from **investments**), and therefore sometimes taxed less heavily. *See also* **unearned income.**

earnest money money paid as a first payment, showing that one means to pay the full amount later.

earnings everything that one earns. *You must declare all your earnings for income tax.*

earnings yield earnings per **ordinary share** (after tax) × 100 and divided by the market price of the

$$\text{share} = \frac{\text{earnings} \times 100}{\text{market price}}$$

ease of prices on the **stock exchange,** to fall a little.

easy money a situation when **interest** rates are low and banks and **building societies** have plenty of **funds** to lend.

ECGD *see* **Export Credits Guarantee Department.**

econometrics the study of the relationships, if any, between **economic** variables (e.g. unemployment, wages) using mathematical and **statistical** methods.

economic (1) most efficient; most profitable; least wasteful. *They decided it was more economic to spend £10,000 on a new salesman than £10,000 on a new advertising campaign.* (2) connected with the **economy** or with the science of **economics**: *economic problems; an economic survey.*

economical cheap to run etc., not wasteful: *an economical car. We try to use economical methods.*

economic depression *see* **slump.**

economic development the **process** of improvement of the wealth of a country or one of its regions, e.g. by increasing the production of food etc., building new roads, docks, railways, etc. *See also* **economic growth.**

economic geography the study of the earth with special reference to the **natural resources** and the development of trade and industry.

economic goods things which are useful but not easy to get when one wants them and therefore the goods have a price.

economic growth the rate at which the **national income** of a country increases, usually measured by the **gross national product** per head of population.

economic order quantity (*or* **EOQ**) the best amount of something to order, considering e.g. the cost of ordering (A); the cost of carrying it in **stock** (R); its annual sales or level of use (S); its unit cost (V).

economic planning a **system** of organising the **economy** (meaning 2) of a country following a plan worked out by the government. *See also* **controlled economy, planned economy.**

economics the study of the use of scarce **resources** in the production and marketing of goods and **services.**

economic system the way in which the industry, trade and commerce of a country is organised. *See also* **capitalism; mixed economy; socialism.**

economic trend the general direction in which the **economy** (meaning 2) of a country is developing.

economic warfare a situation in which countries struggle against each other, using trade and **financial** measures. *See also* **embargo.**

economies of scale ways of making goods more cheaply by making more of them, through the use of machinery, **automation** etc.

economise to try to spend less money and to waste less.

economist a person who writes and lectures on the subject of **economics.**

economy (1) the **financial** state of a country. *The government says it is trying to improve the economy of the country.* (2) the operation of a country's business activities. *There is an article this week on recent changes in the British economy.* (3) not being wasteful. *We must use the utmost economy.*

edge up of prices on the **stock exchange,** to rise a little.

edit (1) to prepare (someone else's writing) for publication in a newspaper, magazine or book. *His job is to edit all new articles before they are sent to the printer.* (2) prepare (a film or tape recording) by cutting or by putting material into a different order.

edition the total number of copies of a book, magazine or newspaper produced at any one time. *The book sold so well that it went into a second edition.*

editor a person who **edits** a newspaper, magazine, book, film, or tape recording; the person in charge of the editing of a newspaper or magazine.

editorial a **column** or columns of a newspaper or magazine giving the editor's opinion on some aspect of the news.

EDP *see* **electronic data processing.**

educational technology modern methods of giving knowledge or information (especially in schools, colleges and universities), using modern equipment, e.g. TV, **video**, film, slides, tapes, **word processors, computers.**

EEC *see* **European Economic Community.**

effect (1) a result. *Our advertising had the desired effect – sales increased.* (2) meaning. *I can't remember the exact words he used but he said we were all first class workers, or words to that effect.* (3) in plural goods or belongings. *He took everything with him – all his personal effects.*
   take effect to come into being, to begin to operate. *The new law takes effect from Monday.*

effective able to bring about the planned result. *Our sales training was effective – all our salesmen reached their sales targets.*

effective date the actual date of the start of a **contract** or agreement.

effective demand the total demand for a **product** or **service** at a certain price.

efficiency the state of being **efficient.**

efficient able to work speedily, or well, without waste or with very little waste. *These new machines are highly efficient.*

EFTA *see* **European Free Trade Association.**

Eight-twenty law *see* **Pareto's Law.**

elastic demand demand which changes greatly as a result of a small change in price, e.g. of sugar, tea, coffee, where a small price reduction can result in a very high sale.

elastic supply supply when a small change in price results in a large change in the supply of the **product.**

elect to choose by voting. *She was elected chairman of the board.*

election the act or **process** of **electing.**

electronic of or using **devices** in which electrons move in a vacuum, gas etc.

electronic data processing (or **EDP**) putting **data** (i.e. facts, numbers etc.) into a **computer** for the purpose of arranging the data into information which can be **analysed.**

embargo (1) an official order stopping the movement of goods, especially ships' **cargo.** *There is an embargo on certain goods going to Russia. See also* **sanction** (meaning 2). (2) the stopping of the publishing of news until a certain time or date. *There is an embargo on publishing the names of the people killed in the accident until their families have been informed.*

embassy the house and/or office of an ambassador; the ambassador and the people who work for him.

embezzle to use (money or property) that does not belong to one. *It turned out that the manager was embezzling the company's money.*

emerging country *see* **developing country.**

emolument (*formal*) a **fee**, pay, salary.

employ (1) to give paid work to. *When the business expands we shall employ more workers.* (2) (*formal*) to use. *Several different methods are employed in this process.*

employee (*or* **employed person**) a person who is working for a company or other organisation (as opposed to a **self-employed person**).

employee benefits things of value apart from wages or salary that an employee may receive, e.g. use of a company car, low-priced meals, or **luncheon vouchers.**

employee handbook a book given to new employees of a company which contains information about the company such as company history, **products, trade unions,** safety arrangements, **dispute** procedures.

employee participation workers sharing in the responsibility of making decisions about the company's future plans, usually with employees having seats on the **board of directors.**

employer a person or company that pays people to do work.

employer's association (*also* **employers' organisation**) a group of owners or directors of companies whose main purpose is to keep good relations between workers and the companies they work for. *Compare with* **trade association.**

employment (1) the state of having a job. *I am in regular employment at last after weeks of being without a job.* (2) the kind of job one is employed in. *My present employment is teaching.*

employment agency a company which supplies workers to other companies for payment.

employment exchange *see* **job centre.**

encash to exchange (a cheque etc.) for cash.

enclose to put (something) in an envelope, parcel etc., along with something else, especially a letter. *I enclose a cheque for £50.*

enclosure (*or* **encl.**) something **enclosed**. *The enclosures with his letter included a cheque for £50.*

end-on course a college or university course made up of six months in college followed by six months in industry. Two new groups of students will thus join the course each year.

endorse (1) to sign one's name on the back of (a **document**, e.g. a cheque). (2) to put a note or stamp on (a driving **licence**) showing that the holder has committed a motoring **offence**. *He had his licence endorsed three times for dangerous driving.* (3) to give one's support to (an action or point of view). *I endorse what you say.* (4) to lend one's name in support of (a **product**). *A well-known actress endorsed their product.*

endorsee a person who is named on a cheque or **bill of exchange** as having rights to it.

endorsement the act of **endorsing**; the signature or other sign that this has been done.

endorser a person who puts an **endorsement** on a **document**, especially a **bill of exchange**.

endowment a gift of regular sums of money to an organisation: *a hospital endowment.*

endowment assurance a **life assurance** where the benefit is payable at the end of an agreed time if the person buying the **policy** is still living, or at the time of death (if he/she dies earlier).

end product a completed **product** at the finish of a production **process**. *In the factory we mix chemicals but the end product is an expensive perfume.*

end user the person who actually uses something. *The buyer of the baby food is usually the mother but the end user is the baby. See* **consumer.**

engaged of a telephone line, toilet etc, already being used. *I can't get through. The line's engaged.*

enlargement a copy larger than the original, especially of a photograph. *Make an enlargement of this picture and we'll use it on the front page of the newspaper.*

enquire (*or* **inquire**) to ask (about something).

enquiry (*or* **inquiry**) (1) the act of **enquiring**. *We have had many enquiries about our new product but so far very few sales.* (2) a careful examination of the facts about something. *There is to be a public enquiry about the spillage of waste into the river.*

enter (1) to go or come in(to). (2) to put (something) into a list, book or record, e.g. an amount of money into an account.

enterprise (1) any type of business. *His firm is quite a small enterprise now though it used to be one of the biggest enterprises in town.* (2) courage or imagination in doing things. *The way he secured those export orders showed great enterprise. See also* **private enterprise.**

entertainment (1) something amusing; something done for amusement. (2) the giving of food and drink, e.g. to business clients: *entertainment allowance.*

entrepreneur a person who owns a business and runs it, and takes the **financial** risks.

entry (1) the act of **entering**. (2) a record that has been **entered** (meaning 2).

environment the outside conditions, especially those in which people work or live. *They claimed that the smoke from the company's factory was harming the environment. See* **external environment.**

environmental lobby a group of people who try to get others in authority (usually members of parliament) to take action to stop damage to the natural surroundings (e.g. trees, land, air, animals). *There is an environmental lobby trying to ban the use of chemicals on the land.*

EOQ *see* **economic order quantity.**

equal pay pay that is the same for men and women who are doing the same work.

equilibrium price the price at which the quantity demanded equals the quantity supplied and where demand and supply are not likely to change.

equipment (1) things which are used in the carrying out of an activity. *The factory needs more equipment.* (2) the act of providing equipment.

equities = **equity** (meaning 3).

equity (1) fairness, justice. (2) the rights of ordinary **shareholders** to a **share** in the profits of a company. (3) the **ordinary shares** in a company.

equity capital that part of the total **capital** of a company which belongs to the owners of the business (the **ordinary shareholders**).

eraser a piece of rubber etc. which can remove pencil, ink or typewriter writing or marks.

ergonomics the study of the relationship between man and his work, his tools, machines, and surroundings, with the aim of improving **output** by improving the design of work **processes**, machines etc.

errors and omissions excepted (*or* **E and OE**) sometimes used in letters, **invoices**, statements to state that the company is not liable for any clerical mistakes or omissions.

escalation clause the part of a **contract** which allows for price rises due to a rise in materials and wages.

escape clause the part of a **contract** which allows one of the **parties** under certain conditions to **withdraw** from the contract without paying any penalty.

establish to set up, to bring into being. *The company was established in 1843.*

established brand a well-known **product** or **brand** which has a high level of sales.

establishment (1) the act of **establishing**. (2) a large business. *Clark and Co is a first class establishment.* (3) the people, buildings and machines within a large organisation.

establishment charges the costs of people, machines, buildings within a large company. The **indirect costs** of a company. *See also* **establishment** (meaning 2).

estate all the property or possessions of a person, especially someone who has died. (2) a large area of land used for a certain purpose; *an industrial estate. They own an estate in the north.*

estate agent a person whose business is to bring buyers and sellers of houses into contact with each other. *I've been to the estate agent to see if he will sell my house for me. See also* **agent.**

estimate *verb* to judge how much something will cost, or to judge the length of time, or the size etc. *Can you estimate the cost of building the factory?*

estimate *noun* a judgement of the cost, time, etc. *I've received three estimates from three different firms. Compare with* **quotation.**

estimator a person whose job it is to **estimate** costs etc.

estoppel (*law*) a rule whereby a person is prevented (or **estopped**) from denying something he has said or written. This rule of law for example could stop a company from denying the authority of its **agent** when it is obvious that such an agency is in existence.

Euro-dollars: dollars in European banks which are used for trade in Europe, e.g. dollars in an English bank which are lent to a company in France.

European Community *see* **European Economic Community.**

European Court of Justice the law court of the **European Economic Community** responsible for putting into effect the rules of the **Treaty** of Rome. It meets in Luxembourg and has a judge from each member state.

European Economic Community (*or* **EEC,** *or* **Common Market**) a group of countries set up by the **Treaty** of Rome in 1957. Its purposes are: to establish a **common market** within its member states; to encourage the development of **economic** activities and to raise the **standard of living** of the member states. Members: Belgium, Denmark, France, Federal Republic of Germany, Greece, Ireland, Italy, Luxembourg, Netherlands, United Kingdom. Headquarters: Brussels. Official languages: Danish, Dutch, English, French, German, Greek, Irish, Italian.

European Free Trade Association (*or* **EFTA**) a group of countries set up in 1960 for the purposes of increasing trade, employment, and the **standard of living** of its members. Membership: Austria, Iceland, Norway, Portugal, Sweden, Switzerland. Headquarters: Geneva. Working language: English.

evade to try to escape or avoid doing (something, e.g. paying tax).

evasion the act of **evading.**

evict to take (a person) away from a house or land by force or law.

eviction order an order by a court of law that a person be **evicted.**

ex (*Latin, meaning* out of; from). For example *ex factory, ex works,* i.e. the price quoted includes all costs up to the point when the goods leave the seller's works. Any charges after that have to be paid by the buyer.

excess *noun, adjective* (an amount which is) above a certain limit, more than is necessary, spare: *excess capacity; excess demand.*

excess supply a situation when the supply of a **product** is greater than the demand for it.

exchange *verb* to give one thing for another. *He exchanged the faulty product for a new one.*

exchange *noun* (1) the act of **exchanging.** (2) the act of **exchanging** the money of one country for the money of another. (3) a building in which things are **exchanged**, bought or sold: *stock exchange.* (4) (*also* **telephone exchange**) a building in which telephone lines and calls are connected.

exchange control a control put by a country on the buying and selling of other currencies and on the way its own currency is to be used to settle foreign debts.

exchange rate the rate (value) at which a currency may be exchanged for another currency, e.g. £1 = $1.40.

exchequer (*UK*) the government department in charge of collecting public money. The **Chancellor of the Exchequer** is the minister in charge of this department.

excise duty a tax put by a country on certain goods produced in that country, e.g. on tobacco and alcohol in the UK.

exclusion clause a clause in a **contract** which states that something is not covered by the contract, e.g. what risks are not covered by an **insurance policy.**

exclusive *adjective* limited to certain people or organisations only. *We have exclusive rights in this market. This is a very exclusive club.*

exclusive *noun* an important piece of news, photograph etc. which is given to one newspaper alone, or to one radio or television company. *I can see the Daily Star has an exclusive on the big fire in the city.*

exclusive agency agreement a
contract with an **agent** giving him
alone the right to sell certain **products**, or to sell certain products
into certain markets.

ex-directory of a telephone number, not in the telephone directory
because the holder does not want the
number to be publicly known.

execute to carry out, to put into
effect. *Smith's the furniture company,
were very quick in executing my order – I
got my new office chair today.*

executive a person having the power
to plan and control certain activities
within a company. *He is an executive in
the sales department.*

executive director a director
working full-time for a company.

executor a person appointed to see
that the instructions in a will are
properly carried out.

ex gratia payment money given in
payment as a favour and not because
one has to pay it. *Although the company
felt it was not responsible for his accident at
the factory nevertheless it decided to make
an ex gratia payment of £100.*

exhibit *verb* to show (**products** or
services) to the public or trade for
the purposes of increasing sales.

exhibit *noun* (*law*) something produced in a court of law as evidence.

exhibition a show of something, e.g.
of goods to try to increase sales; the
place, usually a hall or public area,
where this is held. *See* **trade fair.**

exhibitor a person who or a company which rents space at an **exhibition** and puts goods or **services**
on show.

ex officio (*Latin*) because of one's
position. *As company director he is, ex
officio, a member of the board of directors.*

expand to (cause to) grow larger. *We
are trying to expand our business.*

expansion the act of **expanding**.
*The video market is growing – and this
expansion will continue.*

expenditure (1) the spending of
money. *The company's expenditure on the
new machinery ran into thousands of
pounds. See* **capital expenditure.**
(2) the spending of time or care or
effort.

expense (1) money paid by a worker
in connection with his job, e.g.
money paid for petrol by a salesman
for his car. *You will have £9000 a year
plus expenses.* (2) cost which is related
to marketing goods or **services** or
related to the **administration** of a
company: *selling expense, office expense.*

expense account a statement of
cash spent in connection with one's
business, which the company will
refund, e.g. a salesman's **expense**
account.

expiry the ending (of an agreement
etc.); the date on which this happens.

explore to examine carefully in
order to find out more. *We have to
explore all the possibilities of this company's offer.*

exploration well an oil well sunk in
order to find out if oil is actually
there, and in what quantity.

export *verb* to send (goods) out of the
country for sale. *See also* **exports.**

export *noun* (1) the act of **exporting**.
(2) something **exported**. *Most of our
exports go to the Third World.*

export agent a person who agrees to
sell goods by acting on behalf of a
company in another country. *See also*
agent.

**Export Credits Guarantee De-
partment** (*or* **ECGD**) (*UK*) a
government **insurance** service for
UK **exporters** which can protect
an exporter against certain risks, e.g.
the failure of the buyer to pay.

exporter a person who or organisation which **exports.**

export house (1) (*UK*) a company
which buys goods from a UK manufacturer and then **exports** them at a
profit. (2) (*UK*) a company which
cooperates with a UK manufacturer

in all matters to do with the manufacturer's exports. e.g. getting export orders, holding **stocks** delivery, advertising etc.

export licence a government **document** which is needed before certain goods can be sent out of the country for sale, e.g. drugs, weapons.

ex-rights: shares or **securities** bought or sold with no rights to any **dividend** or new shares (which may be offered at less than the market price). See also **cum.**

external of the outside; outside something; foreign: *the external walls of the building; external trade.*

external environment all these forces outside of the company which a company cannot control but which affect its plans, e.g. politics, legal, social, cultural, **economic** forces.

extractive industry businesses which take materials from the land or sea, e.g. oil, coal, stone, fish.

extraordinary general meeting a special meeting of a company, called by the directors or the **shareholders**, to discuss some urgent matter which cannot wait till the **annual general meeting**.

extraordinary resolution a subject which a company discusses at an **extraordinary general meeting** in order to take a decision on it. For the **resolution** to be put into action the meeting must support it by more than three-quarters of the votes present at the meeting.

extrapolation the act of making an **estimate** of the future (usually to do with figures) using facts already known. *He noted the sales for each of the past nine months and using these figures he extrapolated the sales for the next two months.*

extrinsic value the value of something (e.g. gold) after it has been made into an object for selling (e.g. a gold ring). See also **intrinsic value.**

ex works *see* **ex.**

F

face-to-face selling selling to a buyer in the buyer's presence (as distinct from selling to a buyer by telephone or by letter, or by advertisements).

face value (1) the worth of a coin or banknote as shown on its face. (2) the worth of a **share, product** etc. as stated on it. *The face value of the shares is £1.00 each but they are selling for £1.50.*

facsimile an exact copy of something written (such as a letter or a **document**) or a copy of a photograph. *He took from his pocket the agreement—it was not the original but a facsimile.*

factor *noun* (1) a company which buys or takes over the debts of another company at a price less than the **face value** of the debts. By this means the selling company gets cash from the factor immediately and the factor earns profit by collecting the full value of the debts from the debtors. (2) a type of agent who not only receives orders for his **principal's** goods but who buys the goods from the principal and also stores them (3) a fact, event, or thing which brings about a result. *The main factor in the firm's success was the big demand for its product.*

factor *verb* to carry out the business of a **factor** (meaning 1). *He factors company debts.*

factors of production land, **labour, capital** and management. *For a country to make economic progress all the factors of production must be present.*

factory a building where goods are made by the use of machines, usually in large quantities.

factory acts laws covering the health, safety and **welfare** of workers in factories. The UK Factories Act 1961 brought many of these separate laws together to cover many aspects of the welfare of workers.

factory agreement an agreement reached between a company and all its workers in one of its factories (as distinct from an agreement with only a section of the workforce, or an agreement covering all of the company's factories).

factory costs all the costs of production (materials, wages, power, and factory heating etc.).

failure (1) a company which cannot pay its debts. *The company's a failure—it will close soon.* (2) lack of success; an unsuccessful person or thing. *He never took any risks because he was always afraid of failure. They tried out the new product but it was a failure.*

fair *adjective* (1) just. *This is a fair price we're offering you.* (2) honest. *To be fair, we admit you have never let us down before.* (3) reasonable. *He stands a fair chance of winning.*

fair *noun* (1) a kind of **market** (meaning 2), usually one held in a certain place at a certain time. *The local cattle fair is in September.* (2) = **trade fair.**

fair-trade agreements trade agreements between countries which allow for the **duty-free** exchange of goods between them.

Fair Trading Act 1973 a UK law which gives protection to the public against unfair actions by **monopolies** and against **mergers** which may not be in the public interest. It also promotes greater competition in industry and amongst **retailers**.

fair wear and tear damage to goods brought about by normal use. *This car is guaranteed for one year except for parts which have to be replaced through fair wear and tear.*

fall-back pay a fixed sum of money paid as wages when the full wages cannot be paid due to reasons which are not the fault of the workers. *The building workers who were preparing the ground for new houses will not be able to work because of the flooding and will receive fall-back pay instead of their full wages.*

falling market a situation when the value of goods or **shares** is going down. *Since the decline in trade there is a falling market in oil shares.*

fall into arrears not to keep up one's payment of a debt or one's rent etc. *Could you lend me some money?—I've fallen into arrears with the rent.*

false pretences words or actions intended to deceive. *He got money from customers on false pretences by claiming to be an agent of a well-known company.*

family allowance regular payments by the UK government to the parents of children, related to the number of children in the family below a certain age.

family expenditure survey a yearly survey by the UK government of how families spend their **income**.

family income supplement money paid by the UK government to those families whose **income** is below a certain level.

family life-cycle a theory that different stages of family life cause demand for certain types of **products**. Thus young married people buy a lot of such items as cookers, carpets, televisions, while married people with children of school age buy a lot of do-it-yourself products, games, books.

farm out to have (some work) done by someone else in order to complete a job. *We will do all the brickwork for the new houses but we will farm out all the woodwork—the doors, windows and so on.*

farm subsidies the **subsidies** given to farmers by the government when the market price of certain farm **products** is too low to provide a fair profit.

FAS *see* **free alongside ship.**

fast-moving consumer goods (or **FMCG**) low-priced goods in regular demand such as butter, milk, canned soups, coffee, tea, etc.

father of the chapel name given to a **shop steward** in the printing industry.

favourable balance of trade see **balance of trade.**

feasibility study a close examination of the costs and benefits of a project to decide if a company should undertake it. *We plan to do a feasibility study first before deciding whether or not to buy the £10,000 computer.*

featherbedding employing more workers on a job than is necessary. *When the trade union insisted that three men and not one should operate the new machine the management thought that this was featherbedding.*

feature (1) something which makes one thing or person different from another. *A feature of all products is that they are guaranteed against defects for three years.* (2) a special study or article in a newspaper on some subject. *The Daily News has a feature on the Royal Family today.* (3) full-length film in a cinema. *The feature was about beasts from outer space.*

federation (1) the coming together of various groups which have certain interests in common but which wish also to keep a certain amount of independence; the union thus formed, e.g. the Federation of International Civil Servants' Associations. (2) a form of politics in which a certain amount of self-government is allowed to the states etc. making up the union; a country with this form of government. *The USA is a federation.*

fee (1) money charged for work done by a professional person, such as a lawyer, doctor or accountant. *The dentist's fees are very high.* (2) a sum of money paid, e.g. for entrance to something, for instruction. *We can't afford the school fees any more.* (3) (*law*) a right or **claim** to property that can be inherited.

feed *verb* (1) to cause **data** to be put into a **computer** for **processing.** (2) to give information to (a person). *I'll go to the managers' meeting and feed you with the information that I get there.*

feed *noun* (1) the part of a machine etc. by means of which it is supplied with material, e.g. the **feed** of a **computer** puts **data** into it for **processing.** (2) food for animals. (3) a meal taken by animals or babies: *three feeds a day.*

feedback any kind of **response** which will show whether something will have to be changed and in what way. For example a TV company may try out a new programme but the **feedback** (the viewing figures) may show that the public do not like it. *What's the feedback on the new model which we're trying out?*

felony serious crime.

fiche see **microfiche.**

fidelity bond a type of **insurance** which protects an employer against loss through an employee who is dishonest or who neglects his/her duties.

fiduciary (*law*) a person who acts for the benefit of someone else, e.g. a **trustee.**

field force (**marketing**) a group of researchers who **interview** possible customers near where they live or work.

field organisation a **system** used for arranging the work of a **field force.**

field research a method of finding out about possible customers' attitudes to a **product** or **service** by going out and **interviewing** them. *See also* **desk research.**

field sales manager a person who is responsible for controlling and training a **sales force** (group of salesmen).

FIFO see **first in first out.**

figures *see* **round figures.**

file *noun* (1) a box or folder in which letters and similar **documents** on a certain subject are kept together for reference. (2) a collection of such documents. *We have the case on file.* (3) an organised set of **data stored** in a **computer.**

file *verb* (1) to put (a **document**) on **file.** (2) to record (something) officially. (3) (**computers**) to save and **store (data).**

final demand a last written request for payment before legal action is taken. *I've received a final demand from the rates people.*

final dividend the last **dividend** paid by a company in the **financial year.**

finance *noun* (1) the study of the **management** (meaning 3) of money. *A good manager must understand finance.* (2) money supplied to a company by **shareholders**, lenders etc. *I'm worried about the company's level of finance.* (3) the supply of money for a particular **project.**

finance *verb* to provide money for (something). *The new factory will be partly financed by the government.*

Finance Act a law passed by the UK government (usually each year) which allows the government to get through taxes (e.g. **income tax, corporation tax**) the money it needs for the **financial year.**

finance market a place where bankers and **financiers** arrange the borrowing and lending of money.

financial accounting the **process** of presenting statements to the **shareholders** and/or management of a company to allow them to see what progress it is making.

financial management the **process** of finding money for a company, then planning and controlling the use of it for the benefit of the company.

financial ratios (*or* **accounting ratios** *or* **management ratios**) direct comparison of two quantities within a company to give a measurement or **ratio**. For example, the **current ratio** shows how well a firm's **current liabilities** are covered by its **current assets,** as follows:

$$\frac{\text{current assets}}{\text{current liabilities}} = \frac{\pounds 100,000}{50,000} = 2:1$$

This ratio shows that current liabilities are covered twice over. *See also* appendix 4.

financial risk a danger of loss of money in a business **project**. *To invest in the Brown Company just now is taking a big financial risk.*

financial statement a **document**, such as a **balance sheet**, which describes the **financial** situation and/or performance of an organisation.

Financial Times industrial ordinary share index the average price of thirty of the most important company **shares** in the UK **stock market**, published daily by the Financial Times newspaper, and intended to give an idea of how well or badly the UK stock market is doing. *See also* **Dow Jones Index.**

financial year a period chosen by a company as the one on which it will base its **accounts**: this may or may not be the same as the calendar year (1 January to 31 December). *Our financial year ends on 31 March. See also* **fiscal year.**

financier a person or company that provides **funds** for companies and other organisations. *Three well-known financiers are backing the Bell Construction Company in the building of the new hotel.*

fine *noun* an amount of money which a person is made to pay because a law or rule has been broken.

fine *verb* to make (a person) pay a **fine.**

finished goods completed **products**, ready for sale.

fire insurance one of the main kinds of **insurances** which protects against loss caused by fire and certain other **risks**.

firm *noun* a company or partnership.

firm *adjective* (1) not going to be changed: *a firm offer.* (2) of prices of **stocks** and **shares** on the **stock exchange**, steady, likely to rise.

first in, first out (*or* **FIFO**) a method of valuing **stocks** of goods which have been bought in over a period at different prices: by this method the value of goods in **stock** is based on the value of those which were bought most recently. *See also* **last in first out**.

first-line management (*or* **front-line management**) people who are directly responsible for **supervising** workers on the **shop floor**, e.g. **foremen**. *The boss said we had to support the foremen; they were our front-line managers.*

fiscal connected with public money or taxes: *fiscal year.*

fiscal measures steps taken by a government to control the **economy** of a country, for example by tax changes.

fiscal year a period of twelve months regarded as a unit by the government for the collection of taxes, in the UK for personal tax from 6 April to 5 April the following year, and in the US from 1 July to 30 June. *See also* **calendar year, financial year.**

fixed assets: assets owned by a company which are meant to be used by it in the running of the business over a long period of time, e.g. land, buildings, machinery. *See* appendix 2.

fixed capital the part of the wealth of a company that is **invested** in **fixed assets**. *See* appendix 2.

fixed charge (*or* **fixed expense**) (1) an amount of money which a company has to pay out which does not change no matter how much or how little business the company does, e.g. the repayments of a loan. (2) a **claim** which a person who or organisation which had lent money to a company has on a particular item of the company's **assets** if it cannot pay its debt. *See also* **floating charge.**

fixed cost an amount of money which has to be paid in order to produce goods, and which does not change according to the amount of goods produced, e.g. the rent paid for a factory. *See* appendix 6.

fixed exchange rate a fixed level at which a government tries to keep the value of its currency in relation to other currencies. *See also* **floating exchange rate.**

fixed expense *see* **fixed charge.**

fixed-price contract a business agreement in which the person who has to provide the **service** is not allowed to change the agreed price for any reason.

fixtures and fittings things which are not part of a property (house, factory etc.) but which are attached to it, e.g. an electric light switch, a shelf, a table, chairs etc.

flag of convenience the flag of a country where a ship can be **registered** so that it can be run cheaply without having to follow the regulations and tax-laws that are normal in other countries.

flash pack a type of package which displays information that the contents are being sold at a special low price, as part of a **promotion** to improve sales.

flat rate a payment which does not change, e.g. a worker may be paid at a flat rate of £4 per hour no matter how much he produces.

flat yield *see* **current yield.**

fleece (*informal*) to steal money from (a person) by cheating him. *He fleeced him over the years of £12,000.*

flexible working hours (*or* **flexi-time**) an arrangement by which an employee has some control over his working time, e.g. by being able to start or finish at certain times that are convenient for him, as long as the agreed number of hours are worked.

flip-chart a method of showing information, consisting of large sheets of paper which can be turned down or torn off to show the next sheet.

float *verb* (1) to (cause to) rest on the surface of a liquid. (2) to start (a company), e.g. by offering **shares** in it for sale. *See also* **flotation.** (3) to allow (a currency) to be bought and sold freely, without a fixed **exchange rate.**

float *noun* a small amount of money kept for change or to cover small expenses. *The shopkeeper always started the day with a float of £10. See also* **imprest system, petty cash.**

floating charge a **claim** which a person who has lent money to a company has on all of a company's **assets** (and not just on one asset). *See also* **fixed charge.**

floating exchange rate an **exchange rate** not controlled by the government, but allowed to go up or down, according to demand. *See also* **fixed exchange rate, float** (*verb*, meaning 3).

floating rig a **rig** (meaning 1) which floats and can be moved from one area to another, as it is needed.

floor walker a person employed by a **store** to mix with the customers so as to be able to prevent theft from the store.

floppy disk (**computers**) a flexible **magnetic disk.**

flotation the act of starting up a company, e.g. by selling **shares** in it. *See also* **float** (*verb*, meaning 2).

flotsam (1) parts of a ship or its **cargo** which have been thrown overboard and which are still afloat. (2) wreckage which is afloat from a sunken or damaged ship. *See also* **jetsam.**

flow-chart (*or* **flow-diagram**) a chart or diagram which shows how one stage in a **process** follows another, step by step.

flow-line production a **technique** of producing goods in which the goods, as they are being manufactured, go in a line from one part of the factory to the next until they are complete. *See also* **assembly line, division of labour.**

fluctuate especially of prices, to rise and fall a lot. *Prices on the stock market are fluctuating because of rumours about a general election.*

fluctuation the act of changing up and down: *the fluctuation of prices in the stock market.*

fly-by-night *noun, adjective* (a person who is) not to be relied on; not to be trusted, especially in **financial** matters. *Don't buy anything from him: he is a salesman from a fly-by-night company.*

FMCG *see* **fast-moving consumer goods.**

FOB *see* **free on board.**

folder (1) a cover made from stiff paper used for holding loose papers, notes etc. *He carried his documents in a folder.* (2) a piece of folded paper which advertises something. *They had designed an attractive folder to advertise their services.* (3) a machine that folds envelopes or paper.

folio (1) a sheet of paper of a standard size which has been folded in the middle to give four pages. (2) a book made of such sheets. (3) a sheet of paper which has been numbered on one side only. (4) a printed page number. (5) (**book-keeping**) two facing pages in a **ledger** which both have the same number. (6) (*law*) a unit for measuring the length of a legal piece of writing (in UK, 72 or 90 words, in US, 100 words).

foot the bill (*informal*) to pay the money that is due for something. *Who is going to foot the bill for all this entertaining?*

forecast *verb* to tell in advance what may happen in the future, often by examining what is happening at the present or has happened in the past.

forecast *noun* something told in advance in this way. *We need a forecast of sales for the next six months.*

foreclose to sell an **asset** (e.g. a building, machine) belonging to a person who has **mortgaged** it, because he can no longer pay the mortgage.

foreclosure an action taken against a person who has **mortgaged** his property, but who cannot repay his debt. By this action he is taken to court and (if he still cannot pay) he loses all claim to his property.

foreign bill (*UK*) any bill of exchange that is not drawn and payable in the UK, or drawn in the UK on a person normally living there. (*US* **external bill**).

foreign exchange (1) a **system** by which the currency of a country is changed into the currency of another country. (2) the currency of a foreign country.

foreign exchange broker a person who arranges for the exchanging of the currencies of different countries.

foreign exchange market a group of people who deal with each other in exchanging foreign currencies.

foreign investment (1) the act of putting money for profit into business in another country. (2) an amount of money that has been put into another country in this way.

foreign trade the exchange of goods and **services** for profit between different countries.

foreman (1) a person who is in charge of a group of workers. *See also*

first-line management. (2) (*law*) the chief member of a jury.

forge to imitate the appearance of (something) unlawfully: *to forge a signature/cheque/will.*

forgery (1) the act of **forging** something. *He was arrested for forgery.* (2) something that has been **forged**. *This note looks like a forgery.*

FORTRAN (*stands for* Formula Translation) a widely-used **computer language,** used especially for scientific and technical purposes.

forward contract a promise to buy or sell **commodities** or **securities** at a fixed price at a future date.

forward exchange the buying or selling of foreign currency at an agreed fixed rate but completing the **contract** (the actual purchase or sale) at a future date.

forward integration a situation in which a company takes over the **retail outlets** for its goods so that it has a direct link with its customers. *See also* **backward integration; horizontal integration; vertical integration.**

forward purchasing sales *see* **futures.**

forward rate an **exchange rate** that is agreed for the buying or selling of currency at some future date. *See also* **forward exchange.**

forward sales goods that have been sold with delivery fixed for some time in the future.

four p's *see* **marketing mix.**

franchise (1) a method of selling **branded** goods or **services** by which the owner of the brand name (the **franchiser**) allows someone else (the **franchisee**) to sell the goods/services within a certain area in return for a payment (based e.g. on the amount of goods supplied or sold). (2) (**marine insurance**) part of a **policy,** in which it is agreed that **claims** will only be made above a certain amount, but that successful claims above that amount will be paid in full (to save time and money being wasted on small claims).

franchisee see **franchise** (meaning 1).

franchiser see **franchise** (meaning 1).

franco domicile free of delivery charges between the seller's warehouse and the buyer's place of business. (Commonly used in the **import/export** of goods). See also **Incoterms.**

frank (1) to put a mark on (a stamp) which shows that it has been used. (2) to put a mark on (an envelope) with a **franking machine.**

franking machine a machine which can be used by offices which send out a lot of mail. The machine prints and records the proper amount of postage on the envelope, so that stamps do not have to be used, and at the same time can print an advertisement for the company that is sending the letter or parcel.

fraud (1) the act of getting a person to believe something which is not true, usually in order to get something illegally. (2) (*informal*) a person who is not what he **claims** to be. *He is a fraud – he says he is a lawyer and it is clear he isn't.* (3) a **product** which does not live up to its **claims**. *It is a fraud – it went rusty in a couple of months yet it claimed to be stainless steel.*

fraudulent dishonest; intended to deceive others for **financial** gain etc.: *a fraudulent scheme.*

free alongside ship (*or* **FAS**) (**exporting**) free of delivery charges to a point alongside a named ship. Any costs of loading the goods onto the ship will have to be paid for by the buyer. See also **Incoterms.**

free currency any currency which is allowed to move freely between countries without any rules to stop it. *You can take as much sterling out of the country as you want – it's a free currency.*

freedom of association the right of people to group themselves together for some joint advantage, e.g. the right of workers to group themselves into **trade unions.**

free enterprise an **economic system** in which businesses can compete against one another with very little interference from the government.

free gift something given away without any charge with certain goods so as to improve the sales of those goods. The buyer may receive it with the goods, or he may have to send away for it with proof that he has bought the goods, or he may receive the gift if he agrees to buy or at least examine the goods.

freelance *adjective* working independently without being employed by one organisation. *She is a freelance journalist and you will see her articles in several papers.*

freelance *noun* a person who does **freelance** work. *This is the first time they have employed a freelance.*

freelance *verb* to work as a **freelance.**

free movement of labour a situation in which workers are allowed to move from one country to another to work as in the **European Economic Community.**

free of particular average (**marine insurance**) the **underwriters** are liable only for a total loss and not for for a partial loss, except under certain circumstances, e.g. if goods are washed overboard.

free of tax of goods or **income** etc., on which a tax does not have to be paid.

free on board (*or* **FOB**) in international trade, when the seller's price includes the cost of the goods, packing, delivery to the port and all charges in placing the goods on board the ship (or to the airport if going by air). See also **Incoterms.**

free on rail in international trade, when the seller's price includes any expense in delivery to a railway at a named place. *See also* **Incoterms.**

freepost (*UK*) a **service** provided by the Post Office by which a person can reply to an advertisement etc. without paying any postage (which is paid by the company etc. using the service).

free trade an **economic system** in which the exchange of goods from one country to another is not limited by **tariffs** or by **quotas.**

freight *noun* (1) the transporting of goods by sea, air or (especially *US*) by road or rail. (2) money paid for this: *freight charges.*

freight *verb* to send goods by **freight.** *He was going to freight the goods to major cities in France.*

freight forward any charges for the transporting of the goods must be paid by the person receiving them.

freight inward the cost of **freight** paid on goods coming into a company.

frequency the number of times something happens within a certain time. *The machine is breaking down with increasing frequency.*

frequency distribution (**statistics**) the number of times the units of a certain variable (e.g. salary, examination marks) happens. For example in a test marked from 0 to 10, it would show how many students scored 10, how many 9 etc.

friendly society (*US* **benefit association**) a group of people who make regular payments to a common **fund**, so that they have **financial** protection in case of sickness, death of a wage earner etc.

fringe benefit any kind of extra reward given to an employee in addition to his salary, e.g. cheap meals, use of a car etc. *See also* **employee benefits.**

front-line management *see* **first-line management.**

frozen account money in a bank belonging to a person or company, which cannot be moved because of some legal (or government) rule.

frozen assets things belonging to a company (land, buildings, machinery, etc.) which cannot be sold because of some **claim** against them.

full cost the total cost involved in making something, including the **variable costs** and the current amount of the **fixed costs.** *See also* **absorption costing** and appendix 7.

full employment a situation where there are jobs available for all those who want them.

fully-paid share a **share** of which the full **nominal** (or **par**) **value** has been paid.

functional responsibilities the duties one has in a job. For example, the functional responsibilities of a **sales manager** includes **sales forecasting, sales training**, and reaching the planned level of sales and profits.

fund *noun* an amount of money which has been set aside for a special purpose. *See also* **funds.**

fund *verb* (1) to provide money for (a special purpose). (2) to change a short-term debt into a long-term debt.

funds (1) money available to be spent at any time. (2) all the **assets** of a company. (3) UK government **stocks** and **securities.**

funds-flow analysis a careful examination of the movement of money into and out of a company.

further education (*UK*) a section of the educational system which deals with the needs of students who are above school-leaving age but have not entered a university or **polytechnic.** *See also* **higher education.**

futures (*or* **forward purchasing sales**) **commodities** or **securities** which are bought or sold at a certain price now for delivery at some agreed time in the future.

G

gain (1) an increase, a benefit. *We had a gain of 1% in our market share last month.* (2) a profit. *When costs were taken off the company had a gain of £1000.*

galloping inflation (*or* **hyper-inflation**) very fast **inflation**, e.g. at a rate of about 5% per month.

gamble *verb* (1) to bet, to risk losing money in a game of chance. (2) to take a risk in something: *to gamble on the success of a product.*

gamble *noun* any action which carries a high risk of failure. *Putting a lot of money into something completely new is always a gamble.*

gambler (1) a person who **gambles**.

GATT *see* **General Agreement on Tariffs and Trade**.

gazumping the act of selling a house at a higher price than that previously agreed.

GDP *see* **gross domestic product**.

gearing the relationship between the value of a company's fixed-interest **loan capital** and its **ordinary shares**. If the amount of these loans is greater than the value of the ordinary shares the company is said to be **highly-geared**. If less, it is **low-geared**.

General Agreement on Tariffs and Trade (*or* **GATT**) an international agreement, reached in Geneva in 1947, which tries to lower the **tariff barriers** between countries. Number of countries: 86. Headquarters: Geneva. Official languages: English, French.

general audit a check of **accounts** in a company (usually done at the time of the preparation of the final accounts). *See* **audit**.

general average loss (**insurance**) a deliberate loss of part of a **cargo** of parts of a ship at sea in order to save the ship and the rest of the cargo. When a captain orders goods to be thrown into the sea for this purpose, this loss is called a 'general average loss' and all those who have cargo on the ship or have an interest in the ship would have to pay into a special fund to recover the value of the goods thrown overboard, although they do not own the goods.

general manager (1) a person who controls the work of other managers. (2) a person who decides on the aims of a company and who decides what amount of **personnel**, money and machinery are needed to reach the aims.

general meeting a meeting of all the members of a company such as an **annual general meeting** or an **extraordinary general meeting**.

general reserves that section of the **balance sheet** which shows the profit kept for use within the company. Each year this retained profit goes to the general reserve. *See* appendix 2.

general strike a situation when all the workers of the major **trade unions** stop working as a protest over something which is very important to them.

gentleman's agreement a **contract** which does not have any force in law, but is based on the trust of each party that it will be carried out.

get down to brass tacks (*informal*) to discuss something (e.g. a business deal) seriously; to get down to the real point of discussion. *Let's get down to brass tacks: how much is this project going to cost?*

get the sack (*informal*) to lose one's job. *He got the sack for using company money for his own purposes.*

get-up-and-go (*informal*) great energy and willingness to do one's job. *Our company could use young men with your kind of get-up-and-go.*

ghost to write (an article, story or novel) on behalf of someone else. *The famous actor's autobiography was actually ghosted by a professional writer.*

gift (1) something, such as property or money, given without any payment to someone else. *Before his death the father gave his son the house as a gift.* (2) a natural ability or talent. *He seems to be able to make money from any business he tackles. It's a gift which he has.*

gift voucher (*or* **gift token**) a kind of ticket with the value clearly shown on it which can be bought in a shop then given to someone as a gift. The holder of the gift voucher can exchange it in a shop for something to the value of the voucher.

gilt-edged securities/stocks: securities/stocks issued by the government. There is little risk that the buying of government stocks will result in a loss and so the term 'gilt-edged' or 'gilts' usually means a safe **investment**.

gimmick something new or unusual which catches people's attention. *They've got a good gimmick for selling that new beer – they've sent up a thousand balloons with the beer's name.*

giro a system of sending money from an **account** in one branch of a bank to an account in another branch or bank. This method of settling debts is done by using the specially-printed giro forms available in the branch of any bank.

give-away something given away free with a **product** or **service** to keep increasing the sale, e.g. a gardening magazine may have a give-away of a free packet of flower seeds. *See* **free gift**.

glossary a list of unusual words or terms, usually at the end of a book. *This text book has a glossary of management terms.*

glut more than is needed of something. *There is a glut of oranges at the fruit market and prices are falling.*

gnomes of Zurich (*informal*) powerful Swiss bankers who are said to make large profits from changes in currency rates, and who are supposed to be so powerful as to cause changes in the **financial policies** of governments.

GNP *see* **gross national product**.

go-ahead *noun* (*informal*) permission to do something. *We can't do anything until we get the go-ahead from our financial director.*

go-ahead *adjective* (*informal*) willing to do new things. *It's a very exciting, go-ahead company to work for.*

goal an aim or desire. *Our long-term goal is an improvement in profits but the short-term goal is simply to survive.*

going concern a business which is doing well. *He took over the business as a going concern.*

going price the amount that is being charged for something at the present time.

going public the **process** of changing a **private company** into a **public company**. *I see the Crude-oil Company is going public – their shares are being offered for sale on the Stock Exchange.*

going rate the rate that is being charged at present for wages, or for materials. *The going rate for crude oil is $30.*

golden handshake money given to a senior manager, or a director, of a large company at the end of his **contract of service** (or when his contract of service has been cut short). *He was with them for ten years and received a golden handshake of £5000 when he retired.*

gold reserves a country's **stock** of gold, held in reserve to settle international debts. *See also* **official reserves**.

gold standard the use of gold to **guarantee** the issue of a country's paper money. The UK came off the gold standard in 1931, i.e. its paper money was no longer guaranteed by the full amount of gold.

good faith honesty in dealing with other people in business, e.g. as supposed to exist between all those who have a **contract** between them.

goods things which are offered for sale (but not houses or land). *They have received our order and they say that our goods will be delivered tomorrow.*

goods and chattels (*law*) personal belongings.

goods on approval goods delivered to a person who may buy if he approves of the goods, i.e. if he finds them suitable.

goods on consignment goods sent to an agent for sale.

goods received note a note with the description and quantity of goods received by whoever has bought or ordered the goods. This can then be compared with the **advice note** or **delivery note**, or the **invoice** to check that the goods have all been received.

goods returned note a note with the description and quantity of goods which have been returned by the person who has bought or ordered the goods. The selling company which receives these returned goods needs to record the details so that a **credit** can be given to the buyer.

goodwill (1) benefits that come to a company from being well-known to customers, or being well-placed (e.g. on a busy street) or from being known to be expert in some aspect of business (e.g. a maker of high-quality **products**). *There is a lot of goodwill for the Trent Shipping Company; they are just so reliable.* (2) a **financial** measurement of the worth of **goodwill** in a **balance sheet**.

go out of business to give up one's business, either willingly or by going **bankrupt**. *Many firms round here have gone out of business because of the slump.*

go slow to do less work than normal so as to cause delays in **output**. Used sometimes by workers instead of a **strike** to bring attention to a disagreement with management. Also used a noun: *There was a go-slow at the printing works last week.*

government stock: fixed-interest loans **issued** by the government. In the UK these offers of loans are called **gilt-edged stock** or **gilt-edged securities**.

grading separating something (e.g. wool, grain) into different lots by quality or size etc.

graduated pension a **pension** which is related to the earnings of the person before his/her **retirement**.

graft *noun* (1) getting business, profits etc. by dishonest means, e.g. **bribery**. (2) (*informal*) work. *Coal-mining is hard graft.*

graft *verb* to get business etc. by **graft** (meaning 1).

grant a gift of money, e.g. from the government, especially for education. *Some people say that the grants for students are too low.*

grapevine the way news spreads unofficially. *I heard on the grapevine we're getting a new manager.*

graph a drawing which shows the relationship between two sets of numbers. One set is marked off on an upright line, the other set of numbers is measured off on a line at right angles. The relationship between the two is shown by means of dots or lines etc. *See* **graph paper**.

graphics drawings, diagrams etc. in a newspaper, magazine or book.

graph paper paper on which a **graph** is drawn. The paper is usually divided into small squares each of the same area to help to make the graph clearer.

gratuity (or **tip**) a gift of payment for good service.

graveyard shift (*informal*) a period of overnight work between midnight and eight in the morning.

green card an **insurance document** which a motorist must have when taking his car from the UK to drive in foreign countries. It shows that, if he has an accident, he has **third-party insurance**.

grievance a cause for complaint or protest usually by a **trade union** to a company. *The union leader wanted to see the management so that he could speak to them about the workers' grievances.*

grievance procedure the methods agreed by a **union** and the management of a company for settling complaints.

gross circulation the total sales of a newspaper or magazine (before errors, or **returns** have been counted).

gross domestic product (or **GDP**) the value of all the goods and **services** produced by a country (usually in one year).

gross income earnings before any **deductions** for tax etc.

gross margin a percentage added to the cost of goods: the amount left to cover all other expenses and provide a **net profit**.

gross national product (or **GNP**) the value of all the goods and **services** produced by a country including **income** from its **investments** in other countries.

gross profit sales less the cost of the goods sold, usually expressed in money terms (**gross margin** is usually expressed in percentage terms). *See* appendix 1.

gross sales the total sales before taking off **discounts**, **returns**, breakages, mistakes in delivery etc. *See* appendix 1.

gross weight the total weight of a **product** including its wrapping, packaging, and the weight of the **outer** or **crate**.

gross yield the profit from an **investment** before any deductions for expenses, tax etc.

ground rent the rent paid for land as opposed to rent paid for buildings on the land.

ground rules (unwritten) rules that apply in a special situation. *Be careful what you say at the managers' meetings; Jack will explain the ground rules to you.*

groupage grouping together several different small orders into one load for delivery (usually in a **container**). Groupage is done to get lower delivery rates.

group discussion a research method by which a group of people are encouraged to speak freely on a subject. The subject might be a company's advertisement, **product**, price, label, etc. By giving their opinions the group show what people think and this may help a company to improve their **marketing mix**.

group dynamics the study of how groups of people behave and how persons within the group influence group decisions and actions.

group incentives: incentives given as a result of a group of workers reaching a stated **target** for the group (as opposed to an incentive offered to each worker for reaching an individual target).

growth chart a chart used to plan and control work, e.g. in a factory or on a large **project**. The work is drawn on the chart on a plan of the time to be taken. The stages are then drawn in as they happen.

growth rate an amount by which something has increased (usually stated as a percentage). Often used in relation to sales, **share value**, share of the market, production and other **factors** of business. *Over the past three years our profits have shown a growth rate of 10%.*

guarantee *noun* (1) a firm promise in business (usually in writing or print) that certain agreements will be kept. *If our machine fails within two months of purchase we will replace it free of charge. That's our guarantee.* (2) a promise by one person to pay the loan of another should the latter fail to do so.

guarantee *verb* to give a **guarantee** for. *All our products are guaranteed for three years.*

guaranteed prices: fixed prices which the government offers farmers for certain produce to encourage production. If the market price falls below this guaranteed price the farmers receive the difference from the government.

guaranteed wage an agreement between a company and its workers by which the company promises that the workers' wages will not fall below a certain figure each week.

guardian a person who has the legal right and duty to care for a young person and his/her property.

guesstimate (made up from guess and **estimate**) a statement about the future which is not based on facts, or on very few facts. *They had done no market research so they had no real idea of what the sales would be but their guesstimate was £1 million.*

guillotine (1) a method of stopping a debate in Parliament by fixing a time for taking a vote. (2) a paper-cutting instrument.

H

habeas corpus (*English law*) an order from a court requiring a person to come before the court or a judge as soon as possible, usually used to find out if a person has been lawfully or unlawfully kept in prison.

haggle to argue over a price in a situation where a buyer and seller are both trying to get the best price for himself; common in open street markets. *They haggled over the price for ten minutes then agreed to £5.*

hallmark a special mark put on an article of silver or gold after its quality has been tested. The mark indicates the quality, the maker and the city where the article's quality was tested. *He could see from the hallmark that the ring was 18 carat gold.*

halo effect the result of noting some quality in another person which is greatly liked and has an effect on one's decisions. For example, a manager who interviewed a person for a job might be very impressed by the person's speech and clothing and might decide to employ that person even if these qualities were not necessary for the job.

hammer to announce at the **Stock Exchange** that (a member) cannot pay his debts. *Smith is no longer a member of the Stock Exchange; he was hammered today.*
   under the hammer offered for sale by **auction**. *He's selling all his furniture and it will be under the hammer next week.*

handbill a small sheet of paper with a printed message or advertisement which is handed out to people.

handling charge (1) a charge made for moving goods (by hand or by machine) from one place to another, e.g. for moving goods from the dock-side to a waiting lorry. (2) a charge made by a bank for operating a customer's **bank account**.

handout (1) a sheet of paper or leaflet giving information about something. *The salesman gave the customer a handout on the new product.* (2) something given away free, sometimes to advertise a **product**.

hand over fist (*informal*) especially of making money, very quickly and without problems.

harbour dues sums of money paid by ships for entering and for using a harbour.

harbour-master the person in charge of a harbour and the position of the ships there.

hard cash (*informal*) money that is available now, at once in payment (usually) for something. *He offered the garage £1000 hard cash for the car if he could drive it away at once.*

hard copy printed words or figures on a sheet of paper produced by a machine such as a **photocopier** (and not the words or figures on a **disk** or tape). *Last month's sales figures were on the computer but he had a hard copy made for the sales meeting.*

hard currency any currency that is readily accepted by many foreign countries in payment of debt (without changing it with another currency).

hard disk a hard **magnetic disk**.

harden of a price of **shares** or goods, to rise, or to stop falling. *Shares fell slightly for most of the day until late afternoon when prices hardened.*

hard sell the selling of goods forcefully and with determination. *The manager told the sales force that the new product needed a hard sell to make it a success.*

hardware (1) all the hard parts which make up a **computer** such as the machinery, the wires and so on, but not the **programs**. *See also* **software**. (2) goods (such as hammers, screws, nuts, bolts, etc.) which are sold in a **hardware store** or **ironmonger's** shop.

hatchet man (*informal*) a person who is employed to do things which will not be liked by other workers, such as getting rid of unwanted employees. *They say that he was appointed just as a hatchet man to get rid of some of the older staff.*

haulage (1) carriage of goods by road. *I want you to arrange for the haulage of 1000 cases of whisky to Dover.* (2) the charge for this. *Find out the haulage on a delivery of 1000 cases of whisky to Dover.*

haulage contractor a company which **contracts** to carry goods by road. *See also* **haulage**.

hazard a risk, danger. *The main hazard to Smith's new business was the low prices of the shop next door.*

headhunter a company, or person, that tries to find suitable managers, or people for certain jobs, by approaching the managers direct (as opposed to advertising such jobs in the newspapers). Usually this contact is made without the manager's present company knowing about it. Often the offer of a job by a headhunter is accompanied by an offer of increased salary etc.

heading the word or words which form the title to a section of writing, e.g. the chapter of a book.

head office (*or* **headquarters**) the part of the business where the top managers and (usually) the directors are. *We have branches all over the country but our head office is in Glasgow.*

health hazard any risk or damage to health, in business used to describe those caused by the type of work or the methods of work. *The fumes from the factory were considered to be a health hazard to the workers.*

heavy industry an industry which works with metals, e.g. iron or coal, or with heavy machinery, as in shipbuilding.

heavy user a person or company that buys a lot of some **product** or **service**. *We have all bought brown bread at some time, but the heavy user buys it every day.*

hedging protecting oneself against loss due to price changes, especially by buying at a fixed price for future delivery. This dealing in **futures** can be in currency or **shares** or materials etc. For example, a bank might agree to a contract with a company to sell the company in three months' time a fixed amount of dollars for a fixed amount of pounds. To protect itself from changes in the value of the currencies the bank will hedge, i.e. it will try to buy now, for delivery in three months, at the same price or lower, the same amount of dollars.

higher education education beyond the age of eighteen at a college of **further education** or at a **polytechnic** or university.

high flier a very ambitious and/or very successful person.

high-level language a **computer language** which is used to write **programs** for a wide range of **computers**. Widely-used high-level languages are: **BASIC, FORTRAN, ALGOL, COBOL**.

high-pressure selling forceful selling, when the salesman is only concerned with making the sale, without thought of the customer's real need. High-pressure selling is often accompanied by false **claims** about the **product**, or delivery, or price, all to make sure of the sale. *See also* **low-pressure selling**.

hire to buy the use of (something) for an agreed period of time; to employ (a person). *He hired a van for a week.*

hire purchase a form of payment for goods where the buyer signs a **contract** called a **hire-purchase agreement**. The buyer agrees to pay a small part of the amount due at the time of buying and the remainder in equal parts over a fixed period of time. The buyer is not the legal owner of the goods until the last payment is made. *See also* **instalment purchase**.

histogram a picture, or chart, of how many in a group have a certain characteristic (such as age, height, examination mark) which is being studied. How often a certain age occurs for example will be shown by the length of the thick lines (or bars) on the chart.

historic cost the actual cost of something which has been produced, not what is would cost now.

HMSO (*or* **Her Majesty's Stationery Office**) (*UK*) the official supplier of government books and publications.

hoard to save (money) with no intention of **investing** it or (goods) with no intention of using them. *It's no use hoarding your wealth when it could be put to good use.*

hoarding a large easily-seen surface, usually of wood, on which advertisements are placed. *Every hoarding had an advertisement for their new product.*

holder in due course a person who accepts a **bill** in exchange for value he has given (e.g. goods or **services**), who believes that the bill is in every way a genuine bill, and has therefore the best legal right to the value of the bill.

holder of value a person who possesses a **bill of exchange** for which some value has been given at some time (e.g. goods have been exchanged for it).

holding company a company which controls one or more companies (by owning more than half the **ordinary shares** in them).

holiday pay wages or salary paid to a worker for the time he is on holiday.

home loan a loan of money from a bank or a **building society** when the value of the borrower's home is used to safeguard the loan.

home market trade done by a company in the country where it has its **head office**, and not abroad. *We're a British company but our home market takes only 10% of all the golf-clubs we make; export markets take the rest.*

homogeneous goods goods which have very little difference between them; goods of the same kind.

honorary (*also* **hon.**) of an official of a company or society, unpaid. *He's the new hon. treasurer of the club.*

honour *noun* (1) having honesty, and loyalty; good personal character. *He is a man of honour.* (2) a title of respect used when addressing judges. *Your honour, may I say ....*

honour *verb* to have a high opinion of (a person). (2) to pay (something) when it is due: *to honour a debt/a cheque.*

horizontal integration the joining of two or more companies in the same industry. *See also* **vertical integration**.

horse power (*or* **h.p.**) a unit for measuring the power of an engine. (In making measurement 1 h.p. = 0.7457 kW).

hot money money moved around quickly and/or regularly by its owners into countries, or **investments**, e.g. to get the highest **interest rates**.

hot seat (*informal*) a difficult or dangerous position. *There were very few applicants for Mr Black's job: most people considered it too much a hot seat.*

household all the people that live together in a house.

house magazine a magazine containing news and articles about a company and published by the company. House magazines are usually given free to company workers and sent also to large customers of the company.

house-to-house selling calling direct on homes to try to sell goods. Some cosmetic companies and book companies sell their **products** in this way. *See also* **door-to-door selling**.

hull the body of a ship (as distinct from the masts, funnels etc.). *The ship's hull was rusted from its long sea voyage.*

hull insurance: insuring against damage to a ship (as distinct from its **cargo**).

human relations the study of social problems among people, e.g. those that arise in a company between and among its groups (of workers, **supervisors**, managers) and also between a company and its customers.

hyperinflation *see* **galloping inflation**.

hypermarket a very large **self-service store**, usually over 3,000 square metres, situated out of town, offering a wide range of household goods and groceries, and with plenty of parking space for cars. *See also* **superstore**.

I

IAEA *see* **International Atomic Energy Agency**.

IBRD *see* **International Bank for Reconstruction and Development**.

ICC *see* **International Chamber of Commerce**.

ICJ *see* **International Court of Justice**.

idle capacity machinery or workers not used to the full. *We don't have enough orders so for two days a week we have idle capacity.*

idle money money that is not earning interest, that is not **invested**.

idle time any time when machines or men are not working productively, e.g. due to a machine breakdown, materials not arriving.

IEA *see* **International Energy Agency**.

IFAD *see* **International Fund for Agricultural Development**.

IFC *see* **International Finance Corporation**.

ILO *see* **International Labour Organization**.

image a mental picture that people have of a company, person or product etc. This picture may be formed by the company advertising, or news of its activities in the press. *The* *company's image was harmed by the news of how badly it treated its workers and sales fell.*

IMF *see* **International Monetary Fund**.

impact the effect of something, e.g. an advertisement or a special **promotion** on the public. *The impact of the new advertisement was such that sales increased almost immediately.*

imperfect competition a situation where a company or companies have such an influence over a market (usually because they are so large) that they can affect the price, the supply or the demand.

impersonal accounts (**bookkeeping**) **accounts** which do not deal with people but with things such as goods, machines, cash, wages, rent etc. Impersonal accounts are divided into real accounts and **nominal accounts**.

implied warranty a **guarantee** which is taken to exist although it may not be in writing, e.g. that goods should be fit for use or a new car should be safe to drive.

import *verb* to bring (goods or **services**) into a country, especially for sale. *He was going to import wines from France.*

import *noun* (1) the act of **importing**. (2) something **imported**. *Britain has increased its imports this year.*

import duty a tax on certain goods brought into a country.

importer a person who or organisation which **imports**.

import licence a printed permission from the government which allows certain goods into the country.

import quota a fixed number of a **product** allowed into the country by the government.

import surcharge an extra tax on certain goods which is meant to discourage **importers** from bringing them into the country, usually aimed at protecting an industry, or helping the **balance of payments**.

imprest system a method of controlling **petty cash** in a business. The person in charge of the petty cash must have a **receipt** for each amount of cash given out. These are taken to the company's **cashier** who gives cash to the total of the receipts. By this means the petty cash is brought up to its original amount again.

impulse goods goods which are bought when seen and not as a result of a plan to buy, i.e. bought on the spur of the moment. Impulse goods are usually cheap, and in high demand, e.g. matches, sweets, canned meats etc.

Inc. *see* **incorporated**.

incentive something offered to encourage greater effort. *We will offer extra payment to the salesman with the highest sales for the month – that should be a good incentive.*

incentive scheme a plan of more payment for more effort, e.g. a plan by which a salesman could earn more money if his sales are more than a certain amount. *Our incentive scheme is that each salesman will get £1 for every case which he sells above 100 cases each month.*

incidental expenses small payments or expenses which are in addition to the main expenses. *The business trip cost £1000 in travel expenses and about £50 for incidental expenses such as tips, taxis and so on.*

income money coming in, e.g. from wages or salary (to a person), from sales (to a company), from **investments**. *He had a steady income of £15,000 a year, made up of £12,000 salary and £3000 interest from his savings.*

income and expenditure account a statement of a **non-profit-making organisation** (such as a **charity**) showing the money received during a period of time and all the money paid out in expenses. (It takes the place of the **profit and loss account** for a profit-making organisation).

incomes policy rules which a government lays down in relation to increases in wages or salaries. *The government's incomes policy is based on no one getting a wage increase greater than 5%.*

income statement a written or printed list of money received and money paid out for a period, especially (*US*) a **profit and loss account**.

income tax a tax on money received from salary, **investments**, rent, profits from business etc.

in-company training training of workers which is done inside the company (and not by a business school or college). *I don't have to go away for training because the firm has an in-company training course.*

incompetent not able, not skilled, not qualified. *I don't know why they gave him a job, he's completely incompetent.*

incorporate (1) to make (something) a part of something else. *I have incorporated your ideas in my speech.* (2) to form into a **corporation**.

incorporated (*especially US, also* **Inc.**) formed into a **corporation**.

Incoterms terms used in international trade whose meanings have been agreed by most of the trading countries of the world. These terms and their meanings have been drawn up by the **International Chamber of Commerce**.

increasing returns to scale increasing efficiency by increasing **output**.

increment something added to an existing amount, e.g. a salary increase. *I've had my yearly increment – another 5%.*

incremental cost = marginal cost.

indemnity (1) **security** against loss, or damage. *Your indemnity under this insurance will pay for all damage.* (2) **compensation** for a loss.

indent *noun* an order from an overseas buyer to an **export house** to buy certain goods and send them to the buyer.

indent *verb* (1) to start a line of writing, e.g. on a letter, further into the page than the other lines. (2) **indent for** to put in an order for. *We'll have to indent for some more paper.*

indenture a **contract** between a company and a young worker regarding the number of years he must work to become qualified in a certain trade.

independent (**shop**) a shop owned by a single person or a single company (owning only this shop). See appendix 7.

index (1) a list of names, subjects etc., in alphabetical order, e.g. at the end of a book. *Look up the index and see what page deals with management.* (2) a similar listing but on separate cards and called a **card index**. *The library has all the books listed as a card index.*

index-linked of increases in pay, salary or **pension** etc., related to the **cost-of-living index**. *The cost of living went up 5% this year and so did my pension – it is index-linked.*

index number a number which shows the relative change in prices, wages, **cost of living** etc. over a period of time. For example if a company is measuring its **export** sales it might give its total export sales for 1980 the value of 100. A ten-per-cent increase in sales in 1981 would be represented by the value 110. If in 1982 sales were five per cent up on 1980, then 1982 sales would be indexed 105.

index of retail prices *see* **cost-of-living index**.

indirect cost a cost not related to the making of a **product**, e.g. office costs, rates, rent, manager's salaries etc.

indirect labour costs wages paid to a factory worker who does not actually make the goods, e.g. to a person who keeps the factory clean.

indirect material cost any cost of material which is not used in the making of the **product**. For example the wood used in making a chair is a direct material cost but the materials used up in cleaning the machinery is an indirect material cost.

indirect tax a tax which is not taken directly off **income** or profits, e.g. **value-added tax**.

indorse *see* **endorse**.

induction the act of introducing a person into a new position, in a company.

induction training teaching new workers the method etc. of a job.

industrial accident an injury which happens at work (at the factory or in the office). *See* **occupational accident**.

industrial action action by workers which is intended to slow down, stop or interrupt the work of a company. It often follows on from an **industrial dispute**.

industrial dispute an argument between management and workers over something, e.g. wages, hours of work, new machinery etc. The term is usually used when the disagreement could lead to a **strike**.

industrial estate (*or* **trading estate**) an area in or around a city which has been set aside especially for offices and factories. Usually **sponsored** by the government, and usually the space is given for a low rent. *See also* **advanced factory**.

industrial goods goods that are bought by companies to help them in their own business, e.g. office desks and chairs, factory machinery, raw materials etc. *Compare with* **consumer goods**.

industrialist a person who owns or controls a large factory or factories.

industrial market all the companies that buy goods or **services** to help them in their own business. For example the industrial market for cars is made up of all those companies which buy cars to help them carry on their own business. *See also* **industrial goods**.

industrial relations (*or* **labour relations**) attitudes between management and workers and how they relate to each other. *One thing about the Clyde Works Company, the industrial relations are very good – do you know they've never had a strike?*

industrial revolution (*UK*) the period from the 18th to the 19th century during which certain developments took place, e.g. the coming of power by water and steam, the move by people from farms to factories, the growth of cities, the inventions in spinning, weaving, in coal and steel making, the laying of the railway system.

industrial tribunal a group of three people with the power to settle a **dispute**, if both sides agree to bring the dispute to the tribunal. It usually consists of a lawyer and two people to represent the interest of employers and workers respectively and is used to hear and settle **disputes** on such matters as pay due to a worker, meaning of certain terms in the **contract of employment** etc.

industrious very hard-working.

industry (1) work done in order to manufacture goods; the organisations concerned with this. (2) all companies. *Industry supports the new law on trade union strikes.* (3) work, especially hard work. *The industry of the working man can be seen in the high output figures.*

industry-wide agreement an agreement between leaders of a **trade union** and representatives of all employers in a certain industry. *The print workers have a new industry-wide agreement on hours of work.*

inelastic demand a situation where a large change in price has only a slight effect on people's willingness to buy something.

inelastic supply a situation where the amount of something offered for sale changes very little when the price changes.

inertia selling selling goods by delivering them although they have not been ordered, and then asking for payment. The seller depends on the receiver paying for the goods rather than going to the trouble of sending them back. In the UK, it is quite legal to refuse to send them back and to charge rent to the sender for storage space taken up by these goods.

inflation continued increases in prices and wages which results in the value of money falling.

inflationary spiral a situation when increases in wages causes costs to increase, which causes prices to increase, which causes demands for an increase in wages. *According to some politicians there's only one way to stop the inflationary spiral – no more wage increases.*

information retrieval the **process** of getting information from a source of **data**. The data may be a paper in a filing cabinet or on tapes or **disks** in a **computer**.

infrastructure all the **systems** which support a country's industry and **economy**, e.g. road, rail, post and airway systems; factory, hospital, housing and education systems; radio, television and telephone systems; water, gas and electric systems. *You can tell a country's stage of economic growth from its infrastructure.*

ingot a bar of gold or silver.

inherent vice (**insurance**) a natural fault in the thing insured. For example, all food will go bad eventually, certain metal will rust easily under wet conditions. *Insurance companies will not pay out money for an inherent vice.*

inherit to receive (something, e.g. property, money) which has been left by a person who has died. *He knows that when his father dies he will inherit the business.*

inheritance something (e.g. property, money) which has been **inherited**. *His inheritance was a silver watch and £10,000.*

initial sale the first sale of a **product**. *The initial sale of the new machine makes us hopeful for more sales in the future.*

injunction an order from a court ordering a person to do or not to do, a certain thing. *The customer got an injunction which stopped the company from selling the new baby food until it had further health tests.*

injury benefit money paid to a worker because of an injury, or sickness, at his/her place of work. *He was off work for three weeks because of his injury and received injury benefit of £80 per week.*

Inland Revenue that part of the government in charge of collecting national taxes.

innovate to do something in a new way, e.g. to make new **products** or **services**. *A company has to innovate or its products and its profits will die.*

innovation something which has been made or introduced for the first time. *Video is a wonderful innovation – but then so was the first photograph.*

input something which is to be put into something else, e.g. information into a **computer**.

inquire see **enquire**.

insert written or printed material which is placed inside something else, e.g. a magazine. *To help sales they are putting an insert in the form of an order card in every copy of the magazine.*

insider dealings (*or* **insider trading**) buying or selling **stocks** and **shares** by people who have knowledge of some event which affects the value (when this information is not known to the general public). For example, knowledge is available to a director of the company which is about to make a **bid** for another company. If the director uses this knowledge to buy **shares** in the other company he is engaged in insider dealings.

insolvent of a person or company that is unable to pay debts when they fall due. *He has no money – he is insolvent.*

inst. *see* **instant**.

instalment a regular payment of a debt at certain intervals of time. *We are paying off the office furniture in instalments – £40 per week.*

instalment purchase buying by **instalments** where the buyer is already the owner. *Compare with* **hire-purchase.**

instant (*or* **inst.**) this present month; sometimes used in business letters.

in-store promotion advertising at the **point-of-sale**, i.e. inside the shop or the showroom, e.g. special-price tickets, or a special **display** of the **products**, or the offer of free **samples**.

instrument a legal **document**, e.g. a **contract**.

insurable interest a legal relationship between the **insured** and the subject of the **insurance**. Before one can insure any property or insure against something happening, one must have an insurable interest in the matter; one can't insure against loss or damage of **cargo** unless one stands to lose **financially** from such loss or damage.

insurance a **contract** with an **insurer** to make good any **financial** loss if a certain thing should happen. For example a businessman can protect himself against the financial loss of his factory being burned down or he can insure against loss of or damage to his **stocks**, or **cargo** etc. (The word **insurance** is generally used in connection with something that may happen, for example, a fire and the word **assurance** is used for something that must happen, for example, a death.)

insurance broker a person who offers advice on and may arrange the best **insurance** for certain risks. A businessman sending goods by sea to Brazil may use an insurance broker to arrange the best **cover**.

insurance (*or* **assurance**) **company** a company that offers to make payments if a certain event should happen, e.g. a death, a fire, etc., in exchange for certain payments, called **premiums**.

insurance policy a **document** laying out the terms of an **insurance contract**.

insurance premium a payment which is made by the person who takes out an **insurance policy** or **contract**.

insured a person who or organisation which has taken out an **insurance policy** as protection against the **financial** loss of something happening, e.g. the loss of goods by fire.

insurer an **insurance company** or **insurer** at **Lloyds** which **contracts** to pay the **financial** loss of something happening (e.g. the loss of a ship at sea) in exchange for the payment of a **premium**. *See also* **insurance, insurable interest.**

intangible assets (*or* **invisible assets**) unseen **assets** which are of value of a company, e.g. having the **sole** rights to make a successful **product** (the **copyright**), or **patents**, or **goodwill**.

integrate to bring (parts) together to form a whole. *When forming the company plan he integrated all the suggestions of the managers.*

INTELSAT *see* **International Telecommunications Satellite Organisation**.

intensive selling selling more to the company's existing customers by using more persuasion, e.g. more forceful selling, more advertising, more **sales promotion**.

intercompany comparison (*or* **interfirm comparison**) a method of finding out if a company's performance is worse, as good or better than other companies in the same industry. This is done by matching a company's business results against the published results of other companies. These business results are in the form of **ratios** or percentages and will include for example: the percentage **gross profit**, expenses, **net profit** and **return** on **capital employed**. *See* Centre for Interfirm Comparison.

interest money paid to a lender of cash for the use of it.

interest-free loan money which is lent without the lender charging for its use. *Sometimes people help charities with interest-free loans.*

interest rate a charge for the use of borrowed money. It is usually given as a certain percentage of every £100 borrowed for a year. *He borrowed money from the bank to buy a car and they are charging an interest rate of 20%; so for every £100 borrowed for a year he has to pay the bank £20.*

interface (1) where different interests meet and affect each other, e.g. different jobs, different exports. *In our company we have improved the interface between management and workers.* (2) (**computers**) an **electronic device** for linking a **computer** to **peripheral equipment**.

interfirm comparison *see* **intercompany comparison**.

interim dividend an amount of money paid by a company to its **shareholders** before the end of its **financial year** with the intention of making another payment at the end of the year.

interim report a short statement given before the end of something, e.g. a report to **shareholders** issued by a **public company** before the end of its **financial year**.

intermediary a person who passes proposals between two **parties** in a business deal, e.g. between a **trade union** and a company or between a buyer and a seller.

internal audit a check of one or more of the departments of a company, e.g. sales, production, **finance**, by expert employees of the company. The report which follows such an audit is usually made to the directors of a company.

internal economies of scale savings in costs which a large company can make, e.g. by using up-to-date machinery, improving the training of its workers, cutting material costs by buying in bulk, spreading all costs over a greater **output** etc.

international having to do with more than one country. *If we want to sell more we have to export – we have to sell on the international market, not just the home market.*

International Atomic Energy Agency (*or* **IAEA**) an agency formed in 1957 which has a working relationship with the **United Nations**. Its purpose is to encourage the growth and use of atomic energy for the purposes of peace, health and prosperity throughout the world. Membership: 110 countries. Headquarters: Vienna. Official languages: Chinese, English, French, Russian, Spanish.

International Bank for Reconstruction and Development (*or* **IBRD,** *or* **World Bank**) United Nations bank, set up in 1944 to encourage the flow of **capital** between countries for **economic** purposes, to offer loans at fair **interest rates** to **developing countries**. Headquarters: Washington, DC. Membership: 139 countries. Official language: English.

International Chamber of Commerce an organisation with branches in many countries which aims to help companies with their general business and **economic** problems.

international company = **multinational company**.

International Court of Justice (*or* **ICJ**) the **United Nations** court formed in 1945 to settle **disputes** between members of the United Nations and to advise on legal matters raised by any of its official organisations. Headquarters: The Hague. Official languages: English, French.

International Energy Agency (*or* **IEA**) a group formed by the **OECD** ministers in Paris in 1974 to agree on the sharing of oil between members in times of difficulties over oil supplies. Membership: twenty-one countries, including Australia, Belgium, Canada, Federal Republic of Germany, Italy, Japan, Netherlands, Sweden, United Kingdom, United States. Headquarters: Paris.

International Finance Corporation (*or* **IFC**) a **United Nations** **agency** formed in 1957 mainly to encourage **private enterprise** in member states, especially the **less-developed countries**. Headquarters: Washington, DC. Membership: 118 countries. Official language: English.

International Fund for Agricultural Development (*or* **IFAD**) a **fund** formed by the **United Nations** in 1974 to help **developing countries financially** in all matters to do with food, including production, storage and distribution. Headquarters: Rome. Membership: 131 countries.

International Labour Organisation (*or* **ILO**) an **agency** of the **United Nations** formed in 1946 to achieve **full employment** for its members, to raise their **standard of living** and to improve **working conditions.** Headquarters: Geneva. Membership: 144 countries. Official languages: English, French.

International Monetary Fund (*or* **IMF**) an **agency** of the **United Nations** formed in 1974. Its purposes include: to promote world trade and the employment and **income** of its member states; to try to keep exchange rates steady; to loan money to member states for these purposes. Headquarters: Washington DC. Membership: 141 countries.

International Telecommunications Satellite Organisation (*or* **INTELSAT**) an international organisation of over a hundred countries formed in 1971 to develop, construct, operate and maintain the world-wide system of **communications satellites.** Membership includes: Argentina, Australia, Belgium, Canada, China, France, Japan, Saudi-Arabia, United Kingdom, United States, Vatican City, Yemen Arab Republic, Zaire, Zambia. Headquarters: Washington DC. Official languages: English, French, Spanish.

interview *noun* (1) a formal meeting between (usually) two people where one questions the other about something important, e.g. about a new job, or an increase in salary. *I am going for an interview for a job.*

interview *verb* to hold an interview with. *They are interviewing six people for the job of sales manager. The Prime Minister was interviewed on TV last night.* (2) to try to get opinions from people, e.g. for a research survey. *The* market research company planned to interview 100 housewives to find out what they thought about the new product.

intestate (*law*) of a person who has died, without leaving a will. *He died intestate.*

intra vires (*Latin, meaning* within the powers) (*law*) of an action, e.g. by a representative of an organisation, which is **legally binding** on the organisation.

in-tray a tray on a desk which contains letters, messages, **documents** which a manager has to attend to. (When attended to they will be placed in the **out-tray**.)

in-tray exercise a method of training a person in management by creating a business situation for him to handle. The in-tray exercise is a copy of a manager's busy day at the office. Urgent letters, **memos**, phone messages, **documents** all have to be attended to within a certain time. He has to consider each item in the 'in-tray' and come to a decision about it, then place it in the 'out-tray'.

intrinsic value the worth of something in its natural state, e.g. the price of gold in its natural, unworked form is its intrinsic value. *See also* **extrinsic value**, **market value**.

introductory offer any special price, gift, etc. used by a company to get customers to try a **product** for the first time. *There's an introductory offer on this new toothpaste – you get two tubes for the price of one.*

inventory (1) the value of the **stock** of something, e.g. the value of a company's **raw materials**, or **work-in-progress** or **finished goods**. (2) detailed list of **stock**. *We have to do an inventory of our entire stock of cigarettes and cigars.* (3) **stock**.

inventory control the act or **process** of keeping **stock** to a planned level. Methods of inventory control include **sales forecasts** etc.

invest (1) to use (money) so as to get a profit from it, e.g. by putting it into a bank or by buying **stocks** and **shares**. (2) to put (time, effort etc.) into something. *I have invested a lot of time on this project.*

investment (1) money used by a company to buy **assets**, e.g. land, buildings, machinery. *See* appendix 2. (2) money used to buy **stocks**, **shares**, **securities** or placed on **deposit account** at a bank. *His investments gave him an additional income of £2000.* (3) the act of **investing**.

investment grant money paid by the government to a company to help with its buying of new machinery etc.

investment income money in the form of **interest**, profit or **dividends** from an **investment**.

investment portfolio a list of where a person's or a company's money is **invested**. *His investment portfolio included £5000 invested in a steel company, and £10,000 invested in an engineering firm. See also* **investment**.

investment trust a company which offers its **shares** to the public and whose business is the buying and selling of **securities**.

investor a person who puts money into a company, or who buys **shares** to make a profit, or who paid money on **deposit** at a bank to earn **interest**. *As an investor in gold mines he took many risks. See also* **investment**.

invisible assets *see* **intangible assets**.

invisible exports/imports the **export/import** of **services** such as **insurance**, shipping, banking, tourism, which can earn money without any actual goods being sold.

invoice a printed notice, sent to the buyer of goods which gives the details of the goods ordered (the number, the size, price etc.) and of any **trade discounts**.

I.O.U. (short for 'I owe you') a piece of paper with these letters on it, as well as the amount owed, the date and the signature of the person who owes the money; it can be used as a legal proof of debt. *I loaned him five pounds and he gave me an I.O.U. made out for this amount.*

ironmongers a **retail** shop which deals in goods made of metal such as locks, keys, spades etc. *See also* **hardware**.

irrevocable letter of credit *see* **letter of credit**.

issued capital the value of all the **shares** put out by a company to its **shareholders**.

issued price a price of **shares** etc. when first offered for sale to the public.

issuing house name given to the company or organisation which sells to the public a company's issue of new **shares**. Often the issuing house is a **merchant bank** and often the issue of new shares takes place when a **private company** becomes a **public company**.

J

jerry-built built using low-quality materials, poor workmanship, cheap methods. *You can tell the house was jerry-built, it has only been up a few months and the roof is leaking.*

jetsam (1) goods which have been thrown overboard from a ship at sea in order to make a ship safer. (2) goods thrown over the side of a ship at sea which have been washed up on a shore. *See also* **flotsam**.

jettison to throw goods or part of a ship overboard (e.g. loose timber, torn sails etc.) in order to lighten the ship in a storm, to make the ship safer. *See also* **flotsam**.

jingle a short, repeated, song which advertises something while it is being shown in the cinema, or on television, or which advertises it on radio.

job (1) an occupation, especially one by which one earns one's living. *I am the manager of the factory – that's my job.* (2) a piece of work. *I've been given the job of sorting out the letters this morning.* (3) an order which is being **processed** in a factory. *How is job number 146 getting on, is it finished?* (4) a crime, such as theft or burglary. *He is in prison for a job he did in London.*

job analysis a study of the detail of a piece of work to be done in a factory, e.g. cost of materials, time taken to complete it etc. *See also* **job** (meaning 3).

jobber a person who buys and sells on the **stock exchange**.

job card a card giving details of a **job** (meaning 3) in a factory, e.g. its number, the work to be done, time taken to do it.

job centre (*or formerly*) **labour exchange**) a government office in the main part of a town or city which helps people to find jobs, e.g. by displaying cards with details of jobs which are vacant.

job costing working out the cost of materials, wages etc. for a **job** (meaning 3) in a factory.

job description a list of the important factors of a **job** (meaning 1), e.g. the purpose, the duties and the responsibilities of the job. *The company sent him a job description and after reading it he thought he might have a chance of getting the job, so he applied for it.*

job enrichment the result of re-arranging the methods of working, e.g. re-arranging how the parts of a car are fitted together in a factory, so that the workers are more in charge of how they work, have more responsibility for doing the work, and get more pleasure from the job.

job evaluation a method of judging the relative worth of **jobs** (meaning 1) within a company, deciding how much skill, responsibility, experience etc. they need.

job lot a group of different things bought or sold together usually at a low price. A job lot is usually made up of things left over from other ranges of goods. For example, if the contents of a house were being sold off, a job lot might be made up of unsold kitchen things offered at a low price.

job mobility (*or* **labour mobility**) the extent to which people will move from one part of the country to another in search of **jobs** (meaning 1) or to change jobs. *The job mobility among managers in the UK is quite high.*

job number a number given to each **job** (meaning 3), (or order, or **contract**) inside a company, so that its progress can be checked.

job satisfaction the pleasure a worker gets from his/her work. It may come from the comradeship, the pay, the security, the chances of promotion, etc. in a job. *I know it's not well paid but I get job satisfaction from the job being a very responsible one.*

job security the extent to which a worker feels that his **job** (meaning 1) will last. *Being a football team manager is a terrible job – there's no job security. If your team keeps losing, you are out!*

job specification a detailed description of a **job** (meaning 1), including its responsibilities and the abilities and qualifications needed to do it.

joint account a **bank account** owned by two or more people. *My wife and I have a joint account at the bank.*

joint consultations talks between management and workers before decisions are made on matters which may affect the workers. *If we lay out the machinery in the way you suggest we will improve the output – but we must have joint consultations before we do anything like that.*

joint demand the sale of goods which are closely related, e.g. bread and butter, houses and cookers, cars and car radios.

joint owners two or more people who own the same property. *My wife and I are joint owners of the house.*

joint-stock bank a bank that is a **public company**, that is owned by **shareholders**. Their **financial** responsibility to the bank extends only to the **face value** of their **shares**. *See* **commercial bank**.

joint-stock company a company whose **capital** is made up of **shares** held by a number of people.

joint venture two or more companies or persons coming together for a special purpose (e.g. to get a **contract**). *Since the Jones Company were builders and the L & C Company were electricians they decided on a joint venture for the new hospital contract.*

journal (*or* **day book**) (**bookkeeping**) the book in which all the **debit** and **credit** entries are written as they take place each day. These entries are then written into their appropriate **books of account**.

journey a day of business calls by a salesman. *I have five calls to make on today's journey. See also* **journey planning**.

journeyman a workman who has trained over a period of years to become qualified in his trade. *See also* **apprentice**.

journey planning planning a salesman's daily calls on customers. The plan for each day's calls will include the number of calls, the order in which the calls will be made, the route to be taken and the mileage to be covered.

JP *see* **Justice of the Peace**.

judgement creditor a person who has successfully brought an **action** against someone in a court of law and has 'obtained judgement' for the amount **claimed**, i.e. the law has ordered the debtor to pay a certain amount to the judgement creditor. *See also* **judgement debt**, **judgement debtor**.

judgement debt money which a court has ordered to be paid to a person (the **judgement creditor**).

judgement debtor a person who has been ordered by the court to pay a sum of money to a **creditor**. *See also* **judgement creditor**.

jumble sale a sale of used clothes, books etc. (usually to raise money for a good cause). *The old folk's club could do with a bus outing – let's have a jumble sale to raise the money.*

justice of the peace (*or* **JP**) a member of the public appointed to act as judge in a lower court of law.

K

K (1) short for one thousand. *The advertisement said the salary was £14K per year,* i.e. £14,000 per year. (2) **computer** term for the number 1024.

KD (*or* **knocked down**) goods may be delivered KD, that is, knocked down into parts which can be put together again after delivery. For example, furniture, small sheds, some cars are **exported** on a KD basis, to be put together again when received.

keelage money paid for the use of a port or harbour.

Kennedy round an agreement on **tariff** reductions (named after the US president John F Kennedy), reached in 1964 between the member states to the **General Agreement on Tariffs and Trade**.

keyboard the part of a typewriter, **computer** etc. with rows of letters and numbers, worked by pressing a special key for each letter or number.

keyed advertisement a method of measuring the response to an advertisement in a certain newspaper or magazine. For example an advertisement for jewellery might invite the

reader to write to the company for more information. Included in the company's address might be the words: Dept. (L/T). Anyone answering this particular advertisement will be showing that he saw the advertisement in the London Times (which could be the meaning of the 'key': Dept. (L/T).)

key points (*or* **key factors**) the important points in a task, or a speech, or in a sales message. *The key points in this advertising campaign are three: the product is new, it does what we claim, and it is low-priced.*

kickback (*or* **rake-off**) (*US: informal*) a secret (usually illegal) payment to a person to get an order or a **contract**. *There's a rumour they paid a kickback of 5% of the current price to someone in the company. See also* **bribe**.

kicked upstairs (*informal*) given a better-paid job inside a company but with less responsibility. A person is kicked upstairs to get rid of him usually from a post he cannot manage. *He was really no good at the job of marketing manager so they made him a director of one of our smaller companies: he was kicked upstairs.*

kilometer 1000 metres (or about 0.6 of a mile, or about 1094 yards).

kind: in kind (1) in goods, not money. *The workers on the farm are paid partly in kind; they get free eggs and milk.* (2) in the same way. *He insulted me and I replied in kind.*

kite mark the symbol in the form of a kite which is the mark of the **British Standards Institution**. A **product** which carries this mark has passed the standard of quality set by the institution.

knocked down *see* **KD**.

knock-for-knock agreement (car **insurance**) an agreement between **insurance companies** that if two vehicles suffer damage in a crash each company will pay the insurance **claim** of its **client**. This saves the cost of many minor legal agreements.

knocking copy advertisement which criticises another **product**.

knocking-off time (*informal*) the time at which the working day ends. *I should be home by six o'clock because knocking off time in our office is half-past five.*

know-how (*informal*) skill, knowledge, experience.

L

lab *see* **laboratory**.

label (1) a piece of paper on a bottle or package which describes what is in it. *The label says it is safe for children.* See also **own-brand**.

label *verb* to fix or apply a label to (a **product**, a piece of luggage etc). *In the labelling department the machines labelled the bottles at great speed.*

laboratory (*or* **lab**) a room or a building used for scientific work etc. *Our chemists have produced a new range of cosmetics in the lab.* See also **language laboratory**.

labour (1) work. *Painting this fence is hard labour.* (2) people who do heavy work with their hands (usually) in a factory. *Management and labour are now in full agreement about the wage increase.*

labour agreement a **contract** between a company and its workers, e.g. on payment per hour. *They have reached a labour agreement on the number of holidays per year.*

labour cost (1) wages and other expenses of workers in a company. *Our labour cost is higher now because of the last wage increase.* (2) wages and other expenses of workers on a particular job, or **product**. *The labour cost of this product – not counting the material – is £10.*

labourer a worker who does heavy work with his hands. *He got a job at the factory as a labourer. He worked all day cleaning machines.*

labour exchange *see* **job centre**.

labour force (1) all the workers in a factory. *The labour force agreed to the wage increase.* (2) all the workers in a country. *It is a nation which attracts a lot of foreign firms because it has a well-educated labour force.*

labour-intensive industry a trade where a large amount of money is paid out in wages in relation to the money paid for **assets** (like buildings, machinery). *The retail trade is a labour-intensive industry.* See also **capital-intensive**.

labour market the number of workers in an area. *They decided to build their new factory in Liverpool because of the labour market there.*

labour mobility *see* **job mobility**.

labour relations *see* **industrial relations**.

labour turnover the rate at which people leave a company. Usually measured by:

$$\frac{\text{number of people who left during the year}}{\text{average number of people in the company during the year.}}$$

LAFTA (*or* **Latin American Free Trade Association**) *see* **Latin American Integration Association**.

LAIA *see* **Latin American Integration Association**.

laissez-faire the theory that governments should not interfere with how firms (or people) conduct their business.

lame duck a person or organisation that is weak and unable to manage his/her/its affairs. *The company is now a lame duck – its products are no longer selling.*

landed terms an export price which includes all charges up to the goods being unloaded at the port to which they have been sent.

landing charges the cost of unloading goods from a ship plus the cost of moving the goods into storage plus

customs duties, which have to be paid to the port authority where the goods arrive.

landlady (1) a woman who owns property and rents it to others. (2) a woman who is in charge of a pub, inn, a small hotel etc.

landlord (1) a man who owns property and who rents it to others. (2) a man who is in charge of a pub, inn etc.

land registration the system of putting on record (i.e. registering) the ownership of land in England and Wales. These records help in the buying and selling of land and they are kept in the government department known as the **Land Registry**.

language laboratory a room specially fitted out to allow a person to learn a foreign language by means of tape recordings. The person can learn the language at his/her own pace and can compare his/her speech with the voice on the tape. A teacher can help by listening to the student and giving advice.

larceny (*law*) theft.

last in first out (*oe* **LIFO**) a method of valuing **stock** at the earlier cost (rather than at current cost). *See also* **FIFO**.

last will and testament a legal term for a person's final will which cancels any earlier will.

latent defect a fault which is not seen. *The cars which left the factory in June were recalled because of a latent defect which was found in the steering.*

Latin American Integration Association (*or* **LAIA** *or* **ALADI**) a group of Latin American countries formed at Montevideo, Uruguay in 1980. It replaced the **Latin American Free Trade Association**. The aim is to lower **trade barriers** and thus increase trade between member states. Membership: Argentina, Bolivia, Brazil, Chile, Columbia, Ecuador, Mexico, Paraguay, Peru, Uruguay, Venezuela. Head-

quarters: Montevideo. Official languages: Spanish, Portuguese.

launch (1) to begin something. *He launched into a story about business.* (2) to put (a plan) into action. *Next week we launch the new product onto the market.*

Law Society in England and Wales, the examining body for the profession of **solicitor**. It has authority over all solicitors whether they are working as solicitors or not with regard to conduct and discipline.

lawsuit a non-criminal case in a court of law, i.e. a **civil case**.

lawyer a person whose profession it is to give advice on the law and to speak in court on someone's behalf. *Compare with* **barrister, solicitor**.

lay days (*shipping*) the usual number of days allowed for the loading or unloading of **cargo** from a ship. If the work continues beyond these agreed lay days a **rental** (known as **demurrage**) will be charged.

lay it/something on the line to give clear and strict instructions (about something). *The new manager laid it on the line to the workers: they either had to work harder or the company would go bankrupt.*

lay off *verb* to stop employing (a person). *They had to lay men off at the steel works – there's no work for them.*

lay-off *noun* the act of **laying off**. *There have been too many lay-offs in the coal industry lately.*

lay-off pay payment made to workers who have been sent home because there is no work for them, e.g. builders on a building site (because of the weather) or factory workers (because of a power cut).

layout the arrangement or design of a drawing, an advertisement, or printed material.

L/C *see* **letter of credit**.

lead a person who writes in to a company for more information as a result of seeing an advertisement which offers something for sale. *They spent £10,000 advertising their washing machines and got 1000 leads for their salesmen to call on.*

leader (1) a person in charge, who leads others. (2) a newspaper **column** which is the opinion of the editor on some piece of news. *Did you read this newspaper's leader on the election result? Compare with* **editorial**.

lead time the length of time between ordering something and having it delivered. *When ordering more supplies from the ABC company remember that their lead time is 2 weeks.*

leaflet a small sheet of printed paper, usually given free, which advertises a **product**, **service**, or event.

League of Arab States (*or* **Arab League**) a group of twenty-two Arab States formed in 1945 to strengthen the political, cultural, social and **economic** affairs of its members. Official language: Arabic.

leakage (**retailing**) loss of **stock** from wastage, e.g. bread, milk, vegetables which go bad; loss of stock from theft. *I expect £1000 of stock to be lost from leakage.*

leap-frogging the action of a group of workers when they try to get a pay-rise which matches one given to another group in the same industry. *The engineers now want a pay rise to match the one given to the welders – it is another case of leap-frogging.*

lease *noun* a **contract** for the use of an **asset** (e.g. land, machinery) in return for a rent.

lease *verb* (1) to give a person the use of (something) through a **lease**. (2) to get the use of (something) through a **lease**. *They leased the property for ten years.*

lease back *verb* to sell an **asset** (e.g. land, machinery) and then take a **lease** from the new owner to use the assets in return for rent.

leaseback *noun* such an arrangement.

leasehold property which is held on a **lease**

leasehold land land which is rented from the owner.

ledger a book in which all the **accounts** of a business are kept. Nowadays many businesses keep this information stored in **computers**.

legacy a gift made by a person in a will.

legal holiday a day when public banks are closed for business and when many companies are also closed, e.g. Christmas Day. *See also* **bank holiday**.

legally binding having to be obeyed according to the law: *a legally-binding contract.*

legal reserve the part of a bank's **assets** which must be kept as cash in order to meet the **claims** of **depositors**.

legal tender money which, if offered in payment for something, must be accepted by law.

legatee a person who receives something from a will.

legislation the making of laws by a parliament etc.; laws so made. *There is new legislation about drunken driving.*

lender of last resort the source which can in the end create funds, in the UK, the Bank of England.

less-developed country *see* **developing country**.

lessee a person who **leases** someone else's property.

lessor a person who gives his property on a **lease** to someone else.

letterhead a name, address, telephone number etc. printed at the top of a sheet of writing paper.

letter of attorney *see* **power of attorney**.

letter of credit (*also* **L/C**) a letter from one bank to another which gives the receiving bank authority to pay a certain sum of money to the person named in the letter. This is also a method of payment used by foreign buyers. In this case the UK seller would have to present **documents** to show that the goods have been sent to the foreign buyer. There are various kinds of letter of credit, e.g.:

documentary letter of credit a method of payment used by foreign buyers. The letter is issued by the buyer's bank to the seller's bank giving it **authority** to pay a certain sum of money to the seller. The seller will have to provide documentary proof (i.e. the shipping **documents**) that the goods have been **exported** to the buyer. It is important that every condition in the letter of credit is met by the seller or payment will be withheld. (For example the documents have to be those named by the buyer, the goods, prices etc. have to be as named).

irrevocable letter of credit one that cannot be changed without the consent of the seller. The irrevocable letter of credit contains a promise that the **importer's** bank will pay the seller through the seller's own bank. If the seller is unsure that this promise to pay will be carried out (because, say, of political risks) then he will prefer to have this promise supported by a bank in his own country. This would be a **confirmed irrevocable letter of credit**.

letter of hypothecation a letter from a shipper of goods to a bank giving the bank the rights to these goods in return for a loan of money. In other words the letter of hypothecation acts as **security** for the loan.

letters of administration a **document** given by a court by which a person can be put in charge of the **estate** of a person who has died. *See also* **intestate**.

letters patent an official **document** which gives the right to an inventor to make use or sell his

invention. This document is given by the **Patent Office**. *See also* **patent**.

leverage *see* **gearing**.

levy *verb* to put a tax on (something) *Do you think the government will levy a tax on fires?*

levy *noun* money collected by this means. *There is a training levy to be paid – and a capital levy.*

liabilities the amount of money that a company owes to others. *See* appendix 2.

liability (1) debt; sum of money that has to be paid. (2) the state of being legally responsible for loss, damage, a debt etc. (3) the amount of debt etc. that one is legally responsible for.

licence a printed permission from a person, in authority to do something, e.g. a licence (from the government) to drive a car. *You need a special licence in Britain to sell tobacco.*

licenced trade a general description for companies which buy and sell beer, wines, spirits (for which a special **licence** is needed), e.g. hotels, public houses, restaurants etc.

licensee a person who holds a **licence**, e.g. to sell something such as tobacco, beer, wine, spirits (for which a licence is needed). *Mr Smith is the manager of the pub but the licensee is the owner, Mr Jones.*

lien a right to take goods in order to make the owner of the goods pay a debt.

lieu: in lieu (of) instead of (of); as a substitute (for). *He was given a month's pay in lieu of notice*, i.e. he should have been told the month before that he was to lose his job, but instead he was given a month's salary to leave at once.

life annuity a series of payments made by an **assurance company** to a person during his life but which stops on his death. *See also* **annuity**.

life assurance a **contract** by which an **assurance** (or **insurance**) **company** agrees to pay a certain sum of money when a named person (the **life assured**) dies or at the end of a certain period of time, if he/she is still alive. The person who enters into this contract with the assurance company will have to pay regular sums of money to the company in return for this benefit. *See also* **insurance company**; **insurance premium**; **insured**; **insurer**.

life cycle *see* **family life cycle, product life cycle**.

life expectancy the number of years a person is expected to live. *Life expectancy today is much longer than it was 100 years ago.*

life style a way of living of a society or group of people. *Some say the life style of western countries uses up too much scarce resources.*

LIFO *see* **last in first out**.

lighter a low flat-bottomed boat used for carrying cargo between ship and shore.

lighterage a charge made when goods have to be moved by a **lighter**.

limitation period a period of time, fixed by law, after which legal **action** cannot be taken. *The court had to set him free because he had been held beyond the limitation period without a trial.*

limited (*or* **Ltd**) word which must come after the company name if it is a private **limited liability company**. *See also* **public limited company**.

limited liability company a company in which no **shareholder** can be asked to pay debts beyond the **face value** of his **shares**. **Liability** (meaning 3) is limited to this amount.

limited partner a member of a partnership whose **liability** (meaning 3) is limited to the amount of **capital** he has **invested** in it.

line manager a person in a company who is responsible for carrying

out the orders of his superiors and who has authority over others.

line of command a **system** in a company where each manager is responsible for carrying out the orders of the manager above him.

line of credit a loan made to a foreign firm or authority and supported by the **Export Credits Guarantee Department**.

line organisation a company structure where each manager reports directly to the person above him.

line printer a **device** which prints out information from a **computer** on wide sheets of paper, one full line at a time.

liner a large ship which carries passengers.

liquid asset an **asset** which can be quickly turned into cash, e.g. money owed by debtors.

liquidate (1) to sell (an **asset**, e.g. land, buildings, vehicles, materials) for cash. *He will have to liquidate this old stock.* (2) to sell all the assets of (a company) for cash, and so close the company down.

liquidated damages the amount of money, agreed to in a **contract**, which will be paid by one of the **parties** to the contract if he fails to keep his promise. For example, the contract may state that the Wine Shop Company promises to buy 1000 cases of wine each year from the French suppliers and if orders fall below that figure then £500 must be paid to the French supplier. The £500 is called liquidated damages.

liquidating value *see* **break-up value**.

liquidation the act of **liquidating** (meaning 2). *I believe the newspaper shop has gone into liquidation.*

liquidator a person appointed to sell off a company's **assets** for cash, to share out this money to those owed money by the company, and then to divide up the rest between the owners.

liquidity the state of having cash (or **assets** which can be quickly turned into cash) to pay one's debts. *The company is in a state of liquidity – we can pay all our debts from our cash in the bank plus the amount owed to us by debtors.*

liquidity ratio (*or* **acid test**) this measures how well a company's **current liabilities** (what it owes just now) are covered by its cash (or by **assets** which can be turned into cash quickly, such as debtors).

listed company a company which is listed on a **stock exchange**, i.e. a **public company**.

listed securities shares which can be bought and sold in a **stock exchange**, i.e. they are on the official list of shares which can be so traded.

list price a company's price, as printed in their list of prices. *The list price of this typewriter is £500 but we are selling it for £350.*

litigation the **process** of asking a court to settle a **dispute**.

litre a metric measure of liquid (1.7598 pints).

live account a customer who is regularly buying. *This account, Jones & Co, is no longer a live account because the company has gone out of business.*

living standards *see* **standard of living**.

living wage pay for doing work which is just enough to buy the essentials of life, e.g. food, rent, heat. *The pay in this job is so low it is not even a living wage.*

Lloyd's a world-famous **insurance** centre in London which began in a coffee house run by Edward Lloyd in the seventeenth century. A wide range of insurances are arranged here. Members of Lloyd's are represented by **underwriting** managers, who deal only with **brokers.**

Lloyd's agents people throughout the world appointed by **Lloyd's** to give information on shipping, air-

craft etc., to Lloyd's. Lloyd's agents can also appoint experts to report on damage, or loss, of **cargo** or ships.

Lloyd's Certificate of Marine Insurance a **document** which proves that a **marine insurance** with Lloyd's is in existence. The certificate gives details of the insurance and the goods carried.

Lloyd's list a daily newspaper giving details of arrival, departure and movements of ships, including losses and **claims**.

Lloyd's Register of Shipping a detailed record of ships giving facts on **tonnage**, fittings etc.

load *noun* (1) something being carried or to be carried. *A load of steel bars has just arrived at the factory. This load of goods has to go to a customer.* (2) the weight carried by a wall etc. *That is a load-bearing wall – if you knock it down the roof will fall in.* (3) the power of an electric charge.

load *verb* (1) to put (a **cargo**) onto a ship, truck etc. (2) to increase an **insurance premium** to cover certain expenses. (3) to put (a **program**) into a **computer memory**.

loading the amount by which an **insurance premium** is increased to cover expenses.

loan an amount of money given to a person, to be returned later. *How much of a loan were you looking for?*

loan account an **account** opened by a bank when a person borrows money from it. In the account will be entered the amount of the loan and any payments made by the borrower.

loan capital part of the **capital** of a company, given for a fixed period of time and entitled to **interest** for the loan. *See also* **share capital**.

loan shark (*informal*) a person who loans money at very high **interest** rates. *The man is a loan shark – he wants £30 interest on every £100 borrowed.*

lobby *noun* a person or group trying to influence someone in power (e.g. member of parliament, government minister) by argument or discussion. *A lobby met the minister and tried to talk to him on the matter.*

lobby *verb* to try to get influence in this way.

local authority a form of government of local affairs whereby a group of people are elected by voters of the area to represent them. This group, called a corporation in England, has powers to spend money (given by the government) on such things as education, roads etc. and directs a permanent staff to organise these.

local press area or district newspapers published daily or weekly, giving all the local or area news (as distinct from the **national press**).

location any place in a **computer** store which can contain one unit of information.

lock-out an action by a company to stop workers from going into its factory to work, e.g. closing the factory, or locking the gates; in other words, a **strike** by the company against the workers.

lock, stock, and barrel everything, without exception. *He sold off everything in the shop, lock, stock, and barrel.*

logbook (1) a book kept by the master of a ship in which he writes all of the events during a ship's voyage, especially such things as the weather, ship's speed, etc. (2) (*formerly in UK*) a record of the ownership of a car.

London Bankers Clearing House a group of **commercial banks** which each day "clear" the cheques which have been paid into each of the banks, i.e. they balance out the cheques which are payment to a bank and those that are payment by a bank. As a result a cheque can be written by the banks concerned to settle any debt between them.

long-dated bill a **bill of exchange** due for payment a long-time ahead.

long-range plan one which plans the growth, e.g. of a company over the years ahead (usually five or more years). In making such a plan the company's strengths and weaknesses will be considered by the directors of the company, as well as the opportunities and threats in the market. *See also* **corporate planning**.

long-term liability a debt or loan which has to be paid in a period greater than one year ahead, usually more than five years.

loose tools tools which are small enough to be moved easily within a factory, e.g. small power **drills**, spanners etc. *The value of our machinery is about £150,000 but there is another £20,000 in loose tools about the factory.*

loss a failure to make a profit; a situation when money paid out on a **project** is greater than the money received. *We made a loss on that last contract – the costs were greater than our selling price.*

loss leader a **product** or **service** sold at a very low price, i.e. without making a profit, so that customers will be attracted to other products (or services), which are profitable. *We sell the bags of sugar cheap as a loss leader to get the housewives into the shop to buy all the other lines.*

lost-business report a written explanation to a manager or a director as to why the company did not succeed in getting a **contract**, or why a regular customer is now buying from some other company.

lot (1) a large quantity or number. *There were a lot of people working for the company.* (2) a number or group of similar things sold together at an **auction**. (3) (*mainly US*) an area of land set aside for a special purpose: *a parking lot.*

low-level language (*also* **assembly language**) a **computer** language with simple features.

low-loader a lorry which has been made so that its carrying area is much lower than normal. This means it can carry higher loads without causing obstruction. *We will need a low-loader to carry these new cases from London to York.*

low-pressure selling a method of selling where the salesman joins the buyer in solving the buyer's problem, rather than going after a quick sale. *See also* **high-pressure selling**.

lump sum an amount of money paid all together. *You can either get your pension at so much per week, or you can be paid one lump sum.*

lump system (*UK*) a method of employing workers in the building trade. The worker is not paid wages but is paid a sum of money when his work is done (i.e. he is treated as a separate company). This makes it easy for some workers to avoid paying tax on what they earn, and so attempts have been made to do away with this system.

luncheon voucher a slip of paper with an amount of money printed on it. These vouchers are given by some companies to their office staff and they are exchanged for meals in certain restaurants. *My pay is good and I also get luncheon vouchers.*

luxury a **product** or **service** which is over and above those needed for a normal **standard of living**, e.g. diamonds, furs, beauty treatments.

luxury tax a tax put on **luxuries**.

M

M1, M3 *see* **money supply**.

macadam a type of road surface made of a mixture of tar and small stones which is rolled onto a road to give a smooth hard surface.

machine a man-made **device** driven by power (e.g. electricity) to do work. *With this drilling machine we can drill twenty holes in ten seconds.*

machine code *see* **machine language**.

machine downtime a time when a machine is not working because of a breakdown or because it is being repaired etc. See also **machine idle time**.

machine idle time a time when a machine is ready for work but is out of action because of lack of material, labour, or orders, etc.

machine language (*or* **machine code**) information or **data** expressed in such a way that it can be directly understood by a **computer**.

machine loading planning the work to be done on a machine or machines in a factory so that the best use is made of time, men and machines for the work.

machine shop a place (such as a factory) where machines are at work.

machine tool a large machine for working on metal, wood, etc., e.g. a large **drilling** machine in a factory, a turning lathe, a grinding machine (all used to shape metal, wood, etc.).

machinist a person who works at a machine in a factory.

macro- *prefix* large, great, e.g. **macroeconomics**. *See also* **micro**.

macroeconomics the study of the whole **economy** of a country, i.e. a country's production, demand, prices, **imports**, **exports**, etc. and their effects on each other. *See also* **microeconomics**.

magazine (1) a publication which appears regularly, usually every week or every month (sometimes called a weekly (magazine) or monthly (magazine). It contains news, stories and items of special interest to the reader. Magazines are aimed at special groups of readers' e.g. young girls, golfers, older women, fishermen, etc. (2) a room or store which hold bullets, rifles, gunpowder etc. *On the ship all the guns were stored in the magazine.*

magnate a very rich and powerful businessman, often one who owns a large number of companies: *an oil magnate*.

magnet a material (usually metal) which can attract other pieces of metal to it.

magnetic having the quality of a **magnet**. *He held everyone's attention – he was a magnetic speaker.*

magnetic board a board used for the display of figures, lines, etc. The board and the things on **display** have been specially treated so that they can be moved around the board without falling off. This is done by the use of **magnets**.

magnetic disk (**computers**) a thin flat circular plate on which a large amount of **data** is stored. *See also* **floppy disk, hard disk**.

magnetic tape a long, narrow, thin film of plastic on which sound or other information is stored.

mail *noun* letters, parcels, etc. which are delivered by post. *Has the mail arrived yet?*

mail *verb* (*mainly US*) to send (letters, parcels etc.) by post.

mailing list a list of names and addresses of people or companies with special interests, e.g. managers, fishermen, companies that make cars, home-owners, etc. Such mailing lists are often used by companies who want to contact likely buyers by post. *I must be on the Acme Insurance Company's mailing list – they keep sending me through the post details of their new insurance schemes.*

mail order a form of buying and selling which uses the postal service instead of dealers. Mail-order companies advertise in newspapers and magazines and invite buyers to send off their orders by post. (Goods are often delivered by the same method but sometimes rail or road is used.) *See* **catalogue buying**.

mail-order house a company which sells goods by **mail order**.

main frame name given to a large centrally-placed **computer**.

maintenance keeping something in a good condition, especially machinery. *With that sort of maintenance our machines rarely break down.*

maintenance shift a special period of work, e.g. 6 pm–2 am, for the purpose of checking machines in a factory to make sure that they are in proper working order. *See also* **maintenance**.

major shareholder a person who or organisation which owns more **shares** in a company than anyone else.

make a killing (*informal*) to make a lot of profit in a business deal. *He bought oil shares when the price was low and when the price shot up he sold them and made a killing.*

make good (1) (*informal*) to be a success. *He started off a new business and this time he made good.* (2) to make up for (something that one has lost, damaged, etc.) by some kind of payment. *If any of this equipment is damaged, you must make good the loss.*

make or buy the act of working out the benefits and costs to a company of making a part which is needed (for a machine or a **product**) and of buying in the part from another company. From his examination of benefits and costs a company will decide whether to 'make or buy'.

manage (1) to be in charge of certain activities (or a certain department) in a company. (2) to succeed in doing something which is difficult. *Will you help me to move this desk? I can't manage it by myself.*

management (1) the act of **managing** (meaning 1). *The management of the office is a very important job.* (2) a group of managers, i.e. group of people inside a company who control and direct workers. *The management of the company met the workers to decide on* *their increase in pay.* (3) deciding how **plant**, machinery, materials, men, money should all be used so that a company's **financial** aims can be reached. *The proper management of a firm's resources is the job of the board of directors.*

management accounting a special study of costs and profits by experts in **accountancy** inside a company, in order to give **financial** information to managers in a way which will help them to make better planning decisions on **products** and departments.

management appraisal an examination of a manager's past work for the company so that his training needs and suitability for **promotion**, or increases in pay etc. can be seen. This appraisal is usually done by a superior (usually a director) on a regular basis.

management audit an examination of the ability of **management** in a company, their way of doing their work, their efficiency, etc. This is done so that weaknesses in people's ability do to their job or weaknesses in the methods they use can be seen and corrected.

management by crisis a manager's method – or style – of doing his job. This style of management allows the work done to get so bad (i.e. reach a crisis) that drastic, corrective action is necessary. The manager who manages by crisis does little planning since he waits for events to decide what he should do.

management by exception a method of managing people by which a manager will set out a plan – or a **budget** – for the people who work for him. Only any extreme departure from the plan will be brought to his notice and he will thus have time to deal with other matters. For example, a sales manager sets out a plan of sales for a salesman as follows: Jan 40 units, Feb 50, Mar 45, Apr 60, May 50. If the actual sales were: Jan 40 units, Feb 30, Mar 45, Apr 40, May 50, then the salesman would report to his manager about the sales of February and April at the end of each of these months.

management by objectives (*or* **MBO**) a method of managing people by which a manager agrees with each worker a plan of work to be done in a stated time. These objectives all form part of a plan for the company. At the end of that time the manager and the worker will both decide whether the plan has been achieved. MBO is also used to plan the work of managers. *See also* **management appraisal**.

management consultant a person who is an expert on management. His business is to advise companies on management problems. *The steel company brought in a firm of management consultants to help them get back into profit.*

management development planning the training needs of the managers of a company over the years ahead; especially training managers for future promotion.

management education training managers in the methods of management and in subjects related to managing people and **finance**. Such training can be in-house, or at college, university or a business school.

management game (*or* **business game**) a method of training for management. The people being trained are put into teams, each team representing a company in an industry. Each team receives basic facts about **capital**, sales, **stocks**, cash, **products**, etc., and has to solve its company's problems by making decisions, which affect each company in the industry. This changing pattern of results is meant to copy real life.

management services those parts of a company's organisation which advise and help managers in making decisions, especially about **work study** and **organisation and methods**.

management style (*also* **managerial style**) the way in which a manager gets his workers to do their job, how he behaves towards them, his method of giving orders and of controlling them etc.

management training part of **management education**; improving a manager's ability to do work by giving him the chance to experience problems and to study how to resolve them.

manager (*feminine* **manageress**) a person responsible for the control and training of a group of workers, for planning their work, setting their targets, and helping them in reaching those targets.

managerial style *see* **management style**.

managing director the director of a company responsible for the day-to-day running of the business. (In the UK he is also known as the **chief executive**; in the US he is known as president.) In a small company the managing director is usually the person who set up the company and who is the major **shareholder**. In a large **public company** he is usually appointed to this position.

mandate (1) an authority to act on someone's behalf. *He has a mandate to sign cheques on behalf of the owner of the firm.* (2) an authority to vote on someone's behalf. *The workers gave their shop steward a mandate to vote for them at the meeting.*

manhole an opening in the road, usually covered with a heavy metal plate, down which a worker can go to repair gas and water pipes, etc.

manifest an official list of the items loaded on to a ship, aircraft or vehicle. The manifest also lists the value, origin and **destination** of the goods and a copy is given to the customs.

manpower planning planning the number and type of workers and managers a company will need in the future and planning also how to get them.

Manpower Services Commission (*or* **MSC**) a body set up by the UK government in 1974 to run public employment and training services.

man-profile (*or* **man specification**) a list of the skills needed in a person to do a particular job. *Before they advertised for a sales manager they drew up a man-profile for the job.*

manual *adjective* done with the hands: *manual work.*

manual *noun* a book of instruction about work or machines, or to help in training someone in a job. *For the first week in the firm he studied the training manual.*

manual worker a person who uses his/her hands, often without needing any particular skill.

manufacture to make something, especially using machinery in a factory. *Jim's firm manufactures nuts and bolts but his brother's company manufactures chocolates.*

manufacturer a company which or person who manufactures something. *If the product is faulty send it back to the manufacturer.*

manufacturer's agent (*or* **manufacturer's representative**) a person or company that gets **contracts** for manufacturers. He works on **commission** in a certain area or region. *See also* **agent**.

manuscript (*or* **MS**, *plural* **MSS**) the first copy of a book or article, handwritten (or typed) and not yet printed. *He sent the manuscript to the typist and when it was typed he sent it to the publishers.*

margin (1) the difference between the buying and selling price, i.e. the **gross profit**. *If I sell at £1.50 my margin is 50 pence because my buying price* was £1. (2) the edge of a page where there is no writing. *When you type the letter leave a good margin all round.*

marginal cost (*also* **incremental cost**) the cost of making one more unit. If the total cost of making 100 units is £200 and the total cost of one more (101 units) is £202, then the marginal cost of the last unit is £2. The marginal cost is also known as the **variable** or **direct cost**.

marginal land land which covers the cost of producing crops but which shows no profit.

marginal pricing fixing the selling price of a **product** at the **marginal cost** of making it.

marginal revenue the added **income** from the sale of one additional unit. *See also* **marginal cost**.

margin of safety the amount of sales which are made above the **break-even point**. For example, if total costs are £10,000 and total sales are £10,000 the break-even point is reached (no profit and no loss is made). If total costs are £10,000 and total sales are £15,000 the margin of safety is £5,000. The break-even point and the margin of safety can be shown as a **break-even chart**. See appendix 3.

marine insurance a **contract** between an **insurance company** and the owner of a ship, **cargo** or **freight** against loss at sea. The centre of marine insurance is **Lloyd's** of London.

marine survey an examination of a ship by a **Lloyd's agent** for the purposes of a **marine insurance**.

maritime law (*also* **the law of the sea**) a special area of law relating to ships ports, harbours etc.

markdown lowering the price of something below its usual price; the amount by which it is lowered.

market (1) people with money to buy a **product** and also the desire to buy it. *The market for our cigars is made*

up of males, smokers, earning over £20,000 a year who want a high-quality cigar. (2) an area where things are sold. *We must develop in overseas markets.* (3) special place where buyers and sellers meet to do business: *the fish market, the stock market.*

marketable which can be sold. *The new product seems to me to be a marketable item.*

market analysis examining a market (meaning 1) to find out facts about it, such as numbers, age, sex, etc.

market channel *see* **channel of distribution**.

market coverage the number of likely buyers reached by an advertisement. *I think we should advertise in the Daily News because it is read by most of our customers, so it gives us better market coverage.*

market demand the total sales of a **product** in a period (usually a year). *The market demand for our brand of soup is 12,000,000 cans this year.*

market forces things which affect the sale of a **product**, e.g. price, competition, state of the **economy**.

marketing (1) examining **products** and **markets** so that the right product reaches the right market at the right price and is supported by the right advertising and **sales promotion**. *See also* **marketing concept**, **marketing research**, **marketing plan**. (2) (*US*) shopping for goods. *I do the week's marketing on a Friday.* (3) the department of a company where the marketing staff work. *Take this sample up to marketing and find out what they think of it.*

marketing audit an examination of all the **marketing plans** and actions of a company to find out how well they are being carried out.

marketing concept (*or* **marketing philosophy**) the belief in the following: since a company cannot live without customers it should find out what customers want first, then make **products** or **services** to satisfy them. A great deal of research is needed to find out the effect of any planned decision on the customer. *See also* **concept** (meaning 2).

marketing manager a manager who plans, directs, controls the **marketing plan** of a company.

marketing mix (*or* **the 4 p's**) **product**, price, place, **promotion**. Decisions on these four areas are the most important part of all **marketing plans**. The various decisions (the 'mix' of decisions) will differ for each product. For example, jewellery will have a different price and be sold through a different 'place' (shop) to chocolates.

marketing philosophy *see* **marketing concept**.

marketing plan the written aims of the company for the next period ahead (usually a year). It states which manager is responsible for each part of the plan, what he has to do, when he has to do it. Among the aims in the plan will be the **products** to be sold, total sales, prices, sales by **outlets**, **promotion**, the costs involved, the planned profit and **return on capital**.

marketing planning the **process** of deciding, with the help of **research**, one or more parts of a **marketing plan**. (*See also* **marketing research**.)

marketing research gathering information from inside and outside the company about all aspects of the business, not just the market. By using this information managers should be able to make better decisions. *Compare with* **market research**.

marketing strategy a method used to reach marketing aims. *Our marketing strategy this year is to advertise our new cooker in magazines read by the younger woman.*

market intelligence information from the market of interest to a company. *Compare with* **marketing research**, **market research**.

market leader the company with the largest share of sales for a type of **product** or **service**. *They are the market leader in portable colour televisions.*

market-oriented company a company which allows the market to influence its major decisions, i.e. whose directors and managers believe in the **marketing concept**.

marketplace (1) a place where goods are bought and sold. *Our radio seems to be at the right price but in the marketplace it just doesn't sell.* (2) a special area, or square, for the sale of goods. *Every Saturday morning this whole street is turned into a marketplace.*

market potential all the likely buyers for a **product**. *Our new kind of room heater is not only for homes, but for offices, shops, stores – the market potential is very large.*

market price the price at which most buyers buy – or the price at which most sellers sell. *We would like our shares to be selling at £2 each, but the market price is £1 only.*

market report a report on the state of a market, giving information, e.g. on **stock exchange** prices, **interest rates** etc.

market research finding out all about the people who buy, or may buy, a company's **product** or **service**. This helps to answer such questions as: how many buyers in the market? what do they think of our product? what makes them buy? **Consumer** market research finds out about markets for **consumer goods** and **industrial** market research inquires into markets for **industrial goods**. *Compare with* **marketing research**.

market research agency a company which carries out **market research** for other companies. It will help to identify and solve market problems.

market segmentation dividing a market into separate groups or segments each of which has something in common (which could influence the buying of a **product**). For example, a wine producer might divide the wine market by age, or sex, or area of the country, or **income** etc. New or existing wine products could then be aimed at these specific areas.

market share the proportion of a market which prefers to buy a company's **product**. *Last year only 8% of the people who bought soup preferred ours but this year our market share has gone up to 10%.*

market trend the way a market is changing. *The trend in this market over the past few years is steadily upward.*

market value (1) the price buyers are prepared to pay. *He has had the car for over two years so the market value is much less than he paid for it.* (2) the value of the total market. *Each year the market value of canned meats is £100 million.*

mark-up the difference between the buying price and the selling price. If a shop buys in something for £1 and sells it for £1.50, the mark-up is 50 pence.

mass media ways of informing a very large number of people, e.g. television, radio, newspapers, cinema. *So many people wear jeans that if you want to advertise to them all you have to do is to use the mass media. See also* **media**.

mass production making very large amounts of the same thing, by machinery. *There has been mass production of cars since the days of Henry Ford. See also* **batch production**.

master *noun* (1) the captain of a ship. (2) a male teacher in a school.

master *verb* to become skilled in (something). *He's mastered the computer now.*

master budget a **budget** of **income**, spending, profit, **return on capital** employed etc. for a fixed period ahead, usually six months or a year. It is the main budget for the directors of the company as it is concerned only with the main **financial**, areas, e.g. income, costs, profit, etc. *See* appendix 4.

matched sample (**market research**) a **sample** (e.g. a group of people) which in all respects is the same as another sample. Matched samples therefore could be two groups of people of the same age, sex, income, etc. These two groups could be used to test two different **products**. Answers given about the products will be due to differences in the products because the groups (the samples) are matched.

mate (1) an officer on a merchant ship below the rank of captain. (2) a companion, especially at work. *He likes to have a drink with his mates now and then.*

materials something to be used in the manufacture of goods. *I've ordered the materials for the new garage.*

material(s) control the section of a company which makes sure that the right amount of materials at the right price is in **stock** when needed[1]. *Materials control have found a new supplier of the brass rods which we need for our contract.*

materials handling the study of both the methods and the machines used in moving material in and out of and around a company, so that more efficient methods and machines can be used.

maternity benefit (*UK*) money paid by the government to a woman while she is away from work just before and after the birth of a child.

mate's receipt a written statement given by a **mate** (meaning 1) to an **exporter** as proof that his goods have been put on board a ship.

matrix (1) an arrangement of numbers, letters or signs in rows and columns which make up a square. (2) a mould for casting metal.

mature *adjective* (1) fully developed. (2) of a **bill of exchange, insurance policy** etc., due to be paid.

mature *verb* to become **mature**. *When this insurance matures, I will receive £10,000.*

maturity (1) the state of being **mature**. (2) (*also* **maturity date**) the date when a **bill of exchange, insurance policy** etc. **matures**.

maximum *noun, adjective* (the) largest possible (amount).

MBO *see* **management by objectives**.

MCCA *see* **Central American Common Market**.

mean average. *The mean of 6 + 2 + 4 + 8 is 20 ÷ 4 = 5. See also* **arithmetic mean**.

means test an official inquiry into the amount of money a person has, e.g. to see if he is in need of **financial** help from the government.

measures of central tendency ways of finding out where most of the **values** are in a range of figures. *See* **mean, median** and **mode**, all of which are measures of central tendency.

mechanization the use of machines to help or to replace man at work.

media (*plural of* **medium**) the methods used to spread information, e.g. cinemas, magazines, newspapers, posters, radio, television etc. *They spent over £1 million advertising their new product – they used all the media. See also* **mass media**.

media analysis finding out the value of newspapers, radio, television etc. for advertising purposes. *See also* **media buyer, media planner**.

media buyer a person who buys advertising (in newspapers, magazines, television etc.). He/she works with the **media planner**, e.g. in deciding which **media** should be used.

median the middle value. The median is found by arranging the values from the lowest to the highest and taking the middle value. For example, in the following row of values: 7, 9, 11, 17, 21, 23, 25 the median is 17. *See* **measures of central tendency**.

media owners companies which own the means of advertising to the public e.g. cinemas, magazines, newspapers, **poster** sites, radio stations or TV stations.

media planner a person who decides which advertising **media** (i.e. magazines, newspapers, television, etc.) are best for a particular **product**. A media planner will consider, e.g. the readers of a particular newspaper and the likely buyers of the product, and then decide if that newspaper should be included in the **advertising plan**. *See also* **media buyer, media research**.

media research the study of the people who read newspapers, magazines and posters, or who watch television and cinema, or who listen to the radio, in order to find out their number, sex, **income**, age, and what they think about the **products** and **services** advertised in the **media**.

mediate to help to settle a **dispute** between two other people or organisations.

mediation the act of **mediating**.

mediator a person who **mediates**.

medium *noun* a means by which information can be spread. *Television is a medium we can use to advertise our products. See also plural* **media**.

medium *adjective* of middle amount, neither large nor small. *I take a medium size in suits.*

medium-term liabilities debts which must be paid within the next two to five years. See **current liabilities, long-term liabilities**.

memo (*or* **memorandum**) (1) a note of something from one person in a company to another. *I have a memo here from the works manager asking for a meeting.* (2) a note of something to be remembered. *Make a memo – we have to write to Jones before the end of the month.*

Memorandum and Articles of Association a document drawn up when a company is formed which lists: its name, where the **head office** is, its aims, the amount of **capital**, the directors, etc. This document is sent to the **Registrar of Companies**.

memory a **computer's store** of **data** which is ready for immediate use.

merchandise *noun* = **consumer goods**. *Let's make sure all the merchandise can be seen by our customers.*

merchandise *verb* (1) to put goods on **display** to encourage sales. *If you don't merchandise the goods you won't sell them.* (2) to help **wholesalers** and **retailers** to sell goods which are made by a company, e.g. by **sales promotion, point-of-sale advertising**.

merchandiser a person who **merchandises** (meaning 1). *After we deliver our goods to the shop we always send a merchandiser to put them on show to the customers.*

merchant a person who buys and sells goods. *He's a wine and spirits merchant.*

merchant bank a company which lends money to other companies to help their trade or expansion. Merchant banks also give advice on **mergers, takeovers**, foreign currency, **hire purchase**, etc.

merchantman a ship which carries **cargo** for trade.

merchant navy (1) all of a country's ships which are used to carry trade **cargo**. *Our merchant navy calls at ports all over the world.* (2) the men who work on such cargo ships.

merger the joining of two or more companies to form one company. *Before the merger the two companies used to compete with each other but now they are the same company.*

merit payment an additional payment made to an employee because of the use of special skill or because of special responsibility.

merit rating judging a worker's overall ability to do his job so that the amount of his regular pay can be decided.

meter a machine which shows the amount used of something: *parking meter, water meter.*

method study a close examination of the way people do certain tasks at work so that better, less costly methods can be planned and tried out.

metric system a **system** of weights and measures based on the metre as a unit of length, the gramme for weight, and the litre for liquids.

metric ton (*or* **metric tonne**) 2204.6 pounds (lbs) in weight or equal to 1000 kilograms.

micro- *prefix* very small: *a microcomputer, microfilm, micro-processor.* See also **macro**.

microchip *see* **chip**.

microeconomics that part of **economics** which studies individuals, companies, **products**, rather than the whole **ecomomy**. See also **macroeconomics**.

microfiche a small sheet of 8-millimetre film which has in it information equal to very many full-sized pages. This information can be read using a **microfiche reader**. *He checked the microfiche to see if the library had the book in stock.*

microfilm a roll at 8-millimetre film used for the storage of large amounts of information on a small area. *The last ten years' issue of the daily newspapers are now on microfilm at the library.*

micrometer an instrument used for exact measurement of short distances.

middleman a person or company that links the maker of goods with the buyer or consumer, i.e. **wholesalers**, **retailers** and agents. *It's not true that middlemen simply increase the price and make big profits: they perform a useful task. See also* **channels of distribution** *and appendix 7.*

middle management managers in a company who carry out the orders of a **general manager** (or top management) and who report to him.

mile a measure of length or distance equal to 1609 metres.

mileage (1) the distance travelled in miles. *What's the mileage between Edinburgh and London?* (2) (*informal*) the amount of use of something. *We got a lot of mileage out of the money spent on that sales contest last year – sales are still well up.*

mileage allowance the amount of money given by a company to a person who uses his own car on company business. *The company sent me to London and I had to use my own car, but I was paid a very good mileage allowance.*

mineral natural, solid, non-living material from the earth, e.g. coal, oil.

mineral rights permission to take from the earth in a certain area the **minerals** which lie there, e.g. coal, oil. *He claimed he had the mineral rights to a gold field in Australia.*

mini- *prefix* smaller than normal size: *mini-car, mini-skirt, mini-computer.*

mini-computer a small to medium-sized low-priced **computer**.

minimum *noun, adjective* (the) smallest possible (amount).

minimum stock the smallest amount of goods which a company normally keeps in **stock**. *Compare with* **buffer stock**.

minimum wage the lowest wage by law that can be paid to certain workers.

minor (*law*) a person under the age at which the law judges that he/she is responsible for his/her actions (in the UK, eighteen).

minority interest a person or company that owns less than half the **shares** in a company. *Although his family owned a lot of shares in the business they still held only a minority interest in the firm.*

mint *noun* (1) the place where a country's money is made. (2) looking like new. *He had a 1936 Ford car which was in mint condition.*

mint *verb* (1) to make (coins). (2) (*informal*) to make a lot of (money). *His business is doing very well: he must be minting money.*

minute book a book which contains **minutes**.

minutes a record of what is discussed at a meeting. *He read the minutes of the last meeting.*

misrepresentation (*law*) telling a lie to get a **contract**. If a person signs a contract as a result of being told a lie about the **product** or **service** then he can take action in the courts for **damages**.

mixed economy the **economy** of a country where state-owned industries (e.g. coal, steel) exist alongside **private enterprise**. *France, Great Britain and America all have mixed economies.*

mobile shop a shop inside a van or other type of vehicle which can be driven from place to place.

mobility of labour the extent to which workers will move to find new employment. *The mobility of labour is such that the jobs in the south cannot be filled although there are plenty of people idle in the north.*

mock auction (1) an **auction** in which certain people in the crowd are **bidding** not to own the thing offered for sale but to raise the price of it. (2) = **Dutch auction**.

mock-up a full-size copy of something, e.g. of a new car which a manufacturer intends to build next year. Meantime the mock-up can show the company experts all aspects of the new design.

mode the value which is found most often in a range of figures etc., e.g. the commonest price in a range of prices, commonest age in a group of people. *See* **measures of central tendency, mean, average, median**.

model a copy of something, usually smaller than the real thing. *On his desk he had a model of a new factory.*

modification a small change made to something. *He showed the buyer the plans of the new machine with the slight modifications which he had suggested.*

modify to make a small change or changes in. *Our first plan will cost too much; we shall have to modify it.*

monetarist a person who believes that the **economy** of a country can be managed by controlling the supply of money.

monetary to do with money. *The mark is the monetary unit of Germany.*

monetary policy what the government intends to do in matters related to money, e.g. taxes **interest rates**, borrowing etc. *The prime minister has made a long speech explaining the government's monetary policy.*

money an official way of paying for goods or **services**, i.e. coins, banknotes, cheques, etc.

money at call a debt or a loan which must be repaid as soon as the person who has given the money demands it.

money for jam/old rope (*informal*) very easily-earned money. *It's a very easy job: money for jam, really.*

moneylender a person who lends money at **interest** for a living, or as a business.

money market the **process** by which companies deal in **short-term** loans and foreign exchange.

money-off pack a package with a printed message showing a special low price. *She bought the soap powder in the money-off pack because it was cheaper than the other brands.*

money supply the total amount of money and **near-money** in a country. This amount can be measured in various ways, including **M1** (a narrow measure) and **M3** (a much broader measure). *See also* **monetary policy, near money**.

monitor *noun* (1) a television set used to check and select programmes for broadcasting. (2) = **visual display unit**.

monitor *verb* check, control. *We must monitor the actual sales figures so that we know when each salesman reaches his target.*

Monopolies and Mergers Commission (*UK*) a government body which can inquire into the **merger** or **takeover** of any company where a **monopoly** may result. Monopoly here means where a company or group have control over one-third of the market. After its inquiry, the Monopolies and Mergers Commission can advise the government about whether the merger or take-over should be allowed or not.

monopolise to take or have control of a **product** or **service**. *The government have monopolised the large-scale production of coal.*

monopolist a person or company with the sole right to make or sell a particular **product** or **service**.

monopoly a situation where a company or group of companies has control over a market. *At one time you could buy electricity from different companies but now it's a government monopoly.*

monopsony a situation where there is only one buyer in a market for a **product** or **service** (or for **labour**) although there may be many sellers.

monthly instalment a method of paying for goods or **services** by equal monthly payments for a fixed period. *See* **hire purchase**.

moonlighting having two jobs, e.g. one during the day and another in the evening or during the night. *Yes. He's very rich and very tired; he's been moonlighting for the past year.*

morale the degree of interest and confidence people have e.g. in their job. *I believe the morale in this company is very high.*

moratorium a legal agreement between two persons or organisations to stop the payment of a debt, at least for a time.

mortality rate *see* **death rate**.

mortality table a list showing the expected life of people from the time they take out a **life insurance policy**. This list is used by insurance companies to help them decide the risk involved in any life insurance.

mortgage to give rights to (property), e.g. to a **building society**, in return for a loan of money. Once the money has been repaid the rights to the property are also returned. *The company borrowed £120,000 from the bank but they had to mortgage the factory to get the loan.*

mortgage *noun* an arrangement to hand over property as described above. *They had to take out a mortgage on the factory.*

mortgagee the person or organisation who lends money in a **mortgage contract**.

mortgagor the person or organisation who borrows money in a **mortgage contract**.

most-favoured-nation clause an agreement between countries that each country will give the others to the agreement the best possible **tariff** and **quota** terms.

motion a proposal put to a meeting or a **conference**. If a second person agrees with the motion (or **seconds** it) it is then discussed and voted on.

motion study a detailed study of the movements of a worker doing a particular job. These movements are measured so that wasted movements can be cut down and the work improved.

motivate to give (a person) strong reasons for doing something. *He motivated his salesmen by telling them that the whole company was depending on them to get orders. See also* **motive**.

motivation the state of being **motivated** to do something.

motivational research inquiry into why people behave as they do. Often used in business to answer questions like: why do buyers prefer certain **products** to others?

motive an emotional cause or a reason for acting in a certain way. *His motive for working so hard was his desire to succeed at his job.*

mover a person who makes a proposal, i.e. moves a **motion** – at a meeting or a **conference**.

moving average the average as it changes over time. The moving average of a company's sales can be seen by taking the sales for each of the past twelve months and dividing by twelve. If this is done again when next month's sales are known it will be possible by comparing the two averages to see how the average is moving.

MS, MSS *see* **manuscript**.

MSC *see* **Manpower Services Commission**.

multilateral trade trade carried on between many countries.

multinational *adjective* of many countries.

multinational *noun* a **multinational** company.

multiple a company which owns many **retail outlets** or branches. *The buyer at the multiple head office was offered the very best price if he would allow the salesman to supply all of the multiple's branches.*

multiple bar chart information printed in the form of upright bars on a chart, each bar representing a different thing, e.g. to show the sales of **product** A over the past three years, compared to the sales of product B over the past three years *See also* **bar chart**.

multiple-choice question a question on a form with a choice of answers printed beneath it, one of which is the correct answer, used in **market research** and **surveys**.

multiplier effect the result of e.g. a government **investing** in new roads, factories, machinery etc. This result is usually an increase in **income** (e.g. wages) greater than the amount of the original sum invested, with many people benefitting from a general increase in spending.

municipal of a town or its **local authority**.

Murphy's law (*informal and humorous*) a 'law' seen to operate in offices, factories and homes, on machinery and **projects** which says that if something can go wrong it will go wrong.

mutual shared by more than one person, held in common : *mutual trust.*

mutual company a company owned by **policy-holders** etc. rather than by **shareholders**.

N

nail: (pay) on the nail to pay money at the time of buying something. *He never gives his customers credit ; it has to be cash on the nail.*

name of the game (*informal*) the main part of something ; what something is all about. *You can't succeed in business without taking some risks : it's the name of the game.*

national account a customer (or **account**) that has branches in many parts of the country.

national advertising making a **product** or **service** known all over the country by advertising in the **media**.

national campaign a series of planned actions all over the country. *We are planning a national sales campaign followed by a national advertising campaign for the new product.*

national claim a demand for more pay or better conditions for all its members by a **trade union** in a particular industry. *The steel union's demand for more pay was on behalf of all its members in the industry, and the union said that its national claim was a fair one.*

National Coal Board (*or* **NCB**) a government body which organises the coal industry.

national debt money borrowed by the government to pay those expenses which are over and above the amount of taxes collected.

National Economic Development Office (*or* **'Neddy'**) a UK government unit which gives independent advice on the country's **economic** position and prospects.

National Enterprise Board (*also* **NEB**) (*UK*) a public body set up in 1975 to help the **economy**, e.g. by **investing** government money in industry and commerce.

National Health Service (*or* **NHS**) (*UK*) the medical service for everyone in the country which provides treatment to cure and prevent illness. The service is paid for by companies, workers and the government. *See also* **national insurance**.

national income the value of all goods and **services** produced by a country over a period of time.

national income and expenditure *see* **blue book**.

national insurance payments made by workers and companies to help pay for the **National Health Service**, for **pensions** and unemployment pay.

nationalisation the **process** of **nationalising**. *See also* **nationalised industries**.

nationalise to bring under government control (a company or group of companies). *All of the railway companies were nationalised and they became known as British Rail.*

nationalised industry an industry owned by the general public, i.e. in the direct control of the state. There are no **shareholders** apart from the government. UK examples are: British Rail, British Gas Corporation.

national press newspapers which are sold in all parts of the country. *We can't afford to advertise in the national press. See also* **local press**.

NATO (*or* **North Atlantic Treaty Organisation**) a group of sixteen countries formed in 1949 for cooperation in defence, **economic** policies etc. Membership: Belgium, Canada, Denmark, France, Federal Republic of Germany, Greece, Iceland, Italy, Luxembourg, Netherlands, Norway, Portugal, Spain, Turkey, United Kingdom, United States. (In 1967 NATO military forces withdrew from France at France's request). Headquarters: Brussels. Official languages: English, French.

naturalisation the act of making a person of foreign birth a citizen of a country. *He applied for naturalisation as a British citizen.*

natural resources the materials which are found in nature and can be used, e.g. oil, gold. *With its coal, gas and oil Britain is rich in natural resources.*

natural wastage a normal lessening in the number of people who are working in a company due to death, old age or leaving the job for another one. *Every year the company had to engage about ten more workers just to replace the natural wastage.*

near-money (*or* **near-cash**) something which can be turned into cash very quickly, e.g. **bills of exchange**.

NEB *see* **National Enterprise Board**.

necessaries things which are needed. *He packed the necessaries for his journey: toothpaste, toothbrush, pyjamas, etc.*

necessities things which one cannot do without, e.g. food, clothes, shelter. *He couldn't even afford the necessities of life.*

Neddy *see* **National Economic Development Office**.

negative cash flow a situation when less cash is coming into a business than is going out of it. *He checked over the figures for the company's exports and discovered a negative cash flow for the first six months.*

negotiable instrument a **document** which can be given freely by one person to another, and which can be exchanged for cash, e.g. a cheque, **bill of exchange**, **promissory note**.

negotiate to talk to one or more people with the aim of settling some matter; to reach (an agreement etc.) by discussion. *He wanted to negotiate an agreement with the buyer but he did not want to negotiate a low price.*

negotiation the act of **negotiating**. *At last the contract was signed – it had taken two hours of negotiation with the buyer.*

net (*or* **nett**) with no further reductions or charges. *If she paid for the typewriter now she would get 5% off but if she didn't pay till the end of the month it would be net. See also* **net profit**.

net assets the value of all that a company owns, e.g. land, buildings, machines, **raw materials**, **finished goods** less what it owes, e.g. payment for raw materials, taxes due, **dividends** due, money owed to the bank.

net current assets the value of what a company owns which will be used up over the weeks ahead (i.e. the **current assets**), e.g. **raw materials**, **finished goods**, cash, less what a company has to pay over the coming weeks (i.e. the **current liabilities**), e.g. payment for raw materials, taxes due, money owed to the bank. *See* appendix 4.

net income the amount left after payment of all expenses and taxes.

net loss the amount by which all the expenses are greater than the sales, e.g. total sales £100,000, total expenses £110,000, net loss £10,000.

net margin the **net profit** as a percentage of the sales. *Our profit was £100,000 from £1,000,000 of sales – a net margin of 10%.*

net operating income (*or* **net operating profit**) the profit from a company's main business when all the expenses have been taken off the sales. It will not include profits from **investments** in other companies.

net profit the amount by which the **income** from sales is greater than all the expenses in a **profit and loss account**. *See* appendix 4.

net sales total sales less any goods returned or damaged.

nett *see* **net**.

net weight the weight of the goods less any wrapping or package.

network *noun* (1) any system of lines which cross each other at many places: *the railway network*. (2) a television or radio system where many stations are used to send out the same programme.

network *verb* to broadcast (a television or radio progamme) to many stations.

network analysis a method of planning a complicated job, e.g. building a factory, to find the best order of carrying out the work so that the job will be finished in the shortest possible time within the cost.

net worth the total value of the **ordinary shares** of a company and the **reserves** as shown in the **balance sheet**. *See* appendix 2.

net yield the money from an **investment** less tax.

new issue: shares offered to the public for the first time.

new product development the **process** of bringing new **products** onto the market. *See also* **product development**.

newsagent a shopkeeper who or shop which sells newspapers and magazines as well as other goods, e.g. stationery, cigarettes, sweets.

newsprint a kind of thin paper used in newspapers.

news release *see* **press release**.

new town development (*UK*) towns built since 1946, planned to contain a certain numbers of houses, factories, shops.

NHS *see* **National Health Service**.

night safe a place in a bank where money or other valuable things can be stored when the bank is closed. It is done by using a special opening in the outside wall of the bank.

night-shift overnight working hours, usually between 22.00 hours and 07.00 hours.

no-claims bonus a car **insurance** offered at a special low price because no **claim** has been made to the insurance company in the past year. *I've had two car accidents this year and made a claim each time – so that means I've lost my no-claims bonus.*

nominal accounts: ledger accounts which record the **revenue** and **expenditure** of an **enterprise** (meaning 1).

nominal capital the total **face value** of all the **shares** that a company is allowed to issue. *See also* **authorized capital**.

nominal value the **face value** of something, e.g. a **share** may have a nominal value of £1 but may be sold to someone for £1.25. *See also* **par** (meaning 2).

nominate to name (a person) for some special purpose. *I nominate John Smith to vote on my behalf at the next meeting.*

nominee a person named by someone else to act for him/her in some matter. *See also* **nominate**.

non-contributory pension scheme a **system** of paying for an employee's **pension** where the company pays the full cost of the pension scheme and the worker pays nothing towards the cost.

non-durable goods: products which do not last very long, e.g. shoes, food, drink, sweets etc. *Compare with* **durable goods**.

non-executive director a director of a company who is brought in to advise the other directors. He is not a full-time director and so is not an **executive** of the company. *Compare with* **executive director**.

non-price competition selling goods by means of some benefit other than a low price, e.g. selling canned soup on the basis of how quickly it can be cooked or on how good it tastes, etc. *Their product was of high quality. The manufacturer believed in non-price competition.*

non-profit-making organisation a group or company which has an aim other than making a profit, e.g. a charity, church, social service, school.

non-taxable income money received on which tax need not be paid, e.g. **personal allowance**, **sickness benefit**, **unemployment** pay etc.

non-voting shares *see* **A shares**.

Nordic Council a group of states formed in Copenhagen in 1952, for co-operation in matters of common interest. Headquarters: Stockholm. Membership: Denmark, Finland, Iceland, Norway, Sweden. Official languages: Danish, Norwegian, Swedish.

norm the normal, average, usual. *Some salesmen make 20 calls a day in this firm but the norm is 14.*

normal curve a bell-shaped curve which shows the usual (or normal) distribution of the characteristics of a population; their intelligence; their **income**; their weight, etc.

North Atlantic Treaty Organisation *see* **NATO**.

notary public *(law)* a person usually a **solicitor**, who has the special job of witnessing spoken and written statements and making them official.

note to fix a statement to (a **bill of exchange**) saying that the bill has been presented for payment and payment has been refused. This is usually done by a **notary public**.

notice (1) a statement (usually in writing) by one **party** to a **contract** that he will end the contract at a certain time. *I plan to leave the firm in two months' time so I've handed in my notice.* (2) the period of time before a contract ends. *I gave them two months' notice.* (3) a piece of written news about something. *Did you see the notice about the company dance? It is pinned up on the notice board.*

notice board a board on a wall to which notices may be fixed.

not negotiable words written across the face of a cheque, meaning that it cannot be used by anyone who is not entitled to use it.

null and void with no legal force. *The contract was null and void — a court wouldn't even consider it.*

numbered account a **bank account** where the name of the person using the account is kept secret. Some countries, e.g. Switzerland, have laws which allow people to use such secret accounts.

numerical control control by a **computer** of a machine which makes things.

nuts and bolts *(informal)* the practical details. *I'll tell you about how the office is generally run: my assistant will explain the nuts and bolts.*

O

O and M *see* **organisation and methods**.

OAPEC *see* **Organisation of Arab Petroleum Exporting Countries**.

OAS *see* **Organisation of American States**.

OAU *see* **Organisation of African Unity**.

objective *noun* the aim of something. *The manager explained the objective of the marketing plan.*

objective *adjective* not influenced by personal feelings. *Let's be objective about this and just look at the facts.*

objective test a list of questions to be answered where each question has only one correct answer. Thus the personal feelings of the person checking the answers will not influence the mark or score.

obligation a duty, a state of having to do something, e.g. because one has signed a **contract** to do it.

obsolescence the state of being **obsolescent**.

obsolescent going out of date; hardly ever used any more. *Things are changing so fast that some machines are obsolescent before they are out of guarantee.*

obsolete no longer in use; out of date. *Let's not wait for our machinery to become obsolete — we will renew it now with up-to-date machinery.*

occupancy the state or time of being an **occupant**.

occupant a person who lives in or has the use of a room, building etc.

occupation a person's trade; what he/she works at. *His occupation is salesman.*

occupational accident an injury at work caused by something to do with the job. *He injured his hand in a faulty machine, it was a typical occupational accident.*

occupational guidance advising a person on the sort of jobs he/she is best suited for.

occupational hazard a risk or danger to do with one's job. *Falling off ladders is an occupational hazard of window cleaners.*

occupational pension scheme an arrangement whereby a worker receives a **pension** from his/her company after he/she retires from work.

occupier an **occupant**, especially of a house.

occupy to live or be in (a house, office etc.); to take possession of.

OCDE *see* **Organisation for Economic Co-operation and Development**.

OCR *see* **optical character reader**.

odd-job man man who does various small jobs for payment.

OEA *see* **Organisation of American States**.

OECD *see* **Organisation for Economic Co-operation and Development**.

offence (1) a wrong action which is punishable by law, a crime. (2) something unpleasant or hurtful.

offer *noun* (1) something offered. *I have a special offer on this video: £25 off the usual price.* (2) (*law*) the first step in a **contract**. *He made an offer to sell the goods for £10,000 which the buyer accepted.*

offer *verb* (1) to present (something) for taking or refusing. *They are offering potatoes at £3.00 a bag.*

    offer for sale the advertising of **shares** to the public. A company may sell through an **issuing house** which then offers them for sale.

offeror a person who makes an **offer** (meaning 1).

offer price the price at which a share or goods are offered for sale.

office (1) a place where a company does its paper work, e.g. letters, orders, **invoices** etc. *Our head office is in Lincoln but we have branch offices at every factory.* (2) a room where a person does paper work. *Come into my office, I have the contract on my desk.* (3) a position of trust or **authority**. *He held high office in the government.* (4) a government department, e.g. the **Office of Fair Trading** or the Foreign and Commonwealth Office.

office-bearer a person in an organisation who holds an **office**, e.g. as **chairman, secretary, treasurer.**

office hours hours when an **office** (meaning 1) is open to do business, usually 9 am to 5 pm.

office manager the person in charge of the people who work in an **office** (meaning 1).

Office of Fair Trading (*UK*) a government body set up to protect the public against unfair or illegal business activity.

officer a person with a position of **authority** or trust: *a customs officer.*

official *adjective* said or done with the power of **authority**. *The news that we're closing the Glasgow factory is not official. If we decide to close it we will issue an official statement.*

official *noun* a person who holds a position of responsibility in an organisation, especially a public organisation.

official receiver a person appointed by the government to be in charge of the closing down of a company.

official reserves a country's **stock** of gold and foreign money.

official strike a **strike** which has the support of the **trade union**. When a strike is **official**, the trade union may help its members on strike by making payments to them.

officiate to carry out the duties connected with a particular **office** (meaning 3). *Mr Jones will officiate as chairman.*

off-licence a **licence** to sell alcoholic drinks for drinking elsewhere; a shop which sells alcohol thus.

off-line (**computers**) of a **peripheral**, not directly linked to a **central processing unit**. *See also* **on-line.**

off-peak (1) of a time of day or of the year, less busy. *I prefer to fly during off-peak hours.* (2) existing during off-peak times: *off-peak prices; off-peak holiday.*

off-shore (1) on the sea, at a distance from the land. (2) (*chiefly US*) from or in another country.

off-shore oilfield an area of ground under the sea, **off-shore**, in which there is oil.

off-the-job training training at a college or training centre, away from one's place of work. *See also* **on-the-job training.**

off-trade the selling of alcoholic drinks to **off-licences, supermarkets** etc., rather than to **public houses.**

oil field an area where oil is found.

oil industry all the companies which have the main part of their business in the **processing** and sale of oil.

oil rig a **rig** used for **drilling** for oil.

oil slick a quantity of oil which has leaked from a ship and covers a part of the sea.

oil tanker a long, low ship used for carrying oil.

oil well a hole bored in the ground on land or under the sea to get oil.

oligopoly a market where a small number of producers control a large amount of the supply of a **product** and so can influence the price.

oligopsony a market where a small number of buyers buy a large amount of a **product** and so can influence the price.

one-man business *see* **sole trader.**

one-stop shopping a covered place containing many shops where one can buy many different types of goods without having to move one's car.

on-line (computers) of a **peripheral**, directly linked to the **central processing unit.** *See also* **off-line.**

on-the-job training any learning about a job which takes place at the usual place of work. *They were going to send me away on a course to learn the job but they decided to give me on-the-job training instead. See also* **off-the-job training.**

OPEC *see* **Organisation of Petroleum Exporting Countries.**

open account the most usual method of paying for any goods which are sold to a business. Goods are ordered, delivered and then payment is made at an agreed time, usually four weeks later. *See also* **credit.**

open an account to make an arrangement that one can leave or borrow money, or get **credit** from, a bank, shop etc.: *to open an account with one's local bank.*

open cheque a cheque which is not crossed and therefore does not have to be paid into an **account.** Cash can be received by handing it across the counter at the appropriate bank.

open cover (*or* **open policy**) **(marine insurance)** a method of **insuring** goods when the value of the goods is not known at the time of the **insurance contract.** (A sum is agreed at the time of the contract and this is charged when the actual value of the goods is known). This method is used e.g. when many low-value orders are sent regularly by the same company to the same customer. At the end of the year the real value of all the goods sent can be added up and one payment made to the insurance company.

open-door policy (1) of managers, being prepared to talk to workers in the office at any time. (2) of a country, allowing the goods from all other countries to be **imported** on the same terms.

open-ended question (market research) a question which does not invite one to answer from a given list of answers. For example: "What did you like about the coffee?" is an open-ended question as one can answer it in any way one chooses.

opening (1) a job in a company which needs to be filled. *I hear there is an opening for a manager at Smith Brothers Company.* (2) the beginning of something: *the opening of the new factory.*

open-plan offices offices with no (or very few) walls between one office and another.

open policy *see* **open cover.**

open shop a factory or company where the workers do not have to be members of a **trade union.**

Open University (*UK*) a university which is open to anyone and which teaches its students mainly at a distance, partly by means of television and radio programmes.

operate to (cause to) work or to be in action or to have effect. *That part of the factory is not operating yet.*

operating assets: assets which are in regular use in a company, e.g. buildings, machines, materials, cash etc.

operating budget a plan of **income** and **expenses** for a company covering a period of time, usually a year.

operating costs the normal costs of running a business such as wages, salaries, rent, rates, etc., i.e. the expenses normally found in the **profit-and-loss account**. See appendix 1.

operating profit a gain from a company's normal business over a period of time, usually a year. This profit does not include gains from **shares** or **investments**.

operating statement (1) a statement of the **income** and **expenses** of some part of a business, e.g. of one department of a **department store**, or the income and expenses of one **product** of a company (2) (*especially US*) a **profit-and-loss account**.

operation (1) the way in which something works. *The operation of this machine is not easily explained.* (2) a piece of work to be done. *First you drill a hole in this part and the next operation is to drill a larger hole here* (3) (in) use. *There is a new rule in operation for getting time off work.*

operational research (*or* **operations research** *or* **OR**) using the methods of science on the problems of business so that productivity or profit will be improved, e.g. to get the best use of workers, materials, machines, money and time.

operative (1) coming into effect; coming into force. *The new rule is operative from next Monday.* (2) important, effective: *the operative word in this contract.*

operator a person who operates something: *a machine operator, a telephone operator.*

opinion leaders (*or* **opinion formers**) special groups of people whose opinions on new **products** or new ideas have a great effect on other people.

opinion research finding out what people think of something by questioning some of them (a **sample**).

opportunity cost the value of a certain course of action which one could take but does not. For example, the opportunity cost of using your money to start a business is the **interest** your money could earn in a bank.

optical character reader a **device** which can read specially-printed information and pass it straight into a **computer**.

optimum best, most suitable. *Our optimum level of production is 10,000 units a week.*

optimum order quantity the amount which should be ordered of something which keeps the costs of ordering and holding such **stock** to the best level. *See also* **economic order quantity**.

option (1) a choice. *Have we any other option before we decide?* (2) a right to buy or sell something within a certain time usually at an agreed price. *He took up his option to buy, and bought 600 shares. We can give you a three-month option.*

option dealing (**stock exchange**) the agreement to buy or sell **shares** at a certain price within a certain time. To enter this agreement one has to pay **option money**. If the option to buy (or sell) is not taken up within the agreed time, then one loses the option money.

OR *see* **operational research**.

Oracle (*UK*) a **viewdata system** offered by independent television.

order *verb* (1) to tell (a person) to do something. *He was ordered to stay where he was.* (2) to ask for (something which one wants to buy). *They ordered* *ten more cases.* (3) to arrange in some special way. *The invoices are ordered according to the date they were received.*

order *noun* (1) the act of **ordering** (meanings (1) and (2)). *We have to obey the order. I've got six orders already this morning.* (2) a special arrangement of things. *The names are in alphabetical order.*

on order waiting to be delivered. *We have no shampoo in stock but it is on order.*

order book a special book for writing in the details of any **order**.

order/call ratio the relationship between the number of calls made on buyers and the number of **orders** received. *He called on 40 buyers and got 20 orders so his order/call ratio was 20 divided by 40 or 0.5 : 1.*

ordinary share part-ownership of a company. Ordinary shares allow the **shareholder** to vote at company meetings and to receive a **dividend** (if the company says it will pay one). *See also* **ordinary shareholder, share,** appendix 2.

ordinary shareholder any person or business that owns **ordinary shares** in a company. They are considered to be the true owners of a company with the directors acting on their behalf in the day-to-day running of the business. Ordinary shareholders have no right to a **dividend** unless the company says that it will pay one to them.

organisation (1) an arrangement of parts of a group to form an effective whole; a business, company of other body. *Four units make up the firm's organisation. They are: production, marketing, finance and personnel, and over them all the managing director.* (2) the planning and arranging of something. *The organisation of the conference was very poor.*

organisation and methods (*or* **O and M**) the study of a company's **organisation**, the way it works, the **systems** it uses, so that these may be improved and the company made more profitable.

organisation chart a drawing of how a company is organised showing who is in charge of different parts of it, and how each part is related to the whole. *See also* **organisation, organisation structure.**

Organisation for Economic Co-operation and Development (*or* **OECD** *or* **OCDE**) an organisation founded in 1961 to help the **economic** growth and the **standard of living** of member states; to help the world **economy** and to improve the conditions of the poorest countries. Membership: Australia, Austria, Belgium, Canada, Denmark, Finland, France, Federal Republic of Germany, Greece, Iceland, Ireland, Italy, Japan, Luxembourg, Netherlands, New Zealand, Norway, Portugal, Spain, Sweden, Switzerland, Turkey, United Kingdom, United States. Headquarters: Paris. Official languages: English, French.

organisation man a worker who is very interested in helping his company, even to the extent of harming his home life. *He worked late at the office all of last week — he's becoming an organisation man.*

Organisation of African Unity (*or* **OAU** *or* **OUA**) an organisation of fifty African states formed in 1963, to achieve a better life for the peoples of Africa, to defend their countries, and to promote cooperation between all nations of the world. Headquarters: Addis Ababa. Official languages: English, French, and when possible African languages.

Organisation of American States (*or* **OAS** *or* **OEA**) a group of twenty-eight states formed in 1948, to achieve order, peace and justice among American states and to encourage the **economic**, social and cultural growth of its members. Headquarters: Washington, DC. Official languages: English, French, Portuguese, Spanish.

Organisation of Arab Petroleum Exporting Countries (*or* **OAPEC**) an organisation set up in

1968 for coordination of the petroleum policies of its members and other forms of cooperation. Members include Algeria, Bahrain, Iraq, Kuwait, Libya, Qatar, Saudi Arabia. Headquarters: Kuwait City, Kuwait.

Organisation of Petroleum Exporting Countries (*or* **OPEC**) a union of oil-producing countries formed in 1960 to agree on a basic policy for oil (including prices) and to help the economic growth of member states. Membership includes Algeria, Ecuador, Gabon, Indonesia, Iran, Iraq, Kuwait, Libya, Nigeria, Qatar, Saudi Arabia, United Arab Emirates, Venezuela. Headquarters: Vienna.

organisation structure how a company has arranged its directors, managers and other workers, what their duties are, who they are in charge of, etc. *See also* **organisation chart.**

organise (1) to put (things or people) into order. *Let's get all those orders organised into wholesalers and retailers.* (2) to get (workers) to join a **trade union.** *The workers in the shipyard have been organised for years.*

outbid to offer a higher price than (anyone else), e.g. at an **auction.**

outer a box or outside wrapping in which a number of products are sold. *There are ten packets of biscuits to the outer.*

outgoings money that is being paid out. *If the outgoings are more than the money coming in, you're in trouble.*

outlet a shop; a place where things can be sold. *We don't have enough outlets we have to sell the new razor into more shops.*

out of order (1) not following one another properly. *These numbers are all out of order.* (2) not following the proper rules of the situation. *He lost his temper with a customer he was out of order there.*

output (1) what is made, production. *Today's output was 40,000 shirts well up on yesterday's output.* (2) information from a **computer**, often from a **line-printer.**

output per man what is made divided by the number of men doing the work. For example, if 10,000 pairs of shoes were made by 100 workers, the output per man would be 100 pairs of shoes.

outstanding (1) remarkable, excellent. *His ability as a manager is outstanding.* (2) of a debt etc., not yet paid. *There is still £5.00 outstanding on their account.*

out-tray a tray on a desk containing letters, **documents** etc., that a manager has to attend to. *See also* **in-tray.**

overbook to book more (seats in a plane, rooms in a hotel etc.) than there is space for.

overcapitalise to put more money into (a company) than it can use, e.g. in the form of machines etc.

overdraft the amount of money owed to a bank by a person or organisation, usually an amount agreed by the bank and the customer. This agreement will also state when the money has to be repaid and how much **interest** is to be charged.

overdraw to take out more money from (one's **account** in a bank) than the amount one has in it. *This month my account is £50.00 overdrawn.*

overdue late, having gone beyond the correct or agreed time. *Your account for £10,000 is now overdue. Please pay within seven days. They said our order would be here within a week and ten days have passed. It's three days overdue.*

overhead an expense not directly related to producing a **product** or a **service**, e.g. selling expenses, **rates**, rent, managers' salaries etc.

overhead absorption a method of dividing parts of an **overhead** cost among certain **products** according to particular company rules. For example, a company may decide to allot the cost of advertising to products according to their total sales. Under this method a product that has 50% of the company sales would carry 50% of the total advertising expense.

overhead projector a machine which throws pictures of **graphs**, notes, etc. onto a screen from prepared sheets of clear film, used to illustrate a talk.

overmanning using more workers than are needed to do the work. *The real reason for the company's poor profits was its overmanning in the printing department.*

overproduction making more of something than there is a demand for.

overriding commission a payment over and above the normal **discounts** and **commissions**, paid for some special reason. *If your company buys more than £50,000 of goods from us over the next twelve months, then we will pay an overriding commission of 1% on the value of all goods bought.*

overstock to hold more **stock** of something than is necessary at a given time.

oversubscribed of an issue of **shares** where the number issued is less than the number that could have been sold. *The shares were offered at £1 and were oversubscribed: three times the number offered could have been sold.*

overtime hours worked beyond the normal working hours. *There's been a sudden increase in the number of orders we'll have to ask the workers to work overtime.*

overtime ban a refusal to work **overtime**, sometimes called for by a **trade union** to strengthen the union's position in talks with the management on some matter.

over-trading doing business beyond the limit of a company's **financial** strength, e.g. when it grows too

quickly, or when more goods are being made than the company can pay for.

own brand (*or* **own label** *or* **private brand** *or* **private label**) goods which carry a **retailer's** or a **wholesaler's** name (or **brand**) on the label instead of a manufacturer's brand. Although they are so named, they are made under **contract** by manufacturers for retailers and wholesalers.

P

PA see **particular average loss**, **personal assistant**

package the container in which goods are packed; a number of things packed; a number of things packed together. *Our Christmas cards are sold in packages of twenty-five.*

package deal a number of things offered or put forward for discussion together. *They offered them a package deal: they would build the hospital, put in all the equipment and plant the surrounding trees for a total price of £2 million.*

package tour a holiday with everything (travel, hotels etc.) arranged in advance by the travel agent and all sold at one fixed price.

packaging the covering around goods, sometimes used to advertise them (boxes of chocolates, perfume) and sometimes used to protect them (television, refrigerators). *I'm glad they sent the dishes in strong packaging, there isn't one broken.*

packing material such as straw, paper, etc. used to pack goods.

packing case a strong box used to hold goods either for **storage** or for delivery.

packing list a list of contents of a **packing case** with details of number, weight, etc. of the things in the case. *Look for the packing list. I want to check the contents.*

page rate the cost of a page of advertising in a magazine or newspaper.

paid-up capital the actual amount of money paid to a company for its **shares.**

pallet a square wooden frame on which goods are stored; it can be used, e.g. for quick carrying from a company's store to a company's delivery lorry.

palletisation changing to the common use of **pallets** to help with the delivery of goods.

pamphlet a small book, containing a few pages, sometimes with charts, or photographs. *Have you a pamphlet on your latest cooker?*

panel (1) a group of speakers at a meeting. *Among the panel of speakers was a well-known film actor.* (2) (**market research**) a group of shops or consumers that give information on **products** or **services**. *See* **consumer panel.**

paper currency money that is not in metal form like coins but in paper form like £1 notes, £10 notes, etc. *Compare with* **coin.**

paper profit a gain made when something rises in value but is not actually sold. *My house is worth £30,000 now. Since I paid only £20,000 for it I've made a paper profit of £10,000.*

paperwork any work to do with letters, **memos, documents** etc. *I can't go to the pub tonight: I brought a lot of paperwork home which I must attend to.*

par (1) average or normal. *Joe went round the golf course in 76 strokes. That's par for the course.* (2) of **shares**, the original price, the **face-value** price. If shares are sold at this price, they are sold **at par**, if at a higher price they are sold **above par**, if lower, **below par**. *See also* **parity.** (3) of a currency, equal value. *The US and Canadian dollars were at par at that time.*

paragraph one of the sections into which a piece of writing is divided (by beginning a new line for each section).

parallel import a **product** going into a country by a method not agreed to by the **exporter**. *We send all our goods to our agent in France: now we find that a French store is buying our goods from some other source – and we want to stop this parallel import.*

parameter something fixed; a limit. *The new factory must not cost more than £250,000 and it must be built within nine months: these are the parameters laid down by the company.*

parent company a company which owns more than half the **shares** of another company. *See also* **subsidiary company.**

Pareto's law (*or* **Pareto effect**) the idea that a few important things or people have a great effect. For example, a small number of salesmen will make most of the sales; a small number of customers will create most of a company's profit; in a **retail** shop, a small amount of **stock** will take up most of the money **invested** in stock.

parity (1) equality, being equal. *We want parity of wages with the workers doing the same job in the drilling section.* (2) a situation when a currency's **forward rate** of exchange is the same as its **spot rate**. *See also* **par.**

Parkinson's law the idea that work will always increase to fill the time made available for it. For example, if you give a worker two hours to do a job he will take two hours and not less than this time.

partial loss (**insurance**) not a complete loss, but where damage or loss has occurred to only part of the property **insured**. (But for **marine insurance**, *see* **particular average loss**.)

particular average loss (*or* **PA**) (**marine insurance**) **partial loss** of the property **insured**, caused by something which it was insured against (e.g. a storm, collision) and not shared by the **insurers** of all the cargo (as happens for a **general average loss**).

partly-paid share a share in a company. Only part of **the nominal value** of this share has been paid to the company that issued it.

partner (1) a person who takes part with others in a business. *The four of them set up as partners in a taxi business.* (2) a person who shares in some activity or venture. *Joe is my partner at golf.*

partnership an agreement between two or more people to share in a business together. Unless the agreement says otherwise, each partner shares equally the profits and losses of the business.

part payment part of the full price of something paid to a seller as proof that one intends to buy it. *I'm buying a gas cooker; I paid £20 part payment on it today, I'll pay the rest at the end of the month and have it delivered.*

part-time worker (*or* **part-timer**) a person employed to work less than the usual number of hours in the working week. *They're taking on part-time workers at Clark's shoe factory: I wouldn't mind being a part-timer there.*

party (1) a person or group on one side of a legal **dispute.** (2) a person or group that agrees to a **contract.** *He refused to be a party to the agreement.* (3) a group of people who are together for some purpose, e.g. to go on holiday, to discuss business matters. *When Mr Heller arrives with the German party take them to the manager's office.* (4) a group of people who support a political cause: *the Conservative Party; the Labour Party.*

par value the **face value**; the value of a **share** at its issued price.

passbook a book given by a bank etc. to a customer with details of the customer's **account** with the bank. *He saw from his passbook that he had only £10 left in his deposit account.*

pass off (1) to pretend that (something) is something else. *The company passed off their whisky as a real Scottish whisky when it was actually made in Japan.* (2) to pretend that one is someone else. *She passed herself off as a lawyer but they found she was only an office worker.*

patent (*or* **letters patent**) a legal right given by the **patent office** to a person or company to make use of or sell something new, usually for 16 years. *He took out a patent on his new type of camera.*

patent office a government office which gives **patents** and **trademarks.**

patent rights rights to a **patent.** UK patents apply only to the UK.

patron (1) a person who gives help to something, e.g. a charity, by giving money to it or by allowing his/her name to be used in its support. (2) a person who goes often to a certain shop, theatre etc.

pawn *verb* to give (something of value) to a **pawnbroker** in return for a loan of money. *He decided he would pawn his best suit. Maybe the pawnbroker would give him the £10 he needed.*

pawn *noun* a place where things of value can be **pawned.** *He had to put his gold watch in pawn.*

pawnbroker a person or company that lends money in exchange for goods taken into the **pawn.** The goods may be taken out of pawn when the money is repaid (i.e. within six months). If the money is not repaid within six months the pawnbroker can sell them at an **auction.**

pay *verb* (1) to give money in exchange for something or for work done. (2) to give a profit or advantage. *It pays to make a detailed plan.*

pay *noun* money for work done. *He got his pay for the first week's work.*

Pay as you earn (*or* **PAYE**) a **system** of **income tax** whereby tax is taken off wages or salaries at the time of payment.

pay day the day wages or salaries are paid. *Pay day was on Friday every week for the factory workers and on the 28th of every month for the office workers.*

payee a person to whom money is paid.

payload the total load or weight which a ship, lorry, plane can carry and get money for.

payment the amount of money paid for something; the act of paying. *The firm liked its customers to make payments by cheque.*

payment by results payment made for reaching agreed levels of work. *They had a payment-by-results system, so that the more you produced the more you earned.*

payment on account part payment of a sum of money owing.

pay off to dismiss (a person), i.e. to make up a worker's pay and pay him, and end the agreement to employ him.

pay packet a small envelope containing wages and usually also a piece of paper called a **pay-slip**, with details of how the wages have been made up.

payroll a list of workers employed by a company and the weekly or monthly pay that they earn.

pay-slip *see* **pay packet.**

PDM *see* **physical distribution management.**

peaceful picket a **picket** using non-violent methods, e.g. talking to the people at work, using **leaflets** and **posters** to explain their point of view.

peak the highest point of something. *Sales of our suntan oil reach a peak in August.*

peak demand a time when most people want a **service** or **product**, e.g. peak demand for gas is at breakfast time, for holidays, in the month of August. *See also* **off-peak.**

peddle (1) to go from place to place selling small things. (2) to sell illegal drugs.

pedlar, peddler a person who **peddles** (meanings (1) and (2)). *He was arrested as a peddler of drugs.*

peg *verb* to hold (prices or wages) at a certain level. *The firm planned to peg its price for the new camera at its present level.*

penalty clause a part of a **contract** by which one **party** has to pay a sum of money to the other party if the first party fails to carry out something in the contract, e.g. to deliver something by the agreed date.

pending waiting to happen or to be attended to.

penetration pricing pricing a new **product** at a price well below other similar products so as to get a large share of the total sales quickly.

pension a regular sum of money paid by the government or by a company to a person who has reached the age of retiring from work, or to a widow, or a person who is too ill to carry on working. *See also* **pension fund, pension plan, non-contributory pension scheme.**

pension fund a sum of money which has been collected from people in a **pension plan**. This **fund** is used to provide **pensions** for people who pay into the fund. Another source of money for the pension fund is from **interest** which the fund earns on its money in the bank, or in other forms of **investment.** A company's pension fund can be made up of money paid only by the company, the workers paying nothing towards the cost of their pension. *See* **non-contributory pension scheme, pension, pension plan.**

pension plan (also **pension scheme**) an arrangement by which people agree to pay a certain amount of their wages into a **pension fund** so that they can receive a **pension** when they retire (or when they are too ill to continue working). The UK government runs such a pension plan for workers but some companies prefer to have their own arrangements. See also **non-contributory pension scheme.**

pep talk (*informal*) a talk with a person that gives him/her encouragement, especially when he/she has not been successful so far. *The sales manager gave to his salesmen their weekly pep talk.*

per annum each year. *A salary of £30,000 per annum.*

P/E ratio *see* **price-earnings ratio.**

per capita by (or for) each person in the population. *Germany has a very high income per capita.*

per cent in one or for each hundred.

percentage a rate worked out at so much in a hundred. *In only two weeks we have sold a high percentage of our stock – 87% to be exact.*

perfect competition (*or* **perfect market**) (**economic theory**) the perfect market, i.e. when the price of a **product** is the same to all buyers because buyers and sellers have full information about each other and the product, and there is nothing to prevent anyone becoming a trader in the market.

performance appraisal judging how well a manager or other worker does his job, especially when this is part of a formal appraisal method, e.g. to find out his training needs, whether he should be promoted or have a pay increase. Records are kept of the worker's effort in reaching the aims and finally a discussion of his efforts (a performance appraisal) is carried out. See also **management appraisal.**

performance bond a legal promise (a **guarantee**) given by one **party** to another that the work of a third party will be carried out properly. For example, a company offering a **contract** to a builder may ask the builder to get a bank to give a guarantee that the builder will complete the work properly.

performance review a meeting between a worker and the manager to discuss the worker's progress towards the aims set for the worker at their last meeting. See also **performance appraisal.**

peril serious danger. *He was in peril of losing his job if they found out that he stole the money.*

periodical a magazine.

peripheral *adjective* not central. *The meeting decided not to discuss prices as this was peripheral to the main subject of the bank loan.*

peripheral *noun* (**computers**) a unit of **peripheral equipment.**

peripheral equipment the parts of a **computer system** which are not part of the **central processing unit**, e.g. **visual display units, keyboards, line-printers.**

perishable goods goods which go bad quickly if not sold within a certain time, e.g. eggs, fish, fruit, milk.

perjury (*law*) the act of telling lies after swearing to tell the truth. *The judge asked the witness if he knew the punishment for perjury.*

perks *see* **perquisites.**

permanent lasting for a long time or for ever: *permanent staff. Compare with* **temporary.**

per procurationem (*or* **pp**) power given to sign or to act for another. *The letter was signed p.p. J. Jones & Co., S. Smith.* (S. Smith has the power to sign letters on behalf of the J. Jones Co.)

perquisites (*or* **perks**) benefits (apart from pay) that one gets in a job. *One of my perks is a company car which I can use as my own.*

personal to do with one person. *These are my personal belongings. Compare with* **personnel.**

personal accounts. a company's record of payments to or from people, or companies. *See also* **account, nominal accounts**.

personal allowance an amount of one's **income** which is free of **income tax**. *The governmment said that it would raise the level of personal allowance so that workers would pay less income tax.*

personal assistant a person who helps a manager to do his job. *She got a job as a personal assistant to the sales manager.*

personal call a telephone call for which no charge is made unless a certain person is able to answer it, in which case there is an extra charge.

personal effects goods which one owns that can be moved around, e.g. books, clothes, paper.

personal income tax payment made to the government from the earnings of a person, and not a company. *See also* **corporation tax, personal allowance**.

personal interview (1) a face-to-face talk with a person especially someone in authority. *I have a personal interview with the boss of Brown Brothers Ltd for a job as manager* (2) a talk with a person who is actually present. *The researcher had six interviews to carry out : three personal and three by telephone.*

personality (1) a person who is well known in television, cinema, sport, etc.: *a personality of stage and screen.* (2) the qualities that make up a person's character. *He had a very strong personality.*

personality promotion the selling of goods with the help of some well-known person from television, stage or sport. See also **personality** (meaning 1).

personal loan a loan of money by a bank to a person to allow him/her to buy something, e.g. a car, clothes, a holiday.

personal property all the goods which a person owns, e.g. house, clothes, papers, car etc.

personal selling selling done by a person who is face-to-face with the buyer (as opposed to selling, e.g. by post – *see* **mail order**).

personnel (1) all the people employed in a company etc.; the staff. (2) = **personnel department.** *Compare with* **personal.**

personnel department the department in a company which deals with **personnel management.**

personnel management the selecting, employing and training of the workers and managers in a company. It is also concerned with the **motivation** of individuals and groups within a company, their well-being, and how they can be encouraged to help the success of the company.

personnel manager the person in charge of the **personnel department.**

PERT *see* **programme evaluation and review technique.**

Peter principle the **theory** that over a period of time people will be promoted to the level where, finally, they do not know how to do the job. This theory was put forward by L. J. Peter and R. Hall in the book *The Peter Principle,* published in 1969.

petrodollars US dollars earned by oil-**exporting** countries that are then **invested** in the US and in European countries.

petty cash a small amount of money kept by a company (in the form of coins and banknotes to pay small expenses, e.g. postage stamps.

petty cash book a book in which is recorded all of the small payments that have been made from the **petty cash.**

photocopier a machine which makes **photocopies.** *Go along to the photocopier and run off six copies of this letter.*

photocopy *noun* a photographic copy of a letter, **document**, drawing etc.

photocopy *verb* to make a **photocopy** of (a **document**, letter etc.).

physical distribution means used to move goods from the maker to the user. *Whether you use lorries or the railway the physical distribution costs of moving bricks are quite high.*

physical distribution management (*or* **PDM**) planning and controlling the movement and storage of all materials and goods into and out of a company.

physical stocktaking the counting of the things in a shop, store, **warehouse** etc. by checking each one individually.

picket *noun* a group of people on **strike** who form a group outside a place of work to try to make other workers join or support them; a member of such a group. *See also* **peaceful picket**.

picket *verb* to act as **a picket** at (a place of work).

pictogram a method of showing the differences between things (e.g. the number of cars sold each month) by using drawings.

piece rate a certain payment for each piece of work done (instead of payment by the hour). *The piece rate in this factory is 10 pence for each box completed.*

piecework a method of payment based on the work done (and not on payment by the hour). *They don't have payment by the hour in Smiths Ltd, they're all on piecework there.*

pie chart a method of showing how the total of something (time, materials, **market share** etc) is made up by using a circle which is sliced into various parts. The size of each slice shows the difference in the parts.

pile: make one's pile (*informal*) to make a lot of profit, become very rich.

pilfer to steal a small amount of something. *The wooden case was broken into and some of the goods had been pilfered.*

pilferage stealing in small amounts. *I suppose we lose about £100 a year in pilferage.*

pilot (1) person trained to take ships into or out of a harbour or through a canal. (2) a person trained to fly an aircraft.

pilot *verb* (1) to act as a **pilot** for: *to pilot a ship safely into harbour.* (2) to try (something) out to see if it will be successful: *to pilot a new product.*

pilot *adjective* used as a guide or trial to find out whether something will be successful. *They are going to build a pilot factory in Scotland. We are carrying out a pilot scheme for our new project.*

pilotage a charge made by **pilots** (meaning 1) for their **services.**

pioneer *noun* the first person to go into a country to develop it or to do something new. *As a salesman in this new region you should think of yourself as a pioneer.*

pioneer *verb* (1) to show new methods, new ways, ideas to others. *He pioneered the use of the new product.* (2) to be a **pioneer** in something new.

pioneer selling selling a new **product** to buyers for the first time (or selling an old **product** to new buyers for the first time). *When you are out selling life insurance it is pioneer selling at every call. See also* **pioneer**.

piracy (1) robbery at sea. (2) the use of someone's written work, invention or **patent** without his agreement.

pirate a person who commits **piracy.**

pirate *verb* to steal (**copyright** material). *Their new book has been pirated in several countries.*

pitch (*informal*) the reasons for buying which a salesman gives to a buyer. *The buyer listened to the salesman's pitch but at the end of it he refused to buy.*

placement (1) the act of placing, e.g. workers in jobs. (2) work in a company, or work at a particular job. *They offered Jones a placement in their*

Kent branch and they offered Smith a placement as a salesman.

plagiarise to use (someone else's work, e.g. a book, idea, etc.) as if it were one's own. *He has plagiarised my book – he even has his name on it.*

plagiarism the act of **plagiarising**.

plagiarist a person who **plagiarises**.

plaintiff a person who brings another to court in a case dealing with the rights of private citizens. *See* **defendant**.

plan *noun* a carefully-thought-out course of action. *See also* **marketing plan**.

plan *verb* to prepare a plan (for). *We shall have to plan our sales campaign very carefully.*

planned economy money, goods and other **resources** of a company planned and controlled by the government

planned maintenance (*or* **preventive maintenance**) checking machines, buildings etc. in a regular manner so that they remain free of trouble

planning permission (*UK*) permission from a **local authority** for the way land is used and the types of building built on it.

plant (1) the machinery and other equipment in a factory, office, stores etc. *They are going to sell off the plant.* (2) a factory or building or group of these where work is done. *He has a plant outside the town.*

plant bargaining talks at a factory between workers and managers about wage increases and/or working conditions. *Compare with* **collective bargaining**.

platen the part of a typewriter which holds and moves the paper.

play the market to buy and sell **stocks** and **shares**, hoping for profit (but risking a loss) through a change in prices. *He played the market for a long time but in the end he lost all his money.*

PLC *see* **public limited company**.

pledge *noun* (1) something left with a **pawnbroker.** (2) something given as a sign of love, affection; *a pledge of friendship.* (3) a promise.

pledge *verb* (1) to leave (something) with a **pawnbroker** as a **pledge**. (2) to promise. *He pledged his support for the project.*

plenary session a meeting attended by everyone with the right to be there. *In the afternoon there was a plenary session for the whole conference.*

plough back profits to use profits to buy new machinery, factories etc. instead of paying out the profits to **shareholders**. *We've got the most up-to-date factory in the country because we've been ploughing back the profits.*

plug (*informal*) to advertise (something, e.g. a book, film) by saying its name often in public.

point of order a question at a meeting about how the meeting is being run. *Point of order, should Mr Smith be present at this meeting?*

point of sale (*or* **point of purchase**) the place where goods are bought, especially the shop or shelf from which they are sold. *The point of sale is important because that's where the customer decides to buy or not.*

point-of-sale advertising placing printed cards, pictures etc. near the goods in a **retail** shop to help sell them.

policy (1) a plan of action. (2) a statement of aims. *The company's policy is to keep prices steady.* (3) a **document** which contains a **contract** of **insurance**.

policy-holder a person **insured** under an **insurance policy**.

political to do with a government and how it should govern.

political levy that part of a worker's payment to his **trade union** which goes to support the union's **political** views.

poll (1) to find out the opinions of a large group by asking questions of a **sample.** *They polled a sample of the users of the product.* (2) to receive votes at an election. *He polled 12,000 votes.*

poll *noun* (1) the act of **polling** (meaning (1)); the result of this. *Opinion polls are not always to be trusted.* (2) the number of votes given. *There was a very heavy poll.*

polytechnic a place of higher education which gives **diplomas** and often degrees in science, management, arts etc.

pool *verb* to join (a number of **resources,** e.g. money, **investments**) together.

pool *noun* (1) a joining together, sometimes by several companies etc., in this way. (3) the money etc. joined together in this way. (4) *see* **typing pool.**

population (1) the total number of people who live in an area, city, country, etc. *London has a very large population.* (2) the total number of anything (people, objects, fish etc.) from which a **sample** will be taken. This total number is also known as the **universe**. *There are 20,000 buyers of our product — that's our population and we will sample 200 of them.*

port (1) a place for ships to tie up; a harbour. (2) a town or city with a harbour. (3) the left hand side of a ship. *He turned the ship hard to port.*

portable *adjective* able to be carried about: a portable radio.

portable *noun* something **portable.** *I can bring my typewriter: it's a portable.*

porterage the payment made at a port for the work of moving cargo.

portfolio (1) a large flat container for drawings etc. (2) a list of **shares** which a person owns in companies. *His portfolio was made up of oil shares and retail store shares.*

positive cash flow a situation where more cash is coming into a business than is going out. *I expect we will have a positive cash flow by the end of the year from the new product.*

post *noun* (1) a job, position. *He has a very good post in a car company.* (2) the **system** of delivery of letters, parcels etc. through the **Post Office.** *Has the morning post come yet?*

post *verb* to send (a letter, parcel etc.) through the **Post Office.** (2) to make an entry in a **book of account.**

postage (1) the charge for sending a letter, parcel, etc. (2) the value of the stamps on something to be sent by post. *The postage for the parcel was £2.*

postcode (*US* **zipcode**) the letters and numbers which form part of an address on an envelope to make delivery quicker and easier.

postdate to put a date later than the actual date of writing on (a cheque etc.).

poster a large sheet of paper or cardboard on show to the public. *The poster advertised French perfume.*

poste restante used along with the name of a certain **post office** as an address on a letter etc. to show that it should be kept at that post office until collected by the person to whom it is addressed; the department in a post office which deals with such letters etc.

post free (*or* **post paid**) when the cost of postage is included in the price of goods.

post office (1) **Post Office** a government department which deals with the collecting and delivery of letters, parcels, money, etc. (2) **post office** an office which carries this out in a certain area. *There is a post office in every district.*

Post Office Box (*or* **POB**) a numbered place in a **post office** where mail is kept until it is collected by the holder of the number.

post-test *verb* a test which checks how well something was done. For example, after a company has put on a number of TV advertisements it may carry out a post-test on buyers to see if the advertisements made them more likely to buy the company's **product**. *See also* **pre-test**.

post-test *noun* the act of **post-testing**.

potential *noun, adjective* (something) that can or may come into being. *The potential sales of the new product could be as high as £1,000,000.*

pound (1) a unit of weight equal to 0.454 kilograms. *I lost three pounds in weight last month.* (2) the UK standard of money (**pound sterling**) equal to 100 pence.

pound sterling the basic currency unit of the UK.

power of attorney a legal **document** which gives one person the power to act and sign papers for another.

PP *see* **per procurationem**.

PR *see* **public relations**.

practice *noun* (1) the act of doing something (as compared to thinking about it). *He put the plan into practice,* i.e. he put it into action. (2) the usual way of doing something. *The practice in this firm is for the head cashier to open all the letters each morning.* (3) the work of a doctor, lawyer etc. *He's in practice as a doctor.*

practise *verb* (1) to do (something) over and over to become better at it. *You must practise the piano every day.* (2) to do or work at : *to practise accountancy.*

précis a shortened form of a speech or a piece of writing which keeps all the main points. *Write me a précis of the manager's report. Compare with* **precise.**

precise (1) exact, correct. *These are the precise costs.* (2) taking care to be exact. *He spoke in a very precise manner. Compare with* **précis.**

pre-entry closed shop a company or factory where workers will not be employed unless they are already members of a **trade union**. *There is no hope of me getting a job at Whites. It is a pre-entry closed shop and I'm not in a union. See also* **closed shop, open shop.**

preference shareholder a person who holds **preference shares** in a company.

preference shares: shares which have a right to a **dividend** before anything is paid to the **ordinary shares**. Should a company sell off all its **assets** and close down, preference shares often have the right to be paid at their **face value** before payment is made to ordinary shares. The **voting rights** which come with preference shares are usually less than those of ordinary shares. Such details are given in a company's **articles of association.**

preferred position (advertising) a place in a newspaper or magazine where one wants one's advertisement to appear. The advertiser will have to pay extra (a **premium**) for this preferred position.

preliminary expenses the costs of forming a company such as legal costs, cost of issuing **shares** etc.

premises a building or buildings and the land on which it/they are built.

premium (1) an addition to the usual cost of something because that thing is now of greater value. For example, **shares** are sold **at a premium** when they are sold at a price above their **face value.** Also a banker may offer dollars for sale in four weeks' time **at a premium** if he thinks that the value of the dollar will have risen by then. (2) an amount payable to an **insurer.**

premium bond *see* **premium savings bond.**

premium offer something extra which is offered to a buyer to make him/her buy more of a **product**, e.g. a silver spoon offered by a sugar manufacturer to buyers who send in a certain number of empty sugar bags.

premium savings bond (*or* **premium bond**) a **bond**, issued by the UK government (sold in blocks of £5). Each bond sold is numbered and these numbers are put into a total pool of numbers. From this pool at regular intervals numbers are drawn. These numbers are given prizes of £25 up to £100,000. At any time the bonds can be exchanged for their **face value**.

prepaid expenses costs which are paid although the goods and **services** are not yet used. For example, a company may pay its rent or rates for the period July to December in June of the same year.

presentation (1) the act of putting before a meeting a carefully thought-out course of action or proposal, usually with the help of charts, film etc. *The advertising agency were asked to make a presentation of their planned campaign.* (2) the act of offering a **bill of exchange** for payment. (3) the act of offering a gift to someone. *Are you going to Bill's presentation? He's retiring today.*

present value today's value of money which is due to be paid at a certain date in the future.

press newspapers and other news **media** (TV, radio) in general. *When the company announced it was going to close down, the press was at the door for more news.*

press conference a meeting at which the news **media** (newspapers, radio, TV etc) have been invited to hear some special news from a person or organisation and where the media can ask questions. *The company held a press conference to explain the reasons for the air crash.*

press cuttings pieces of news about something cut from newspapers and magazines. *See also* **clipping service.**

press release (*also* **news release**) a special item of news about something written and sent to the **press** in the hope that it will be used by them. *The company issued a press release about the take-over.*

Prestel a **viewdata** system offered by British Telecom.

prestige advertising (*or* **corporate advertising**) putting information into newspapers, radio, television etc. which will improve the **image** of a company in the mind of the public.

pre-tax before the amount of tax to be paid is taken off: *pre-tax profits.*

pre-test *verb* to test (something) before it is carried out in full. For example, a newspaper advertisement may be pre-tested, so that its effect on likely customers will be checked before it is put into the newspaper.

pre-test *noun* the act of **pre-testing.**

preventive maintenance *see* **planned maintenance.**

price a sum of money asked for something which is offered for sale. *What's the price of that dress? See also* **cost, value.**

price control action by the government to stop prices rising so that the **cost of living** will not increase.

price-cutting offering something for less than its usual price, usually in order to increase sales. *I see Macy's have started price-cutting again.*

price discrimination setting different prices for the same **product** in different markets. *British cars are cheaper in France – do the British car companies use price discrimination?*

price earnings ratio (*or* **P/E ratio**) the current price of one **share** in a company related to the part of the profits (i.e. the **earnings**) that it gets. This **ratio** is worked out by first dividing the total profit by the number of **ordinary shares**. This will give the earnings per share. The earnings per share is then divided into the **market price** of one share to give the price earnings ratio.

price fixing an agreement between companies which are selling the same type of **product** or **service** on the price which should be charged. (Such an agreement is often against the law unless it can be proved that the public gains by it.)

price index a method of measuring the rise or fall in prices by giving to the first year a value of £100. The following years are then shown as a percentage increase or decrease of this first (or 'base') year. For example:

Year:	1981	1982	1983
Price:	£1,000	£1,200	£1,400
Index:	100	120	140

price leader a major company in an industry whose price sets the price level for all the companies. An increase or decrease in price by the price leader is usually followed by the other companies in the industry moving their price up or down by the same amount.

priceless so valuable it cannot be priced. *The ancient Greek vase was priceless.*

price list a printed sheet showing the selling prices of various **products** of a company. *We bring out a new price list every month.*

price range the variety of prices for a **product** from the lowest to the highest. *The price range for these goods is quite large this year.*

price-sensitive used to describe a **product** or **service** for which the demand falls when the price is increased.

price ticket a piece of paper etc. on which is printed the price of a **product.**

price war a situation when two or more companies continue to cut the price of a **product** or **service** in an attempt to increase their sales. *There is a price war in air fares to the USA.*

primary data information from an original source. For example, if a company makes a list of its own customers this is primary data, or if it questions its own customers the answers are primary data; but if it uses information which is published by others it is using **secondary data.**

primary products: products from natural sources, e.g. of agricul-

ture (wheat, etc.), forestry (trees, etc.), fishing, mining (coal, etc.).

prime cost *see* **direct cost.**

prime time on television and radio, the time which attracts the biggest audience. *Television companies charge more for advertisements at prime time because there are more people watching.*

principal *adjective* chief, main, most important. *Our principal customers are car owners.*

principal *noun* (1) the sum of money on which interest is paid. *I pay back £20 interest each month and another £20 to repay the principal.* (2) the company, or person that an agent works for. *I'm an agent for Scotch whisky and my principal is S. McNab Limited, of Glasgow.* (3) the head of a college, school or university. Compare with **principle.**

principle (1) a basic rule of personal conduct. *He is a man of very high principles.* (2) a basic rule which applies to something. *A basic principle of democracy is free speech.* Compare with **principal.**

printer (1) a person employed in the trade of printing (e.g. the printing of books, newspapers, etc.). (2) (**computers**) a machine which changes computer information into printed form on paper sheets.

print-out (**computers**) printed information on paper sheets which comes from a **printer** (meaning 2).

prior charge the **security** for a loan to a company made with the condition that the money must be repaid before other loans.

private brand *or see* **own brand.**

private company *see* **private limited company.**

private enterprise the owning and controlling of companies by private individuals and not by the state. *See also* **public ownership.**

private label *see* **own brand.**

private limited company a company whose **shares** cannot be bought on the **stock exchange.** Private companies are often small, two-people or one-family firms. A UK private limited company is a **registered company** with a **Memorandum and Articles of Association** which state the rules and conditions under which it carries out its business. It must not have more than 50 **shareholders.** The letters Ltd after a business name mean that it is a private limited company.

private property land or buildings owned by ordinary people or companies, i.e. not owned by the state.

private sector of the economy all the property and business activity in a country which is controlled by ordinary people and companies and which is not owned by the state or local government. *See also* **public sector of the economy.**

probability the likelihood of something happening. *If you toss up a penny one hundred times the probability is it will come down heads about fifty times.*

probate *(law)* the **process** of proving that a will is **valid.**

probationary period a short time at the start of a person's employment during which his/her ability to do the job will be tested. *My probationary period finishes next week; then I'll know if I'm still in a job or not.*

procedure a way of doing something. *We always try to follow the correct procedures.*

proceed (1) to go on (with whatever one is doing). *Please proceed with your talk.* (2) to take legal action (against a person). *See also* **proceedings** *and compare with* **proceeds.**

proceedings (1) how something is done: *the proceedings of the meeting* i.e. the way the meeting was carried out. (2) taking legal action. *I have started proceedings against the canned meats company.* (3) the reports of the meeting(s) of a society, conference etc.: *Proceedings of the Marketing Group. See also* **proceed** *and compare with* **proceeds.**

proceeds money gained from the sale of something. *The proceeds from the new line helped the finances of the company.*

process *noun* (1) a number of actions to get something done: *the manufacturing process.* (2) a special method of doing something. *We're using the silk-screen process.* (3) the whole action in a legal case: *the process of the law.*

process *verb* (1) to deal with (something) in some organised way: *to process an order.* (2) to treat or prepare (something, especially food) in a special way: *processed peas.* (3) (**computers**) to carry out some operation on (**data**) in order to get certain information etc.

process chart a drawing which shows the order of events of a piece of work to be done, i.e. making, moving, storing, etc. Since the process chart is a picture of the way the work is done, it can lead to better methods of doing it. *See* **process** *(noun:* meaning 1).

process industry a group of companies in the business of changing liquids, powder, grains etc. into finished or partly-finished form, e.g. the oil industry, the sugar industry, the wheat industry.

procurement the act of buying; purchasing. *His job was the procurement of the best materials for the product.*

produce *verb* (1) to make, manufacture, bring into being. *We produce steel plates.* (2) to show, to be examined. *He produced his visiting card.* (3) to prepare (a play, film etc.) for showing on the stage, TV, radio etc. *He will produce Macbeth in London.*

produce *noun* what is made.

producer (1) a person or company that makes or grows something. (2) a person who **produces** (meaning 4) a play or film.

product anything made by man or nature.

product acceptance how much buyers prefer a certain **product.** *It has 15% of the market – that shows some product acceptance.*

product development making present **products** better in some way, e.g. in design, colour, more uses etc. See also **new product development.**

product differentiation making a **product** which might have many **competitors**, e.g. toothpaste, soup, etc., different in some way, e.g. by the **package**, the advertising, the price, the colour, the name, etc.

product feature (or **sales feature**) a benefit which a company tries to point out to its buyers to make them buy. For example, benefits of a new soap may include: clear skin, attractive smell, freshness all day etc.

production (1) the act of making a **product.** (2) the quantity produced. *Production of coal has greatly increased.* (3) the way a play, film etc. has been produced: *a new production of Hamlet.*

production control managing materials, people, machines and methods so as to provide the planned **output** in the most profitable way.

production line a method of producing goods in a factory where the various stages of making the **product** follow each other in order. See also **assembly line.**

production manager a person who is in charge of the **process** of making goods in a factory.

production-oriented company a company which thinks more of how it makes its **products** than its customers' needs. See also **marketing concept.**

production overheads the **indirect costs** of running a factory area compared to the **direct costs** of actually making the **products,** e.g. heating costs, rates, cleaning costs, manager's salary etc.

production planning that part of **production control** to do with **estimating** the materials, men and machines needed to satisfy future sales.

production platform a raised metal or concrete floor though which oil can be pumped. It can be positioned on long metal legs resting on the sea bed or it can float above an **offshore oilfield.**

productivity relating **input** to **output** within a company. Input is measured in the amount of people, machines, material and money put in, and output is measured in the amount of products or **services** produced. *We can increase our productivity by producing more with the same inputs.*

product liability insurance having a **policy** (meaning 3) which will protect a company from claims in the event of any harm to a customer caused by a fault in its **product** or the **packaging.**

product life cycle the **theory** that **products,** like people, are born, some die soon afterwards, others grow, get old and then die. If this is so, then new products must be made ready to provide the profits as the old products fail.

product mix all the different **products** which a company offers for sale. *Our product mix has too many slow sellers.*

product-plus (*informal*) something about a **product** which in the buyer's opinion makes it better than others of the same type. *This new golf-ball is made to go further – that's a great product-plus.* See also **product feature.**

product test a way of finding out what users think of a **product.** One method is to ask a section of all buyers (a **sample**) what their views are on the various **product features** and compare this with their views on other products of the same type.

profession a job which needs study for several years in a special branch of knowledge such as law or medicine. *The teaching profession claim that their job is not all holidays.*

professional *adjective* (1) working in one of the **professions.** *He guessed that the other was a professional man: a* *doctor or a lawyer.* (2) showing or having skill in something which needs a long period of training to reach. *The way he handled the men showed that he was a very professional manager.* (3) doing or working at something for money (which others do for pleasure alone): *professional football player.*

professional *noun* a person who is **professional**, especially someone who takes part in sport for his/her living and not just for pleasure.

proficiency test a test of how well a person can do a certain job.

profit the result of more money coming in from the sale of a **product** or **service** than all the costs related to it. *See also* **earnings, income, margin, profit margin.**

profit *verb* to get profit or advantage (from something).

profitability the measure of the profit of a **product** or **service** in relation to the money **invested** in it. For example, it may take £100,000 to buy a factory, machines, materials, etc. to make something and the profit at the end of the year may be only £1,000. The product will have made a profit but its profitability will be seen to be very poor. Profitability is the measure of the **return on capital** employed.

profitable of a **product** or **service**, having an **income** greater than its costs. *Selling crisps is a very profitable business.*

profit and loss account (*or* **operating statement**) a record, which usually covers a year, of a company's total sales, total expenses, and showing either a **net profit** or a **net loss.** *See also* **gross profit, net profit** *and* appendix 1.

profit centre a unit or department of a company which has,to be responsible for its costs and its profit. *We run all our hotels on a profit-centre basis.*

profit margin the difference between a maker's selling price for a **product** and the cost of making it or between a **retailer's** or **wholesal-**

er's selling price and what he paid for it, e.g. buying price £1, selling price £2, profit margin £1 (i.e. the profit margin is 50% of the selling price).

profit sharing an agreement by which workers in a company each year get a certain part of its profit in addition to their normal wages or salaries.

profits tax payment to the government of a certain part of a company's profits. *See also* **corporation tax.**

profit-volume chart a drawing showing: the number of a certain **product** sold, the total value of these sales, the **fixed costs**, the **variable costs,** and the total profit reached. The chart shows how variable costs increase with each product sold and at what level of sales all costs are covered (the **break-even point**). *See also* **break-even chart** and appendix 3.

pro-forma invoice a copy of an **invoice** sent to a buyer who may buy the goods; it gives all the details and the cost of the goods and is issued before an order is placed.

program a set of instructions for solving a particular problem by a **computer.**

program *verb* (1) to write **programs** for a **computer.** (2) to prepare (**data**) to be handled by a computer. (3) to put a program into (a computer).

programme (*US* **program**) (1) a list of actors and actresses and the parts they have in a play; a list of programmes in a concert. (2) a (complete) show in a hall, theatre, etc. or on radio or television. *We waited till we had seen the complete programme.* (3) a list of duties or activities. *This is today's programme for our visitors.*

programmed instruction (*or* **programmed learning**) learning by small amounts (from a special book or **computer program**) with the student's knowledge of each stage being checked before he moves on to the next part of the program.

programme evaluation and review technique (*or* **PERT**) a method of checking the times taken to finish important parts of large, complex jobs such as making aircraft, ships, bridges etc. It helps the planning and control of such large **projects** and is closely related to **critical path analysis.**

programmer a person who plans, writes and tests complete **programs** for a **computer.**

progress chaser a person in a company whose work is to see that orders get through their various stages in the factory, get finished and delivered on time.

progress payments payments made to a manufacturer (e.g. a builder) as each stage of a **contract** is finished, common in the cases of very large **contracts** such as ships, planes, etc.

project *noun* (1) something carried out according to a plan. *How is the new factory project coming along?* (2) something which is put forward as a plan but on which no work has begun. *Let's have a look at this project of yours for a new product.*

project *verb* (1) to stick out. *The window projects over the street.* (2) to plan; to say that something will happen. *We are projecting a large expansion next year.*

projected planned, proposed, expected. *These are the projected costs of the new model.*

project group a small number of people who come together to solve a particular set of problems. For example, the head of a company might tell three of his managers to form a project group to solve the problems arising from moving to a new factory.

projection (1) the act of **projecting.** (2) something which **projects.** 3) a guess of future sales, future **output**, future profits etc., based on present and past figures. *My projection for next year is total sales of 10,000 units.*

project manager a person in charge of solving the problems of one particular **project** (noun: meaning 1).

promissory note a promise in writing to pay, without any conditions, a certain sum of money to the holder of the note or to some other named person, either when the money is asked for or at some other named date.

promote (1) to bring (goods or **services**) to the notice of buyers to increase sales. *It is a brand new product so we will have to promote it strongly.* (2) to help in the setting up of a company or some public event, e.g. a play, concert, boxing match. *Who is promoting the new company?* (3) to advance (a person) in a job, give (him/her) a better job with more pay; to advance (a person) in rank. *I think he is doing so well we could promote him to manager.*

promoter a person who **promotes** (meanings (1) and (2)). *He is the main promoter of our sales in France.*

promotion (1) action to help the sales of a **product** or **service,** e.g. a salesman making a sale; advertising a product in the press or television, radio, posters, cinema etc.; showing special tickets and displays at the **point-of-sale** to sell the goods. *We must make certain that all our promotion activities take place in the order that we planned.* (2) advancement in a job (or rank). *I'm doing so well I feel I'm due for promotion in this job.*

promotional mix methods used by a company to help the sale of its **products** or **services.** It includes advertising, personal selling, **sales promotion, publicity.**

proof (1) showing that something is true. *Have you proof that our profits are falling?* (2) a first copy made of a piece of printed matter so that any mistakes can be put right before printing takes place. *I'm checking the proofs of my new novel.* (3) a measure of alcoholic content in a drink (e.g. gin, whisky). *It's 70 per cent proof.*

proof of delivery usually a signature on a **delivery note** which is asked for by the firm sending the goods. Having such a signature is considered proof that the goods actually have been delivered and received.

property (1) something which is owned. *That suit is my property.* (2) land, buildings which are or can be owned. *This looks like a very valuable piece of property.*

property tax money asked for by the national or local government from a person because of the value of the land, buildings etc. which he/she owns. *See also* **rates**.

proposal something **proposed**; the act of **proposing**.

propose to put forward (a plan, suggestion etc.) for consideration.

proprietary goods: products owned by a company (i.e. only they have the right to make them).

proprietor an owner, especially of a business. *Who is the proprietor of this hotel?*

pro rata in proportion; at a certain rate. *Those who sell £100 of goods will get £1 bonus, those who sell £200 will get £2 bonus, and the rest pro rata.*

prospect *noun* (1) a person who may become a customer. *I want you to list all the prospects in your area.* (2) a hope (of something). *No, there's no prospect of that happening.*

prospect *verb* to search for gold, silver or other valuable things: *to prospect for oil.*

prospectus a printed notice which gives details about something, e.g. a college (what courses can be studied there), a company (its aims, the amount of money it needs, and which asks the public to buy **shares** in the company).

protectionism a **system** of helping trade inside a country by stopping goods entering the country which may harm that trade.

protective practice *see* **restrictive practice**.

protest *noun* a **certificate** (which is proof) that a **bill of exchange** has not been paid as ordered (has been **dishonoured**).

protest *verb* to make a **certificate** that a person has refused to pay a **bill of exchange** (has **dishonoured** it). The certificate is usually written by a **notary public.**

protocol a **system** of rules of speech and behaviour which should be followed on certain important occasions such as when heads of state meet each other or when royalty is meeting someone.

prototype a first example of a **product** or machine from which other improved ones will be made. *Well, this is just the prototype, but it proves we can make a new computer at less cost than our present one.*

provident fund a source of **finance** for sickness, **insurance** and **pension schemes** etc.

province (1) a division of a country, often for the purposes of government. *Canada is divided into provinces.* (2) **the provinces** the areas of a country away from the capital and other large cities.

provincial of a **province** or **the provinces**.

provision (1) (**accounting**) an amount of money set aside for renewing an **asset** (such as a building, machinery etc.) (2) an amount of money set aside for some known need: *provision for bad debts.* (3) *in plural* **provisions** food or food supplies. *We will need to get some provisions for our trip.* (4) a condition in some legal **document**, e.g. a clause in a **contract.**

proxy an authority to act or sign for another person, e.g. to vote for him/her at a meeting or at an election.

PSV *see* **public service vehicle.**

public (1) people in general. *The great British public.* (2) a particular group of people: *the cinema-going public.*

public *adjective* connected with people in general or with the government; open to people in general: *a public park; a public library; public ownership of the mines.*

public authority a public body employed to do work of benefit to the public and not for private profit. *The town council is a public authority. See also* **local authority.**

public company a company whose **shares** can be bought or sold on the **stock exchange**. *See also* **public limited company**.

public house (*or informal* **pub**) a building where alcoholic drinks can be bought and drunk.

publicise to make widely known.

publicity any action to attract the public's notice to something, especially by reporting in the **media.** *They had a lot of publicity for the launch of their new product.*

public limited company (*or* **PLC**) a limited liability company whose **shares** can be bought by the public.

public ownership ownership of a business or property by the state. *The whole railway is in public ownership. See also* **private enterprise.**

public relations (*or* **PR**) any actions by an organisation which will improve relations between it and people who are important to it, including the general public. *I think we should improve our Report to our Shareholders – it would be good PR.*

public relations officer a person employed by a company to help its **public relations.**

public sector of the economy the property and business activity in the country which is controlled by the state or local government. *See also* **private sector of the economy.**

public service vehicle (*or* **PSV**) a vehicle which has a **licence** to carry passengers in return for payment, e.g. a bus, taxi.

public utility a **service** (e.g. British Gas) or supply **system** (e.g. gas, water) which is used by the general

public. In the UK such services are controlled either by the state or local government.

public works work paid for by the government to give **services** of use to the general public, e.g. building motorways, hospitals, schools etc.

publish to print and offer (a book, magazine, newspaper etc.) to the public (or to some special group). *We will have to publish a new price list for our buyers.*

publisher a person whose business is the **publishing** of books. *He's in the publishing business – he's a publisher of children's books.*

punch *noun* a tool or machine for making holes in something.

punch *verb* to make (holes) with or as with a **punch.**

punched card a card on which there is information in the form of holes which can be read by a variety of machines.

purchase *verb* to buy. *We have to purchase a new machine.*

purchase *noun* something bought. *He carried in all his purchases.*

purchase officer (*or* **purchasing officer**) a person in a company in charge of buying the things the company needs, e.g. materials, oils, paint, machines etc.

purchase order a form used by a buyer (see **purchase officer**) to detail the goods which a buyer wants from a seller and which is then given to the seller as an order.

purchaser a person who buys.

purchasing agent a person who buys goods on behalf of someone else for a payment (called a **commission**).

purchasing office an office in a company where all the buying for the company is carried out.

purchasing officer *see* **purchase officer.**

purchasing power the value of money measured by the goods or **services** it can buy. *The purchasing power of the £1 is much less today than ten years ago.*

Q

qualified acceptance a **bill of exchange** which has conditions attached to it, e.g. as to where it is to be paid or the amount to be paid.

qualified accounts *or* **qualified report** a report by an **auditor** stating that he/she is not satisfied with something in the **accounts** which he/she has **audited.**

quality control a method of making sure that goods being produced are of the planned standard, usually done by taking **samples** of the goods (and possibly the materials they are made from) and examining them very carefully.

quango a group of people set up by the government, but not directly controlled by it, with a special responsibility to advise on such matters as the countryside, prices, wages.

quantity (1) an amount. *They ordered a quantity of wool from the suppliers.* (2) a large amount or a large quantity of something. *It is often cheaper to buy in quantity.*

quantity discount (*or* **quantity rebate**) an amount by which a price is lowered when a large amount of goods is ordered. *If you buy 600 we can offer you a quantity discount.*

quantity surveyor a person whose job is to find out how much **labour** and materials will be required to build something.

quarantine *verb* to force (a person, animal or thing) to remain separated from others to prevent the spread of disease. *The ship was quarantined.*

quarantine *noun* the state of being **quarantined.** *The ship spent ten days in quarantine.*

quarter-days (*UK*) the days which come at the end of the four quarters of the year when certain rents or **interests** may become due. In England, Wales and Ireland the days are: 25 March (Lady Day), 24 June (Midsummer Day), 29 September (Michaelmas), 25 December (Christmas Day); in Scotland: 2 February (Candlemas), 15 May (Whitsunday), 1 August (Lammas), 11 November (Martinmas).

quarterly *adjective* happening every 13 weeks: *quarterly payments.*

quarterly *noun* a magazine which is published four times a year.

quartile (**statistics**) the value that lies midway between the lowest value and the middle value in a series of values, e.g. in a list of **accounts** arranged by value; or the value that lies midway between the highest value and the middle value. In other words the quartiles will divide a list of values into four equal parts.

quarto (1) a size of paper 10 in. × 8 in. (254 mm × 203 mm). (2) a size of paper obtained when a sheet is folded twice, giving eight pages.

questionnaire a list of questions used to find out information from people, especially about their likes and dislikes, their opinions and ideas etc.

queuing theory a **technique** which is used to find out about and thus lessen the amount of time that customers have to queue, e.g. in a bank, **supermarket.**

quick ratio *see* **liquidity ratio.**

quid (*informal*) a **pound (sterling).**

quid pro quo (*Latin* meaning something for something) especially with reference to **negotiations,** something that is given in exchange for something else.

quire formerly 24, now more usually 25 sheets of paper or one-twentieth of a **ream.**

quorum a number of people who have to be present at a meeting for its decisions to be effective according to the rules of the meeting.

quota (1) an amount or share of something which someone is allowed to have. *The goods are in short supply and no one can be allowed to receive more than the quota.* (2) a limited amount (of people, goods etc.) allowed into a country by government regulations.

quota sampling a method of **sampling** in which the population is divided into certain groups (of the same age, sex, income etc.). The number of people in each group is decided and then people are chosen for interview on the basis of convenience. *Compare with* **stratified sampling**.

quotation (1) a statement of how much certain goods or a certain **service** will cost, made by the person who will provide the goods or service in response to an inquiry by a possible customer. (2) a statement by a person trading in a certain market (e.g. the **stock market**) of how much something (e.g. **shares**) will cost either to buy or to sell.

quoted company *see* **listed company**.

R

racket a dishonest way of making money in business. *They force the hotels to pay protection money or else they complain loudly about the food in the hotel's restaurant: it's a racket.*

rack jobber a **wholesaler** or manufacturer who puts a selection of his goods on show in a shop or store, calling from time to time to replace things that have been sold and collecting his share of the money from the sales.

railhead (the place at) the end of a railway line.

raise (1) to move to a higher position. (2) to arrange to get (money, a loan etc.). *They were not able to raise enough capital for the new project.*

rake-off (*informal*) a share of the profit from a deal, especially a deal which is illegal or when the share is in the form of a **bribe**.

rally *noun* a recovery in the price of **stocks, shares** or **commodities**.

rally *verb* to make a **rally**.

R and D *see* **research and development**.

random done by chance without making a deliberate choice. *He tested the goods by selecting a few random examples for close examination.* See **random sampling**.

random access *see* **direct access**.

random sample a group of people or things which have been selected by **random sampling**.

random sampling a **sampling procedure** in which every individual member of the group being **sampled** has an equal chance of being chosen. *See also* **quota sampling**.

range *noun* (1) the amount by which things vary from the smallest to the largest. *We are looking for suits in the £100 to £150 price range.* (2) a number of different articles that are for sale. *He sells a very wide range of goods.*

range *verb* (1) to vary in price, quantity etc. between certain limits. *Their tyre prices range from £25 to £40.* (2) to go freely from one place or subject to another. *The discussions ranged over a variety of problems.*

rank *noun* the position which a person has in an organisation, especially a military or similar organisation. *He holds the rank of general.*

rank *verb* (1) to arrange (people or things) in order according to some principle (usually so that one can choose among them more easily). *The applicants for the job were ranked according to their exam results.* (2) to come into a certain class, above or below other classes. *He ranks as one of the best salesmen we've got.*

ranking the act of **ranking** (meaning 1).

rate *noun* (1) an amount that is paid in exchange for some fixed amount of goods or **services**. *We pay our engineers at a rate of £10 per hour.* (2) a speed; an amount within a certain period of time. *His rate of travel was 50 miles per hour. We make machines at a rate of six per day.* (3) the amount of tax one pays as a percentage of one's **income**. *The tax rate has been lowered from 33⅓% to 30%.* See also **basic rate.** (4) the amount of tax one pays for certain public services: *the water rate. See also* **rates.** (5) the amount of **premium** paid or charged for **insurance** as a proportion of the total amount insured.

rate *verb* (1) to place at a certain level when compared to others. *This is rated to be one of the most successful businesses in the country. He is not highly rated as a businessman.* (2) (UK) to give a certain value to (a property) for the purpose of paying local taxes. *See also* **rates.**

rateable value (*UK*) the amount which might reasonably be charged for the yearly rent of a property: used as the basis for fixing the amount of **rates** (local taxes) which a property owner has to pay.

rate card a **document** which shows how much it will cost to advertise (depending on size of advertisement, time of advertisement etc.) in newspapers, radio, television, posters etc.

rate of exchange *see* **exchange rate.**

rate of return an amount of money (**income**, profit) that is gained from an **investment**, usually expressed as a percentage of the investment. For example, if a person invests £200 in a bank for a year and gains £20 at the end of that time his rate of return is

$$\frac{20}{200} \times \frac{100}{1} = 10\%.$$

rates (*UK*) local taxes paid on both private and commercial property. *See also* **rate, rateable value.**

ratification the act of **ratifying** a **contract.**

ratify to agree to, and take responsibility for, the conditions of (e.g. a **contract** that has been **negotiated** on one's behalf). *The new contract will have to be ratified by the Board of Directors.*

rating a number value which a person or thing has been given in a **rating scale.** *See also* **ratings.**

rating scale a method of comparing things, usually by giving each thing a number value. *On this rating scale each employee is given a number from 1 to 5 for the various aspects of his work. See also* **rating.**

ratings the **estimate** of the audience of a television or radio broadcast, of special interest to advertisers who buy time on television or radio. *The comedy series has not been doing very well in the ratings. See also* **rating.**

ratio an amount of one class of people or things, when compared to another. *They produce cars and lorries in a ratio of three to one. See also* **current ratio.**

ratio analysis using the **ratio** method to make various **financial** measurements of a company *See* appendix 6.

ration *noun* an amount of something which a person is allowed to have in a time of shortage.

ration *verb* to limit the supply of (goods etc.) in this way. *See also* **rationing.**

rationalisation the act of **rationalising.**

rationalise to make (something, e.g. a company) more efficient by organising it in a less costly way. *We are rationalising production by having it all done in one larger factory.*

rationing a **system** of making sure that there is a fair distribution of goods which are in short supply by limiting the amount that can be got by any one person, usually done by governments in time of crisis, e.g. war. *See also* **ration.**

rat

rat 140 recommended

rat race an organisation, group or society where everyone is in fierce **competition** with everyone else. *Jack is very unhappy with his present firm: he feels he's in the rat race.*

raw materials materials which have not yet been manufactured or **processed** in any way. *Industry needs a constant supply of steel, coal and other raw materials.*

readership the number of people who actually read a publication as distinct from those who get a copy of it. *It has been found that on average three people read every copy of our magazine and so our readership is three times our circulation. See also* **circulation**.

real accounts: ledger accounts which record **assets**, **capital** equipment etc.

real estate *(mainly US)* things which are owned but which cannot be taken away by the owner, e.g. houses, land.

real income the amount of **income** which a person has available to buy goods and **services**.

realisation of assets the act of selling the **assets** of a company for cash. *See also* **realise** *(meaning 2)*.

realise (1) to be sold for (a certain price). *His property realised several thousand pounds.* (2) to sell (property, **assets** etc.) for cash. *When he died, the other partners realised the company's assets.*

real time a period of time in which a **computer** is actually **processing data** as it receives the data. *The airline booking system uses a real-time system to make sure the flights are not overbooked.*

ream a number of sheets of paper, formerly 480, now more usually 500, equal to twenty **quires**.

rebate a return of part of a sum of money which one has paid. *I've just had an unexpected income tax rebate. See also* **discount**.

receipt *noun* a piece of paper which states that something has been paid for. *I'll pay you now but I must have a receipt.*

receipt *verb* to give proof that (something) has been paid, e.g. by giving one's signature. *Could you receipt this bill?*

receivable (1) acceptable for payment. (2) owed, but not yet paid: *accounts receivable.*

receiver (1) a person who is officially appointed to take over the property of a debtor until as much as possible of his debts have been paid. *A receiver has been appointed in the Brook Shipbuilding Company. See also* **offical receiver.** (2) a person who accepts stolen goods. *See also* **fence.**

receiving order an instruction from a court appointing an official receiver to take over the property of a person or company that cannot pay his/its debts and to call a meeting of the **creditors**. *See also* **bankruptcy**.

reception (1) the act of receiving. (2) the place in a hotel, office etc. where visitors are received. (3) a formal party.

recession a fall in business activity causing unemployment and other hardships, but not so serious as a **depression**. *See also* **boom; depression; slump; trade cycle.**

recipient a person who receives something.

reciprocal trading a situation where a person who supplies certain goods or **services** to a company promises to buy from it other goods and services in return.

reclaim to make (an area that is not productive, e.g. a desert) into an area that can grow crops etc. *In the Netherlands, a lot of land has been reclaimed from the sea.*

reclamation the act of **reclaiming**.

recommended retail price *(or* **RRP**) the amount which a manufacturer of **consumer goods** suggests that the goods should be sold for to the consumer. *Compare with* **resale price maintenance**.

record *adjective* the greatest or best ever. *Our factory has achieved record output this year.*

record *noun* (1) written account: *a record of these events.* (2) a **disk** for playing music etc. on a record-player. (3) a list of things which someone has done. *He had a good record while he was working for us.* (4) the best or greatest amount. *Our sales have reached a new record. Sales have broken all previous records.*

　　for the record so that something can be recorded as having been done. *Just for the record, we should not forget the wonderful job the staff have done.*

　　off the record not for publication, to be kept secret. *I don't think much of his management style, but that's off the record.*

　　on record publicly known or stated. *He's on record as having actually admitted the results were down.*

record *verb* (1) to put down in writing for future use. *All his decisions have been recorded in these notebooks.* (2) to put (sound) onto a **disk.** *The poet's voice was recorded before he died.* (3) to show on a scale. *The thermometer recorded 30° centigrade.*

recorded delivery the **Post Office** service by which, for an extra charge, an official record is made of the sending and delivery of a letter or package.

recourse (1) the right of a person holding a **bill of exchange** to ask for payment for the bill from the **drawer** or **endorser** if the person who has accepted the bill cannot pay. This right does not exist if the drawer or endorser has written **without recourse** or **sans recours** (*French*) beside his signature. (2) a source of help in time of difficulty. *As a last recourse to get money we had to sell some assets,* i.e. there was no other source of help available. *They eventually had recourse to the stock market.*

recruit *verb* to take on (new soldiers in an army, new workers in a company etc.). *We have started to recruit for our new London store.*

recruit *noun* a soldier who has just joined the army; a new worker in a company etc.

recruitment the act of **recruiting**.

rectify to put (something) right.

red: in the red (*informal*) owing money, in debt. *In spite of all the economies we've made, we're still in the red.*

redeem (1) to become the owner of (something) by paying off money owed on it. (2) to pay off (a loan, etc.): *to redeem a mortgage.* (3) to sell (**shares** etc.) for cash. (4) to keep (a promise). (5) to make up for (something one has done wrong or badly).

redeemable (*or* **callable**) (1) with reference to **bonds, shares** etc., able to be bought back by the person who issued them, usually within certain time limits. (2) of bonds, able to be exchanged for cash.

redeemable preference share a type of **preference share** which can be exchanged for cash or for another share by the issuer at some time in the future.

redeploy to give (workers) new tasks to do which may sometimes involve **re-training** them. *There is no longer enough work in the department and so some people will have to be redeployed.*

redeployment the act of **redeploying** workers.

redevelop to rebuild, replan (a building, an area).

redevelopment the act of **redeveloping**.

redraft *verb* to write something again. *I shall have to redraft this letter.*

redraft *noun* (1) a foreign **bill of exchange** which is drawn by the holder of a **dishonoured** bill on the person who issued or **endorsed** the dishonoured bill. The new bill is for the amount of the dishonoured bill plus any expenses that have been involved in **protesting** it. (2) a letter, report etc. which has been written again with some changes.

red tape time-wasting rules or **procedures** (especially with reference to government departments). *We've lost two weeks on this delivery because of government red tape.*

reduce to make smaller; to make less: *to reduce prices.*

reduction (1) the act of **reducing**. *We are trying to achieve a reduction in the rate of inflation.* (2) the amount by which something is less or smaller. *I could offer you a slight reduction in price if you pay cash.*

redundancy (1) the state of being **redundant**. (2) (**computers**) *see* **redundancy check**. (3) (**computers**) the unnecessary keeping of copies of **data**.

redundancy check (**computers**) the use of extra **characters** or **bits** to find mistakes.

redundancy payment the extra money given to workers who have been made **redundant**.

redundant (1) unnecessary; not needed, especially with reference to a worker or workers whose **labour** is no longer needed. *The factory closed down and hundreds were made redundant,* i.e. they were unemployed because their labour was no longer needed. *See also* **redundancy payment.** (2) (**computers, communications**) not strictly necessary but useful for checking for errors. *See also* **redundancy check.**

re-export *verb* to send abroad again (goods which have been **imported**).

re-export *noun* (1) something which has been **re-exported.** (2) the act of **re-exporting.**

referee *noun* (1) a person who is given the power to decide in a **dispute.** (2) a person who is named by someone applying for a job, loan etc. as one

who can give opinions on the **applicant's** ability, honesty etc. *See also* **reference** (meaning 2). (3) in sport, a person who decides whether a game is being played according to the rules.

referee *verb* to act as a **referee**.

reference (1) a (usually) written opinion on a person's character, ability, honesty, etc. in support of someone's application for a job or a loan etc. *I sent a copy of the reference from my last employer when I wrote my application for the job at the bank.* (2) a person named by the **applicant** as one who will provide such support. *I named my last boss Mr Ford as a reference. See also* **referee** (meaning 2). (3) the act of referring to a book or an article, or part of a book, or article. (4) numbers and/or letters put at the top of a business letter so that it can be filed or found in a file. *The reference for this letter is JWB/757/4.*

refer to drawer a note stamped or written on a cheque by a bank which is refusing to **honour** the cheque for a certain reason (e.g. there is not enough money in the **account** of the person who signed the cheque); the person wishing to cash the cheque must refer to the person who has signed it to find out what the reason is.

refinancing a method of repaying a loan by taking out another loan.

reflate to **stimulate** (the economy) by increasing the money supply and so increasing employment and business opportunities. *See also* **inflate**.

reflation the act of **reflating**. *See also* **inflation**.

regional development grant (*UK*) an amount of money given by the government to encourage business development in poorer areas of the country.

regional employment premium (*UK*) an amount of money given by the government to employers to lessen the cost of employing workers in certain areas of high **unemployment.**

regional planning courses of action by the government to improve jobs, housing, education in certain parts of the country.

register *noun* (1) an official list: *register of shareholders.* (2) a special kind of **memory location** in a **computer** where information can be stored for a time, and/or processed.

register *verb* (1) to put in a **register** (meaning 1). *His name has been registered on our list of members.* (2) to send by **registered post.** *We had better register this parcel.*

registered company a company which is on the official list of the **Registrar of Companies.**

registered mail *see* **registered post.**

registered office the official head office of a company as given to the **Registrar of Companies.**

registered post (*or* **registered mail**) (*UK*) the **Post-Office** service by which, for an extra charge, letters and parcels are specially delivered and signed for on delivery; **compensation** is paid for loss. *See also* **recorded delivery.**

registered trademark the official **trademark** of a company which has been listed so that no one else can use it.

register of directors a list which must be kept by every company, giving the directors' names, addresses, nationalities and other information.

register of members a list of those who belong to an organisation.

registrar (1) a person who is in charge of official lists and records. *The Registrar of Companies.* (2) an official who keeps the list of births, marriages and deaths in a particular area. (3) (*mainly US*) an employee of a company who keeps a record of the

ownership of the company **shares.** (4) a hospital doctor who is next in **rank** to a **consultant.**

registry (1) a place where records are kept. (2) (*shipping*) the **registering** of a ship's country of origin etc.

regression analysis (statistics) a **technique** by which one kind of change (or changes) can be used to predict another kind of change (or changes). For example, using this technique it might be possible to predict from the increase in **incomes**, the likely increase in video sales.

regressive taxation a method of raising taxes which results in lower-paid workers paying a higher proportion of their wages in tax than higher-paid workers.

regulate to control, to make or keep correct.

regulation (1) the act of **regulating.** (2) a rule as to how something should be done. *That is against the regulations.*

reimburse to repay (a person) for money already spent. *You will be reimbursed for all expenses.*

reinstate to employ (a person) again in a position after he has been **sacked** or **suspended** from it.

reinstatement the act of **reinstating.**

re-insurance an arrangement by which an **insurance company** will lessen its own risk in an insurance by sharing the risk with another insurance company or companies. A common arrangement for example when extremely costly things are insured, e.g. large aeroplanes, ships, oil wells, where one insurance company might judge that the risk is too great for that company to take on its own.

reliability the state of being **reliable.** *These engines are well-known for their reliability: they hardly ever break down.*

reliable able to be trusted; able to be depended on with confidence: *a reliable company; a reliable machine; a reliable worker.*

relief *see* tax relief.

remit *verb* (1) to send (money etc.) to a person by post. *He used to remit £50 to his parents every month.* (2) (*law*) to send (a case) to another court. *His case was remitted to the local court for a decision.* (3) to send (something) to a person for the necessary action. *This problem has been remitted to Mr Smith and he is working on it.* (4) to free a person from a debt or punishment. *His sentence to life imprisonment has been remitted.*

remit *noun* (1) (*law*) the act of sending a case to another court. (2) (*mainly Scottish*) a matter on which a person is expected to act. *This problem is not within my remit.*

remittance (1) the act of sending money etc. by post. (2) the amount of money sent by post, often on a regular basis. *He receives a weekly remittance of £50 from his family. See* **remit** (verb: meaning 1).

remunerate to pay (a person) for something he has done. *He has been well remunerated for his services.*

remuneration (1) the act of **remunerating**. *Does he expect remuneration for these services?* (2) the amount of money paid to a person for something he has done: *very good remuneration.*

rent *noun* the amount paid, usually regularly, for the use of a person's property, especially land and buildings. *I've let my house to a student for a very low rent.*

rent *verb* to pay a person for the use of (property). *He rented the house for £100 per month. See also* **hire.**

rental (1) the amount of money paid in rent: *a rental of £100 per month.* (2) the amount of **income** which is received from a property. *These flats have an annual rental value of £10,000.* (3) the amount of money paid for the **hire** of goods: *TV/telephone rental.*

reorder level the level at which a fresh supply of a particular kind of **product** held in **stock** must be ordered.

repeal *verb* to **cancel** (a law). *This Act of Parliament will probably be repealed if the opposition ever gets into power.*

repeal *noun* the act of **repealing.**

repeat purchasing the act of buying goods which are in frequent daily or weekly use (e.g. newspapers, bread, cigarettes, etc.) and which therefore have to be bought often.

replace to put a new or different thing or person in place of (an old one).

replacement cost the present-day cost of **replacing** an **asset** such as a building, machine, car etc.

replacement demand the level of sales of a **product** to replace old or worn-out products. For example, the present-day sales of videos are to first-time buyers. When most homes have videos the demand will be mainly for replacement models. *Sales of radios are to satisfy a replacement demand.*

replacement value (**insurance**) the amount it would cost at current prices to buy the thing insured.

reply-paid postcard a type of card which can be posted without having to put a stamp on it, used by companies to make it easy for customers to reply to advertisements etc.

repossess to take back (property, especially property given under a **hire purchase** agreement), when the conditions of the agreement have not been met. *If you don't pay the rest of the money within a week, the television set will be repossessed.*

representative *adjective* being an example of a group or class. *This is representative of the quality of product which we can deliver.*

representative *noun* a person appointed to act for others. *We will send a representative of the company to the* *creditors' meeting. See also* **sales representative.**

repudiate (1) to refuse to accept the conditions of (e.g. a **contract**). *The Board of Directors repudiated the contract which their negotiators had agreed.* (2) to refuse to pay (a debt).

repudiation the act of **repudiating.**

reputed ownership a situation which can happen in case of **bankruptcy,** where someone (A) has been allowed to keep goods belonging to someone else in his possession, with the result that A's **creditors** think that the goods really belong to A: if A then becomes bankrupt, his creditors are allowed to have those goods considered as among A's possessions, and so they may be used to help pay his debts.

requisition *verb* (1) to make an official demand for the use of (something that is needed) with or without payment. *During the war many cars were requisitioned by the military.* (2) to make a request for (the supply of materials etc.). *We shall have to requisition some more typing paper.*

requisition *noun* (1) the act of **requisitioning.** (2) a **document** which requisitions something.

resale price maintenance (*or* **RPM**) a system by which the minimum price for a class of goods is decided by the manufacturers (perhaps in agreement with **retailers**), and no **retailer**/shopowner or dealer is allowed to sell below that price. *In Britain, resale price maintenance is illegal as far as most goods are concerned.*

rescind (*formal*) to make no longer effective, **cancel** (a law, **contract**).

research and development (*or* **R and D**) part of a company's activities concerned with discovering new **products** for the company and for making **technical** improvements in existing products. *See also* **new product development, product development.**

reserve currency a currency which can easily be changed into other currencies without loss and therefore can be used as a part of a country's **official reserves.** *The US dollar, the British pound, the German deutschmark and the Japanese yen have all been used as reserve currencies at some time.*

reserve for bad debts an amount of money set aside to cover debts which are expected not to be paid. *The reserve for bad debts in the profit and loss account of most companies has increased because of the poor economic situation.*

reserve price (*UK*) the lowest price which a person who has put something up for **auction** is willing to accept. (*US and Scottish* **upset price**).

reserves that part of the profit of a company which is not paid out to the **shareholders** but which is kept by the company for use for its **fixed** or **current assets.** *See also* **reserve currency, official reserves** and appendix 2.

reserve stock *see* **buffer stock.**

residue (1) what is left of something. (2) what is left of a dead person's **estate** after all debts, expenses and special **bequests** have been paid. *The residue of his estate was divided equally among his children.*

resolution a formal decision taken at a meeting. *A resolution was passed that all fees would be doubled. See also* **motion.**

resources *plural* (1) the source of wealth in an area, e.g. agriculture, materials etc. *South America has vast natural resources.* (2) anything which belongs to an area, a company or a person and which can be used to advantage. *We shall have to make full use of our financial resources in the development plan.*

respondent (1) a person who has to answer to a **charge** that has been brought against him in law. *He was named as the respondent by someone who is* suing him for £100,000. (2) a person who answers questions in **market research.**

response (1) the act of replying. *I called but there was no response.* (2) a showing of interest (in buying a **product** etc.). *We advertised our product on television but so far there has been very little response.*

responsibility (1) the state of being **responsible.** (2) something that one is **responsible** for. *His new job carries heavy responsibilities.*

responsible (1) in charge (of). *You will be responsible for the conduct of the new sales campaign.* (2) capable of being blamed. *If anything goes wrong, you'll be held responsible.* (3) reliable: *a responsible worker.* (4) needing the ability to made decisions which one will be held responsible for: *a responsible position.*

restraint of trade a situation in which an employee is forbidden by **contract** to use knowledge got in his present employment for the benefit of another competing firm that he might work for in the future.

restrictive endorsement a special kind of **endorsement** written on a cheque, **bill of exchange** etc. which restricts the rights of the person being given the cheque etc. (the **endorsee**).

restrictive trade practice (or **restrictive practice**) an arrangement among companies about prices, production, shares of the market, etc. which means that there is less **competition** between them in these areas and (usually) more profit. *See also* **ring.**

retail *noun* the sale of goods direct to the general public, especially in shops, stores and by **mail order.** *You can buy it retail.*

retail *verb* (1) sell goods directly to the public. *He retails cigarettes and cigars.* (2) to be sold to the public (at a certain price). *These chairs retail at £50 each.*

retail *adjective* connected with the sale of goods directly to the general public: *the retail trade, retail prices. See also* **wholesale.**

retail audit (or **shop audit**) an examination of a **sample** of **retail** shops to give information on sales, **market shares**, prices, **distribution** etc.

retailer a person who sells goods directly to the public, e.g. a shopowner. *See also* **wholesaler.**

retailers' co-operative a number of **retailers** who group themselves together in order to keep costs down, e.g. by buying goods in **bulk**, by advertising together.

retail outlet a place where goods are sold direct to the public, e.g. a shop or **supermarket.** *We are trying to increase the number of retail outlets for this new brand.*

retail price the price at which a **product** is sold by a **retailer.**

retail price index a measure of changes in the price of goods from a certain point in time: if the average price of a range of goods at that point = 100, then changes in prices can be stated above or below that figure (usually above, because of **inflation**). *The retail price index has gone up from 100 to 174 in the past ten years.*

retained earnings (or **retained income** or **undistributed profits**) profits which are not paid out to **shareholders** but are kept within a company so that they can be used if they are needed. *See also* **reserves.**

retainer (1) money paid for **services** to be used when needed. (2) money paid to a **barrister** for his **services.**

retire (1) to (cause to) stop working, usually because one has reached a certain age. *In Britain, most men retire at the age of 65.* (2) to leave a position one has been elected to, either by choice or because one has to. *The chairman and secretary have to retire at the* end of this year, as they are only allowed to serve for two years. (3) to pay (a **bill of exchange**) on the due date or earlier.

retirement the state of being **retired** from work. *His colleagues wish him many happy years of retirement.*

retrain to train (a person) to do a new job, use new skills, or enter a new profession. *It is thought that in the future people may have to be retrained for new jobs two or three times in their working life.*

return (1) the amount of money which is gained on an **investment**, often expressed as a percentage. *These bonds guarantee a return of 10%.* See also **return on investment**. (2) a report, especially one with facts and figures. *I want the sales returns for the last six months,* i.e. details of what we have sold in that period. *Have you sent in your tax return?* (3) *in plural* **returns** goods which haven't been sold and which are sent back to the manufacturer or **wholesaler**.

return on investment (or **ROI** or **return on capital**) profit expressed as a percentage of the amount of money that has been **invested** in a company; often used as a method of judging how successful a company has been. *We are not expecting a very good return on investment this year.*

revaluation an increase in the value of a currency with regard to other currencies. The term is used when **fixed exchange rates** are in use, and the increase in value is decided by the government. See also **devaluation**.

revenue (1) **income** from the sale of a company's **products** or **services**, from the sale of **assets**, or from **investments**. *Our revenue this year is up 10%.* See also **sales revenue**. (2) the amount of money a government raises by taxes. See **inland revenue**.

revenue account (**book-keeping**) a statement showing the **income** (**revenue**) and expenses of a business.

revenue expenditure money spent on running a business (compared with money spent on buying **assets**). See also **capital expenditure**.

reverse takeover a situation in which a smaller company makes a **takeover bid** for a larger company.

revoke (*formal*) to **cancel**. *This regulation has now been revoked.*

revolving credit (or **continuous credit**) a **system** by which the borrower borrows money up to a certain limit, and while the loan is being paid back, may borrow up to that limit again without **negotiating** a new loan.

rig *noun* a special large platform and **drill** used for getting oil and natural gas out of the earth or from the sea bed.

rig *verb* (*informal*) to control prices, **shares** etc. in a **fraudulent** way. *It is said that the prices of some of these commodities have been rigged, so don't buy them.*
   rig the market to cause the prices of **shares** etc. to go up or down so as to make an unfair profit. *He rigged the market by buying so many shares that their value went up to far more than they were worth.*

rights issue the act of allowing **shareholders** to buy extra **shares** in a company at a cheaper price, usually according to the number of shares they already hold, e.g. one share for every two shares held. *The shares of that company have risen in value because a rights issue is expected.*

ring a group of businessmen who agree not to compete with one another but to keep prices at a level which allows them to make a large profit. See also **restrictive practice**.

risk *noun* (1) a danger. *If you invest your money in that company there is a risk that you might lose it all.* See also **calculated risk**. (2) a type of loss than can be **insured** against: *fire, injury and other* *risks*. (3) a thing or person considered in terms of a possible **insurance claim**. *He is a good risk*, i.e. it's not likely that a **claim** will be made because of him.

risk *verb* to take a chance with. *He risked his whole fortune to save the company.*

risk analysis a **technique** of judging the likely good and harmful results of management decisions, especially in terms of how the various harmful possibilities might affect the company.

risk capital (1) the money **invested** by the **ordinary shareholders** of a company; **equity capital**. (2) the money invested in a **project** with a high risk of failure but with very high profits if successful, e.g. mining shares, oil shares.

risk manager (**insurance**) a person who examines various risks which his company is engaged in (**insuring** against fire, death, accident etc.).

rival brand a competing make of goods. *We have to sell these beans cheaply because there are several rival brands.*

robot a machine used to do work usually done by a person and which acts like a person, e.g. in its range of activities. *See also* **automation**.

robotics the making and using of **robots**.

ROI *see* **return on investment**.

role conflict a situation when a person, e.g. a manager, is expected to carry out two different kinds of activity which interfere with one another. *You may find that being a foreman and also being the trade union representative will give rise to some role conflict.*

role-play exercise a method of training in which the **trainees** take the parts of various people involved in a business situation, e.g. customer and salesman.

rolling plan a plan for a certain period of time (e.g. five years) which is examined and brought up to date at regular intervals, e.g. every year.

rolling stock the engines, carriages, vans etc. used by a railway.

ROP advertisement *see* **run-of-paper advertisement**.

round: in round figures (*or* **in round numbers**) to the nearest 10, 50, 100 etc.; roughly correct(ly). *Could you give me the year's trading results, in round figures?*

route card (*or* **route sheet**) a **document** which goes with something that is being manufactured and shows the different **processes** which it has to go through and where it has to be taken to for these processes to be done.

royalty an amount of money paid to an author etc. for the use of his **copyright**, to the owner of an invention for the use of his **patent**, usually a certain amount for each thing sold. *The author gets a royalty of 10% of the selling price of each book sold.*

run: run on a bank a situation where a bank's customers lose confidence in a bank and therefore all try to take out their money at the same time.

run on the pound a situation where people want to change the pound into other currencies as quickly as possible.

runaway inflation *see* **galloping inflation**.

running costs (1) money that is needed to keep a business going from day to day, e.g. wages, heating etc. *Highly-automated factories are usually expensive to buy but have low running costs.* (2) money needed to keep machinery of any kind in use. *This car uses very little petrol so the running costs are low.*

run-of-paper advertisement (*or* **ROP advertisement**) advertisement that can be put anywhere in a magazine or newspaper and therefore should cost less.

S

sack a large bag made of coarse cloth, plastic etc., especially one used for holding grain etc. (2) **the sack** the act of **sacking**.

sack to dismiss (a person) from a job. *When the theft was discovered he got sacked from his job as a manager.*

safe deposit (*or* **safety deposit**) a place (often a bank) where valuable things may be left and kept safe for the person leaving them (the **depositor**).

safe deposit box (*or* **safety deposit box**) a box in a **safe deposit** in which things are kept for the **depositor**: he is usually given a key to open the box.

safety officer an employee in an organisation who is responsible for making sure that the health and safety of the workers are protected as far as possible.

safety stock *see* **buffer stock**.

salaried paid by means of a **salary** (rather than **wages**).

salary a fixed regular payment for work done, usually paid monthly but often expressed as so much per year. *Her salary was £20,000 per year. See also* **wages**.

salary review an examination of the amount of money which an employee earns in terms of his work, the rate of **inflation** etc., to see whether he should be paid more and, if so, how much. *Many workers have an annual salary review.*

sale (1) the act of giving goods in exchange for money. *There are laws which apply to the sale of food within certain times. He made a sale every five minutes, on average.* (2) the selling of goods at lowered prices. *This store holds a sale in January.* (3) an **auction**. *Some goods have been damaged by fire so we are holding a sale to see how much we get for them.* (4) the amount of goods sold. *The sale of television sets has been falling over the last few years.*

sale and lease back to get **capital** (cash) for one's business by selling one's business property and then renting it from the new owner for a certain period.

sale or return a method of selling where a **retailer** or a **wholesaler** receives goods for sale on the basis that he will pay only for goods that are sold, the unsold goods being returned within a certain agreed time.

sales aid any material which a **sales representative** can use to persuade customers to buy his goods, e.g. leaflets, **display advertising**.

sales analysis (1) the act of carefully examining all the details about the sale of goods. *A careful sales analysis will show us which markets to concentrate on.* (2) a table or diagram showing the main facts about the sale of goods within a certain period. *The sales analysis indicates that sales have been steadily improving since January.*

sales audit an **analysis** of sales according to type of goods sold, areas where the sales have been made, type of **distribution channel** etc.

sales budget an **estimate** of the amount of goods which will be sold over a certain period of time, and also an estimate of the cost of reaching this level of sales; actual sales and costs will be measured against the **budget** at regular intervals.

sales campaign planned activity to increase sales, usually for a certain **product**, area or type of customer. *Our customer is going to be mounting a big sales campaign in the London area next August. See also* **sales drive**.

sales conference a formal meeting of all the employees of a company connected with the selling of the company's **products**, in order to discuss past achievements, future **targets**, new sales **techniques**, and so on. *See also* **sales meeting**.

sales control the **process** by which the success of **sales representatives** is measured (e.g. the average value of sales, new **accounts** opened etc.).

sales costs expenses which come directly from the attempt to sell goods to customers. *We are trying to cut down on sales costs by making fewer sales calls, but selecting our possible customers more carefully.*

sales drive a greater-than-usual effort to increase sales over a certain period. *Sales have been falling recently, so we shall be mounting a big sales drive soon.* *See also* **sales campaign**.

sales engineer a person with specialised **technical** knowledge of machinery etc. which helps him to sell **products** of that type.

sales feature *see* **product feature**.

sales figures a list of numbers of sales along with their totals, averages etc.

sales folder a file or similar container which contains a collection of sales material.

sales force the **sales representatives** of a company.

sales forecast an **estimate** in advance of the amount of likely sales of a company's **products**.

sales incentive something which will encourage a **sales representative** or a **wholesaler** or a **retailer** to sell more. *As a special sales incentive, all retailers who increase their sales by 10% will be given special discounts.*

sales inquiry a request for further information about a **product** from a possible customer.

saleslady *see* **salesman**.

sales literature anything printed which helps to sell a **product**. *I always carry some pamphlets and similar sales literature.*

salesman/saleslady/saleswomen/salesperson (1) a person who sells goods direct to customers in a shop or store. *Ask the salesman at that counter over there: I'm sure he'll be able to help you.* (2) = **sales representative**.

sales manager a person in charge of a group of **sales representatives** and responsible for all aspects of selling a company's **products**.

salesmanship the **technique** of persuading possible customers to buy something; the ability to do so. *His salesmanship has been the main reason for our increased success.*

sales manual a book or booklet given to a **sales representative** which contains information that will be useful to him in performing his duties.

sales meeting a regular coming together of a group of **sales representatives** in order to review past sales and discuss plans for the future. *We hold our sales meetings usually every month. See also* **sales conference**.

salesperson *see* **salesman**.

sales planning the **process** of deciding on the details necessary to achieve sales **targets**.

sales promotion methods of encouraging sales, e.g. by using **competitions**, free gifts etc.

sales prospect a person or company that is likely to buy a certain product. *The sales manager gave his representatives a list of sales prospects.*

sales quota the amount of goods that should be sold within a given period of time by a **sales representative**, or within a certain area, or with regard to a certain **product** etc. *All the salesmen exceeded their sales quotas last month.*

sales representative (*or* **representative**) a person whose job it is to sell a company's **products** to possible customers.

sales revenue money received for goods sold over a certain period of time. *Compare with* **sales volume**.

sales tax a type of tax which is collected on behalf of a government by the person selling the goods: the tax is added to the price of the goods. *See* **value-added tax**.

sales territory the area of the country or part of the market within which a **sales representative** has to work. *We have divided the country into eight sales territories, with a sales representative in each.*

sales volume (*or* **volume of sales**) amount of goods sold. *Our sales volume has doubled since last year. Compare with* **sales revenue**.

saleswomen *see* **salesman**.

salvage *noun* (1) the act of saving ships and/or their **cargoes** from destruction at sea. (2) the act of saving any goods from destruction, e.g. by fire. (3) money paid to a person who rescues a ship and/or its **cargo** from destruction. (4) goods rescued from destruction at sea or from fire, flooding etc. *There is a sale of fire salvage lines being held tomorrow.*

salvage *adjective* connected with saving goods etc. in this way: *a salvage operation; salvage money.*

salvage *verb* (1) to save (ships, their **cargoes** or other goods) from destruction. *The ship was salvaged even while the storm was still raging.* (2) to save from any kind of danger; to make good any kind of loss. *The failed businessman tried to salvage something of his reputation by repaying some of his debts.*

sample *verb* (1) to take (a small part of something) in order to judge the whole thing. *Would you care to sample this fruit?* (2) to test a small number of people who are typical of the whole group being examined.

sample *noun* (1) a small part of something which can be taken as typical of the whole thing. *Sales representatives often take samples of products to their customers. A chemist analysed a sample of the goods to see if the customer's complaint was true.* (2) a

(usually small) amount of a **product** given free to possible customers to encourage them to buy. (3) (**statistics**) a number of people who are typical of the whole group being investigated.

sample survey a type of investigation in which only a typical part of the total group to be examined is investigated. *See also* **random sampling**, **quota sampling**, **stratified sampling**.

sampling frame information about a group (i.e. **universe**) that is to be **sampled**, which will make it easier to identify which members of the group will be **surveyed**.

sampling procedure a method of finding out information about a large group of people by actually questioning only a small number of them. *See also* **quota sampling**, **random sampling**.

sanction *noun* (1) permission (to do something). *You can only export these goods with the special sanction of the government.* (2) *in plural* **sanctions** actions taken against a country, usually by a group of other countries, in order to force the country concerned to do something. *The country was subjected to economic sanctions because it was encouraging terrorism.*

sanction *verb* to allow, permit. *The committee has sanctioned our use of the building until midnight.*

sandwich course a method of organising studies so that the students spend part of their time at a college or university and part of their time in a place of work (office, factory, etc.). *My son is doing a sandwich course in accountancy at the local polytechnic.*

sans recours *see* **recourse**.

save (1) to avoid wasting; to avoid using up. *Save fuel! Save time by using the phone.* (2) to put (money) into a bank etc. instead of spending it. *I try to save 10% of my salary.* (3) (**computers**) to **store** (**data**) in such a way that it can be used again later.

savings money which has been saved. *His savings amounted to over £50,000.*

savings account an **account** for personal savings, sometimes with a slightly higher **interest rate** than a **deposit account**.

savings bank a type of bank which is intended to help ordinary people to save. *See also* **trustee savings bank**.

scab *see* **blackleg**.

scarcity value a situation where something is valuable or expensive simply because it cannot be easily got. *Sometimes useless things are sold for high prices simply because of their scarcity value.*

scatter diagram a chart on which the frequency of the occurrence of **data** is recorded as points or dots (small round marks): it can be seen at a glance what sort of pattern is formed by the data.

scenario (1) a short description of a play, film etc. giving the main details about what happens, where the action takes place, and so on. (2) an imaginary description of what might be the situation if certain possible things happened. *Let's try a scenario of what would happen if our sales doubled.*

schedule *noun* (1) a list, especially one showing when certain things should be done or should happen; a timetable: *an airline schedule. You must follow this schedule exactly. Our visitor is behind schedule/ahead of schedule/on schedule* (i.e. late/early/exactly on time). (2) a list, added to a legal **document**, listing things which are mentioned in the document but which may be changed from time to time.

schedule *verb* to arrange for something to happen at a certain time. *You are scheduled to speak at the Town Hall tonight.*

scheduled flight a flight which is on the regular timetable of an airline.

scientific management a **system** of applying scientific rules to management. *See also* **operations research**.

scrap *noun* (1) a small piece of something: *a scrap of paper.* (2) used metal etc. which is available to be used again. *These old cars are only fit for scrap.*

scrap *verb* (1) to destroy; do away with. *We are going to scrap all these old ways of doing things and try some new techniques.* (2) to make into **scrap** metal. *Just scrap these machines and see what you can sell them for.*

screen *verb* (1) to decide which people who have applied for a post should be **interviewed**. *After we've finished the screening, we'll draw up the interview timetable.* (2) to check on (employees or possible employees) in defence or similar occupations where security is important to make sure that they are loyal (faithful to their country) and dependable. (3) to check (a new **product** or idea) against certain **criteria** at an early stage so as to check whether it is worth spending time and money on developing it.

scrip issue *see* **bonus issue**.

script *noun* (1) handwriting: *a very clear script.* (2) a method of writing or printing: *Roman script, Arabic script.* (3) the words of a play, speech, etc. to be spoken by actors, politicians, etc. *He writes scripts for television.* (4) an answer paper written by someone in an examination.

script *verb* to write a **script** for: *to script what someone will say.*

seal *verb* (1) to put one's **seal** on (something) to show that it has one's approval. (2) to close up (an envelope etc.) to make it impossible to get at the contents without tearing or breaking.

seal *noun* (1) a mark made on material (usually red wax) to show that the **document** it is attached to has been written with the approval of the person making the mark. *The King's seal was attached to the letter.* (2) a special mark made on certain **documents** from a company to show that they have been **issued** by the company: it is known as the common seal or company seal and a record of all such documents must be kept. (3) a solid thing such as a ring or stamp which makes such a mark. *He kept the company seal in a safe.* (4) something which keeps a letter or parcel etc. closed until it reaches its destination. *This glue will make a good seal.*

sealed-bid tender a method of offering to perform a **contract** by which each offer is put in a **sealed** envelope; at a certain fixed time all the offers are opened together and the best offer can be accepted.

seasonal adjustment the act of allowing for **seasonality** e.g. in **sales figures**. *Sales have remained very steady this year, after seasonal adjustment.*

seasonal discount a lowering of the price of **products** to **retailers** at times when sales are usually low in order to encourage business. *We are trying to even out our sales over the year by offering seasonal discounts.*

seasonality changes in sales for a **product** which happen at the same time every year. *Seasonality is a major factor in the tourist industry.*

second *verb* to support (a **proposal** put forward by someone else) at a meeting. *Will you second the motion?*

secondary data: **data** taken from published sources of information and not gathered specially for the purpose. *See also* **primary data**.

secondary picket a group of **strikers** who try to stop other workers from going into a factory, office etc. which is not directly involved in the **dispute**. *The coalminers decided to set up some secondary pickets outside the electricity generating stations.*

secondary picketing act of setting up **secondary pickets**.

seconder a person who **seconds** a **proposal** at a meeting.

second-hand owned or used already.

second mortgage an agreement by which a person borrowing money gives his property as **security** for a second time, on the condition that the holder of the first **mortgage** has first claim if the borrower cannot pay his debts.

secretary (1) a person who handles the paperwork for a person or company by typing letters, filing correspondence etc. (2) a person who does similar work for a club or society. (3) the minister at the head of some government departments: *the Home Secretary.* (4) a high-ranking civil servant. (5) *see* **company secretary**.

sector a division of something. *See also* **private sector**, **public sector of the economy**.

secured creditor a person who is owed money but has a legal right to an amount of the borrower's property which is equal to (or more than) the amount of money he is owed.

security (1) the state of being safe from danger or loss: *to be in the security of one's own home.* (2) protection against criminal acts, e.g. theft. *My firm has to spend thousands of pounds on security every year.* (3) property which is promised to a person lending money if the borrower cannot pay. *He put up his house and car as security for the loan.* (4) a **certificate** of ownership of **stocks**, **bonds** etc. for which repayment is **guaranteed**: *government securities.*

security of tenure the right to keep one's job or property provided certain conditions are met. *Any lecturer in this college who is employed for more than two years has automatic security of tenure.*

segmentation (*or* **market segmentation**) the dividing of a market into various groups (or **segments**), which will make it easier to direct a **product** at that section of the market, e.g. the age of the customers, their leisure interests, their occupations. *After putting segmentation into effect, we decided on two entirely different advertising campaigns to sell our product to different parts of the market.*

selection board a group of people who have been given the duty of choosing the best person (or persons) for a job. *I have been given an interview for that job I wanted: I come up before the selection board on Monday.*

selection interview a meeting between the person (or persons) applying for a job and the person (or persons) who have to decide on who is the most suitable.

self-assessment questions a type of question used in some learning situations, in which the student can check on his own progress by checking his knowledge against certain questions which he corrects himself.

self-completion questionnaire (**market research**) a method of getting information in which the answers to a list of questions are filled in by the customer, member of the public etc. himself and not (as is usually the case) by an **interviewer**.

self-employed person a person who is working for himself and is not the employee of someone else. *In Britain, being a self-employed person means that you are taxed in a different way from those who work for someone else.*

self-financing of a business, **operating** in such a way that the costs of buying new equipment, **shares** in other companies and similar **expenditure** are paid out of **revenue** (and not e.g. by borrowing).

self-liquidating (1) of a loan, being able to be paid back with **interest** from the profits of whatever business the money was borrowed for. *He had to borrow the money to buy his stock, but the loan was self-liquidating: in six months he had repaid it from his profits.* (2) of a **sales promotion**, where something is offered at a price which covers the cost of the promotion.

self-service store a type of shop where the customer picks up his/her own choice of goods from the shelves, and pays for the goods when leaving. *See also* **supermarket, superstore, hypermarket.**

sell *verb* (1) to give (something) to someone else for money. *He's sold his house for £50,000.* (2) to be bought. *These goods are selling well*, i.e. many people want to buy them. (3) to deal or trade in. *Do you sell furniture in this store?* (4) to persuade people to accept. *He sold the government the idea of building a canal.* (5) to be employed in the selling of. *He sells cars.*

sell *noun see* **hard sell, soft sell.**

sell-by date the date by which a **product**, especially food, should be sold before it becomes unfit for use.

seller's market a situation where there is a great demand for some **product**, giving an advantage to anyone selling it. *This is a good time to put your house up for sale: it's a seller's market.*

selling cost an amount of money which has to be paid out, e.g. for advertising, in order to sell a **product**. *See also* **distribution cost.**

sell short to enter into an agreement to sell something now which one does not yet possess, because one expects to be able to buy it more cheaply than the agreed selling price. *I'm selling these shares short: the agreed price is £10 per share but I expect to be able to buy them at £9 before then.*

seminar a meeting of an educational nature in which ideas are exchanged and discussed.

semi-skilled worker a **manual worker** who has had a limited amount of training but not enough to qualify him as a craftsman.

semi-variable cost a type of cost which increases only if the amount of goods produced or sold increases by a large amount, e.g. the cost of **supervising** groups of workers.

sentence completion (market research) a **technique** by which people being **interviewed** complete a sentence in any way they like e.g. 'I like X brand because ...', and which sometimes gives information which could not otherwise be predicted.

sequence *noun* (1) a number of things which follow one another: *a sequence of events*. (2) (**computers**) a set of items or instructions which have been put in a certain order.

sequence *verb* to put (things) in a certain order, e.g. alphabetical order.

sequential access storage (computers) a **system** of **storing** and retrieving **records** in a certain order (or **sequence**).

serial number a number given to one thing in a series.

service *noun* (1) something done by one person for another: *to thank someone for his services*. (2) a department of government; people employed in a government department: *the civil service*; *the services* (i.e. Army, Navy and Air Force). (3) a supply of something (e.g. transport) for general use: *a good train service*. (4) *in plural* (**economics**) a class of things which can be bought and sold, but which are not manufactured goods, such as special knowledge, experience, and skills. *Banking and medicine are services for the public.* (5) the way in which one's needs are attended to. *The service in this restaurant is terrible.* (6) the act of regularly checking up on a machine to make sure that it is working properly. *This car should have a service every 6000 miles.* (7) a set of dishes: *a tea service.* (8) the length of time someone has been employed. *My father was given a gold watch for his years of service in the company.*

service *verb* (1) to check up on (a machine) to make sure it is in proper working order. *You should get your dishwasher serviced at least every three years.* (2) to pay the **interest** on (a loan).

service charge (1) an amount added to a bill in a hotel or restaurant (usually 10% to 15%) which is then shared among those who have given the customer **service**, so that a **gratuity** need not be given. (2) a bank charge. (3) an amount paid by those living in properties (e.g. in a block of flats) which share certain **services** (e.g. keeping a garden in order, cleaning etc.).

service department a part of a company which deals with the needs and complaints of customers to whom goods have been sold. *See also* **after-sales service**.

service industries businesses which do not manufacture goods but which provide customers with **services** which they are willing to pay for, e.g. the hotel trade, the insurance industry.

set (1) a grouping-together of things which have some feature(s) in common: *a set of even numbers*. (2) (*psychology*) a state of mind which will make it likely for a person to behave in a certain way: *a learning set*. (3) the scenery used in a film or play to show where the action takes place: *a film set*.

set of bills an original **bill of exchange** and its copies: if any one is cashed, the others are automatically **cancelled**.

settle (1) to pay (a debt). (2) to give legally by means of a will or **contract**. *He settled all his property on his wife.* (3) to go to live somewhere; to cause (others) to do so. *They settled in Australia.* (4) to decide (something) by agreement: *to settle an argument*; *to settle out of court*, i.e. to solve a legal quarrel before it is decided by a judge.

settlement (1) the act of settling. (2) a collection of houses, especially where people have not lived before. (3) a legal agreement by which money or property is given to a person; *a marriage settlement.* (4) an agreement which ends a legal quarrel: *an amicable* (i.e. friendly) *settlement.*

settlement discount *see* **cash discount**.

set-up cost an amount of money which has to be paid in making changes in machinery, when one type of **product** is stopped and another one has to be manufactured. *We don't switch products very often, so set-up costs are not significant.*

severance pay money paid to a worker by his employer when the worker is dismissed from his job through no fault of his own. *See also* **golden handshake**.

shake-out (*or* **shake-up**) (1) the **process** of lowering costs by lowering the number of people employed by a company. (2) the **process** of completely changing the way a company is run, which usually includes changing the top management of the company.

share one of the equal parts into which the money (**capital**) needed for starting or running a company is divided. For example, if a company needs £100,000 for its development, it can offer 100,000 £1 **shares** for sale, but the actual price of the shares will go up or down according to how well or badly the company is doing. *See also* **ordinary share**, **preference share**.

share capital an amount of money which a company needs for carrying on its business, and which is related to the **shares** it offers for sale to the public. *See also* **issued capital**, **nominal capital**, **paid-up capital**.

share certificate (*US* **stock certificate**) a **document** given by a company to a person who buys one

or more **shares** in the company as proof that he/she is the legal owner of the shares.

shareholder (*also, especially US,* **stockholder**) a person who owns **shares** or **stock** in a company. *The shareholders will be invited to a meeting next month to meet the new members of the board.*

share index a type of **index number** which takes the average rise or fall in the price of certain selected **shares** to show whether the price of shares in general (or a certain type of share) is rising or falling. *See also* **Dow Jones index**; **Financial Times industrial share index**.

share issue the act of making **shares** available for buying.

shelf life the length of time that a **product**, especially food, can stay on the shelf of a shop, store etc. before it becomes unfit for sale. *These tins of soup have a shelf life of three months.*

shell company a type of company that exists in name only and does not do any actual business, useful, e.g. to a person who wants to start a business but wants to save himself the expense of setting up a company from the beginning.

shift *noun* (1) a movement; a change. *There has been a slight shift upwards in share prices.* (2) one of the periods of time (usually lasting about 8 hours) that the working day of a factory or other business is divided into, each period having a different group of workers. *In this factory, people work three shifts: 8 am to 4 pm, 4 pm to midnight, and midnight to 8 am.* (3) a group of workers who work during a certain **shift** (meaning 2). *The next shift will be starting in about an hour. See also* **night shift**, **shift working**. (4) (**computers**) an instruction which **shifts** (meaning 3).

shift *verb* (1) to move. *Could you shift these cases to the other end of the store, please?* (2) to pass on (the cost of a tax) to someone else. *The shopkeepers will shift this tax on to their customers.* (3)

(**computers**) to move **bits**, **characters** etc a certain number of places to the left or right.

shift in demand a change in the kind of thing that customers want, or the amount of what they want. *We do our best to anticipate shifts in demand.*

shift key a key on a typewriter or **computer keyboard** which changes the position of the keys, e.g. to type capital letters.

shift working a method of organising work so that it is done by different groups of workers at different periods of the day. *The factory will be in use 24 hours a day from now on, so we shall have to start shift working. See also* **shift**, **night shift**.

ship *noun* a larger type of boat.

ship *verb* (1) to transport (something) by ship. *We'll ship the supplies you need immediately.* (2) (*especially US*) to transport by other means. *We can ship your goods either by road or rail.*

ship-broker a person who acts for a shipowner, by getting **cargo** and passengers for his ships, but also handling **insurance** and other matters.

ship chandler a person or company that provides the things that are necessary for a ship.

shipment (1) the act of shipping goods. (2) a quantity of goods shipped.

shipper a person or company whose business it is to send goods abroad by ship.

shipping note (1) a note which gives the official in charge of the docks that a ship is leaving from, details of the goods which are to be shipped. (2) *see* **mate's receipt**.

ship's articles a type of **contract** by which sailors agree to the conditions, payment and so on for the ship they are going to work in.

ship's certificate of registry a **document** which contains all the necessary details of a ship: its name, owner, weight (**tonnage**), and the country where it is **registered**.

ship's manifest a detailed description of a ship's **cargo**, to be sent to the agents abroad who will receive the cargo, and also given to the customs at the port that the ship leaves from.

ship's report information which must be given about a ship to the customs officials of the port it has arrived at, giving details about the **cargo**, passengers, crew and any other matter that information is asked on.

ship's stores goods (such as food and drink) which will be needed by a ship's crew and passengers while at sea, but which are not part of the **cargo**. Such goods are noted by customs while the ship is in a foreign port and are put under **seal**.

shop *noun* (1) a place where goods are sold, usually **retail**: *a butcher's shop*; *a bookshop.* (2) a place where a certain kind of work is done: *a workshop. See also* **talk shop**.

shop *verb* (1) often **shop for** to go to one or more shops with the aim of buying something. *My wife is shopping for things for our new house.* (2) **shop around** to go to various shops or other businesses to buy something at the best value. *If you're buying a new car, it pays to shop around.*

shop assistant a person who serves customers in a shop.

shop audit *see* **retail audit**.

shop floor (1) the part of a factory etc. where the machines and the workers who run them are. (2) ordinary workers, especially when organised into a **trade union**.

shopper a person who is buying goods, or about to buy goods, from a shop. *The town was crowded with Saturday morning shoppers.*

shopping (1) goods that have been bought from a shop or various shops:

the week's shopping. (2) the act of buying goods from a shop or shops.

shopping centre an area where there are a number of shops together. *They are building a large shopping centre near these new houses.*

shopping goods a type of goods (usually more expensive) which are bought after the customer has given some thought to the matter, e.g. after comparing prices.

shop steward a person **elected** by the workers in a factory, shop etc. to put their complaints to their **trade union** and the management.

shop window (1) the window of a shop where goods are on show. (2) = **showcase** (2).

short *see* **sell short**.

short bill a **bill of exchange** which is payable at **sight**, on **demand**, or within less than ten days.

short-dated securities (*or* **shorts**) certain types of **securities** which are repayable in less than five years.

shorthand a method of writing things down quickly. *He took notes in shorthand and typed them later.*

short-term (1) lasting for a short time. *This investment has some short-term benefits but will not pay you much in the long run.* (2) having a **maturity date** that will come soon (e.g. in less than a year): *short-term credit*; *short-term debt*.

short-term planning the act of making plans for things which will happen soon (e.g. within about a year). *Compare with* **long-term plan**.

short-time working a situation where an employer lowers the number of hours in the week that his employees can work (perhaps because of lack of orders, or because certain necessary supplies are not available).

showcard a card put near a **product** in a shop etc., giving information to help to **promote** it.

showcase (1) a container, usually of clear plastic or glass, which allows goods to be seen by possible customers, but keeps them safe from being damaged or stolen. *We have a showcase displaying our range of scarves in the main reception area of the hotel.* (2) any situation which allows a company's goods or **services** to be shown in a way which should make them attractive to possible customers. *The international meeting will be a showcase for the town's hotel facilities.*

shrinkage the amount by which anything becomes smaller. *If you buy this cloth, remember to allow for some shrinkage when it is washed.*

shrink-wrap to cover goods (e.g. food etc.) with a thin clear plastic covering (**shrink-wrapping**) which is then **sealed** tightly round the goods by the use of heat.

shut-down the closing of a factory etc. for a certain length of time.

sickness benefit (*or* **sick pay**) (*UK*) money paid by the government (under the **National Insurance scheme**) to a worker who is too ill to work.

sight: at sight of a **bill of exchange**, payable at once on presentation.

significant (1) important; worth noting: *a significant drop in profits.* (2) (**statistics**) not to be explained by chance. *The difference between the results of the experiment and what was predicted is statistically significant.*

sign on (1) to begin work etc., especially by signing one's name. (2) to register one's name in order to **claim unemployment benefit**.

silent partner (*or* **sleeping partner**) a **partner** in a business who does not take an active part in running the business, but shares the profits, usually because he or she has **invested** money in it.

silicon chip *see* **chip**.

simple interest: interest which is paid on the **principal** (amount of money borrowed) alone. *See also* **compound interest**.

simulate (1) to pretend. (2) to imitate (a **process**, situation etc.) so as to find out more about it. *This wind-tunnel simulates the conditions that the aircraft will be flying in.*

simulation (1) the act of pretending or imitating. (2) imitation of a **process**, situation etc. (usually involving mathematical calculations) so as to find out more about it. *In our business school, we do simulations of various business situations, using a computer to check on the results of our decisions.*

sine die (*Latin, meaning* without a day) without a date being fixed (for another meeting, for something to be done, etc.). *The judge adjourned the case sine die.*

single-entry bookkeeping a very simple method of recording **accounts**, now seldom used, by which each business **transaction** is recorded only once.

sinking fund an amount of money built up out of profits (or, in the case of a government, out of taxes) so as to meet some payment which has been foreseen, e.g. renewing a **lease** on some property.

sit-down strike a kind of **strike** in which workers refuse to leave the place where they work until their demands are met. *See also* **sit-in**.

sit-in a form of protest, in which the people who are protesting occupy some place, e.g. an office, and refuse to leave it. *The students are staging a sit-in in the library. Also used as a verb*: **sit in**. *See also* **work-in**.

situation report an account of how things are, e.g. in any part of a business. *The sales manager will be giving a situation report with respect to the new sales drive at today's meeting.*

skill ability to do something as a result of training or practice. *These young people are being trained in the skills of management.*

skilled worker a type of **manual worker** who, as a result of training, can do certain jobs which need a certain amount of skill and judgment; a craftsman.

skills analysis a method of examining in detail the different **processes** involved in performing some task for which training is needed, so that the training can be more effective.

skimming price a price of goods fixed at a level which will probably be attractive only to customers with high **incomes**. *See also* **penetration pricing**.

sleeper (1) a manager who is not active in doing business and looking for new business. *See also* **thruster**. (2) an address which is used to check that **direct mail shots** are reaching their **targets**. (3) a part of a train which is used for sleeping in during the journey; a train which has such compartments.

sleeping partner *see* **silent partner**.

sliding scale a method of deciding the amount of tax, **duty** or other payment to be made on something, by which the amount of tax etc. varies according to the value of the thing on which the tax is due. *See also* **pro rata**.

slogan a word, phrase or sentence which is related through advertising with a particular **product**. *In this competition, you get a prize if you can think of a good slogan for this new product.*

slot machine a machine with a special hole (or **slot**) for coins by which one can buy e.g. cigarettes, sweets, a spell at a game (operated by the machine).

slump *noun* (1) part of a **trade cycle** when unemployment is greatest and opportunities for business are at their lowest. (2) a sudden lowering, e.g. in prices, sales, production etc. *There has been a slump in the sales figures over the last few months.*

slump *verb* of prices, profits, employment etc., to become suddenly much lower or smaller. *Our profits have slumped considerably since last year.*

slush fund an amount of money which has been set aside for paying **bribes** and similar illegal or improper business or political activities. *He set up a slush fund for paying bribes to politicians.*

snip (*informal*) something very cheap; bargain. *You should buy that car: it's a snip at £500.*

social insurance a method of providing **insurance** which is organised by the government.

socialism any of the various kinds of belief related to the ideas of property, factories, transport, and so on being owned by the state for the benefit of everyone, not just by certain people for their own benefit, and equality in society rather than **competition** for wealth. *See also* **capitalism**.

social responsibility a duty which a person or business owes to the society of which it is part: the person or business should not do anything which is harmful to society, and should even use some of its profits to improve society if it can.

social security a **system** by which the government pays money to certain groups of people who need it, e.g. the unemployed, the old.

socio-economic grouping the division of society into social classes, e.g. from A (highest income, highest social position) through B, C1, C2, D and E (lowest income, lowest social position).

sociology the scientific study of human society.

soft currency the money **system** of a country which is likely to fall in value usually because of an **adverse trade balance**, and is therefore not in demand by those who buy and sell currencies. *See also* **hard currency**.

soft furnishings household goods made of cloth of any kind, e.g. curtains, cushions.

soft goods cloth of any kind.

soft sell a method of persuading people to buy goods without putting much direct pressure on them to do so. *See also* **hard sell**.

software: programs that can be used in a **computer**. *See also* **hardware**.

sole only; for or by oneself alone. *The agency has the sole right to sell the goods in France.*

sole trader a person who runs his own business by himself, and not in **partnership** with anyone else.

solicitor (1) (*UK*) a lawyer who handles general legal matters, and who can also represent his clients in the lower courts. *See also* **barrister**. (2) (*US*) a lawyer who advises the officials of a town or city on legal matters. (3) (*US*) anyone who goes round looking for trade, business etc.

solus position of an advertisement e.g. in a newspaper, in a separate position, away from other **competing** advertisements.

solvency the state of being **solvent**.

solvent having enough money to pay one's debts.

source the person, thing or place from which something comes. *What is the source of your information?*

source language a **computer language** in which it is easier for the user to write **programs** but which has to be translated by the computer into **machine language** before the instructions to the computer can be put into effect, e.g. **BASIC, CO-BOL, FORTRAN**. *See also* **machine language**.

source program (**computers**) a **program** which has been written in a **source language** and not in **machine language**.

sovereign *noun* (1) the king or queen of a country. (2) (*UK*) a coin formerly in use when it was worth one **pound sterling** but now no longer **legal tender**, although it is still **minted** and exported to certain countries, especially in the Middle East.

sovereign *adjective* (1) having the greatest authority: *my sovereign lord.* (2) independent, not ruled by another country: *a sovereign state.*

sovereignty (1) power. (2) independence. (3) the idea that the **consumer** has choice in the market and can reject goods or prices which are not found acceptable.

space in newspapers and magazines, the pages or parts of pages which can be used for advertising when everything else is printed.

space bar the bar on the **keyboard** of a typewriter or **computer** which causes a move to the right.

space buyer *see* **media buyer**.

span of control the range and number of **subordinates** that a manager at a certain level is directly in charge of. *According to our theory, the higher a manager's position, the wider his span of control should be.*

spare part a part of a machine etc. which can be bought separately in case that part should fail.

special deposit (*UK*) an amount of money which a **clearing bank** has to leave with the Bank of England and which can be used by the government to lower the amount of money the clearing banks have available for lending, and therefore to lower **credit** generally.

special endorsement a statement on a **bill of exchange** which states to whom, or on whose order, the bill is payable.

special feature a section in a magazine or newspaper, or in a special issue of a magazine or newspaper, which is concerned with a certain subject, often one which will attract advertising related to it.

speciality goods types of goods which are often sold, e.g. through advertisements and/or **door-to-door selling** rather than through shops or stores, e.g. double-glazing, encyclopedias.

speciality salesman a type of salesman who is concerned with the sale of **speciality goods**.

specification a detailed description. *These tools that you have provided do not meet our specification.*

speculate (1) to think about something without knowing all the facts; guess. *We can only speculate about his early life, since he never discussed it with anyone.* (2) to be involved in some kind of risky business operation in the hope of making a large profit, e.g. by buying property, **shares** etc.

speculation (1) the act of **speculating**. (2) a business operation which carries high risks but also hopes of great profits. (3) in the **stock exchange**, the act or an example of dealing in **futures** (where the dealer sells a **commodity** at a certain fixed price on a certain date, hoping that he will be able to buy it at a lower price before then).

speculative (1) of **speculation**. (2) related to any business operation where there is some degree of risk of failure. *Speculative builders often build houses in the hope that someone will want to buy them.*

splash story the main news story in a newspaper, usually appearing on the front page.

split shift a type of **shift** (meaning 2) which is divided into two parts, so that workers are there when they are needed. For example, in a bus company, the drivers may work from 6 am–10 am and from 4 pm–8 pm, if these are the busiest times.

split the difference (*informal*) to **strike a bargain** by choosing an amount exactly half-way between what each side has previously offered. *I'm asking £300 and you're offering £200: let's split the difference and agree on £250.*

sponsor *noun* (1) a person or group that supports some activity, e.g. a **competition**, performance, either for charity or as a form of advertisement. *The sponsor for this event is a local factory.* (2) (*especially US*) a business which pays for radio or television time to advertise its **product**. *We interrupt the programme for a message from our sponsor.* (3) (*US*) a **guarantor**; a person who **guarantees** a person or thing.

sponsor *verb* to act as a **sponsor** to. *The company has sponsored various events, including a golf competition and an athletics meeting.*

spot a single period of time on television or radio used for advertising. *Our new product will be featured in two television spots every evening this week.*

spot price a price for goods, especially **commodities** that can be sold immediately.

spot rate a type of **exchange rate** for currency that can be sold and delivered immediately.

squeeze the controlling by a government of the amount of money used, e.g. to stop the rise of **inflation**: *credit squeeze.*

stabilisation the **process** by which a government stops sudden large-scale changes in the **economy**, e.g. by controlling **money supply** to prevent **inflation**, or by buying or selling currency to prevent large changes in the **exchange rate**.

stabilise to (cause to) become steadier; to stop changes in (something).

stabiliser any means which a government uses to **stabilise** the **economy**, e.g. control of the money

supply to prevent **inflation**, or making new government jobs to lessen unemployment.

stable market a type of market where the amount of goods sold is not usually seriously affected by price-changes. *See also* **staple product**.

staff *noun* a group of people employed by an organisation. *Our staff are well paid and work hard. There is an annual football match between staff and students.*

staff *verb* to hire employees for (an organisation): *to be fully staffed/understaffed,* i.e. to have all the employees one needs/not enough employees.

staff association a group formed to represent the views of the employees of a particular company or organisation (usually **white-collar workers**); similar to a **trade union**, but not linked to any other group outside the company or organisation.

stag (**stock exchange**) a person who buys new **share issues** in the hope of selling them quickly for a profit.

staggered working hours an arrangement for working by which the employees arrive and leave at a time which is different from the other offices, factories, etc. in the area, usually to make travelling to work easier because fewer people will be using transport.

stagnation the state of not growing or developing. *The economy has reached stagnation level.*

stale cheque a cheque which has been held for a long time without being handed over to a bank for payment; banks can refuse to cash cheques beyond a certain time, usually three months or six months.

stamp duty the amount of money that must be paid to the government before certain **documents** are **valid** (recognised as legal), e.g. documents about the sale of **shares** and property.

stand (1) something on which something else stands. (2) a place with shelves etc. where goods are shown, especially at an exhibition. *Come round to our stand and I'll show you our new products.*

standard costing a method of checking on the cost of producing something, by **estimating** how much it should cost (**standard cost**) and then comparing this to the actual cost; if there is a difference between the two figures, then the reason for this difference should be found out.

standardisation the act of **standardising**.

standardise to cause to be made or done in the same way or according to some rule. *We are trying to standardise the design of all our goods.*

standard of living the level at which a person, group of people generally within a country can afford to live; one way of measuring this is by finding out how many hours a person has to work in order to buy a certain amount of certain goods. *Heavy increases in taxes are bound to affect everyone's standard of living.*

standard rate the basic rate of **income tax** which one pays on **income** after **allowances** have been taken off.

standard time the official local time for a country, or an area within a country. *Before you phone a foreign country, it is best to check what the standard time is there.*

standby *adjective* ready to be used if needed: *standby arrangements.*

standby *adverb*: **go standby** to travel at the last minute on an aircraft at a lower fare, using a seat not already booked.

standby pay money given to workers who have to make themselves ready for work in case their **services** are needed.

standing committee a group of people set up on a **permanent** basis to deal with a certain subject. *He is a member of the Standing Committee on Foreign Affairs.*

standing order an instruction to a bank to pay out a certain amount of money at certain regular times (e.g. once a month). *I pay my rates by standing order. Compare with* **standing orders**.

standing orders rules which have been drawn up for the proper running of the meetings of an organisation. *According to the standing orders, there must be at least one meeting of the executive committee each month. Compare with* **standing order**.

standstill agreement an arrangement between two countries when one country cannot pay its debts to the other, that it will be given a certain fixed period of time to repay the debts.

staple = **staple product**.

staple product (1) a main **commodity** produced in a country or region. *The staple products of this region are wheat and dairy products.* (2) essential goods, for which there will always be a demand, e.g. in UK, bread or milk. *See also* **stable market**.

stapler a **device** for joining pieces of paper together by means of small pieces of metal.

statement (*or* **statement of accounts**) a **document** which is sent to a customer at a certain time, e.g. at the end of each month, to show him how much money he owes for goods or **services** received; it usually lists **invoice** numbers and amounts. *See also* **invoice**.

statistic *singular form of* **statistics** (meaning 1).

statistical of **statistics**: *a statistical report.*

statistics (1) (*plural*) facts given in the form of numbers. *These statistics* show that our share of the market is increasing. (2) (*singular*) the science of collecting and understanding **statistics** (meaning 1). *Some knowledge of statistics is necessary for the study of market research.*

status inquiry the act of checking on an order or a possible customer, e.g. to see whether he will be able to pay his debts and whether he has failed to pay his debts in the past.

status symbol something which is meant to show how important or wealthy its owner is and to make people think highly of him/her. *Some expensive cars are more than just a way of getting from A to B: they are status symbols.*

statute a law passed by a law-making body.

statutory meeting a meeting that is required by law, e.g. of the **shareholders** of a new company.

sterling UK money: *one pound sterling; to have one's reserves in sterling.*

stet an indication that something on a **document** (a word, phrase, number etc.) has been crossed out by mistake and should in fact remain as it was before.

stevedore a person whose job it is to load or unload ships.

steward (1) a person who runs a property for someone else. (2) a person who is in charge of the food and other things needed on a ship. (3) an official who helps with organising a crowd of people attending a meeting of any kind. (4) a person who acts as a waiter on an aeroplane or ship, and has certain other duties.

stewardess a female **steward** on a plane or ship.

sticker a piece of paper which can be stuck onto some surface, e.g. window, envelope etc. for advertising purposes.

stimulate (1) to excite; to make (a person) become interested. *We are*

trying to stimulate public interest in our new product. (2) to make more active. *News of the recent oil discoveries has stimulated the stock market.*

stimulation the act of **stimulating**.

stipend a salary, especially of a priest or minister.

stock *noun* (1) the amount of goods in a **store** or ship that have not yet been sold. *I don't know if we have any of these goods left: I'll check my stock.* (2) the amount of **raw materials** which are available for use. *The country has built up large stocks of coal.* (3) *in plural* **stocks** = **shares**. (4) = loan **stock**, **securities** issued to raise loans for the government at a fixed **rate** of **interest**, and which may or may not be **redeemable**. *See also* **gilt-edged securities**. (5) film material that has not yet been exposed: *film stock.*

stock *verb* (1) to keep (goods) for sale. *We stock all kinds of wood.* (2) **stock up** *or* **up on** to get supplies of (something): *to stock up on food for the winter.*

stockbroker a person who is an agent in the selling of **stocks** and **shares** to the public for a **commission**. *See also* **jobber**.

stock certificate *see* **share certificate**.

stock control the practice of keeping enough **stocks** (meanings 1 and 2) of goods or materials to meet the possible demands, but at the smallest cost in terms of **storage**, **bulk-buying**, etc. *See also* **buffer stock**, **economic order quantity**.

stock cover the time that **stocks** (meanings 1 and 2) will last if sales and/or use of goods and materials continue at the usual rate.

stock exchange (*or* **stock market**) a place where **stocks**, **shares** and government **securities** are bought and sold. *See also* **bourse**.

stockholder *see* **shareholder**.

stockholding cost money that has to be spent to keep a **stock** (meanings 1 and 2) or supply of goods or materials, e.g. by paying rent on **storage** space. *The problem about keeping large stocks is that it increases the stockholding costs.*

stock-in-trade (1) goods or materials which a business has for sale; **stock** (meaning 1). (2) anything which a person or company normally does as part of their business. *As a successful hairdresser, being charming with women is part of his stock-in-trade.*

stockist (*UK*) a dealer.

stock jobber *see* **jobber**.

stock level the amount of goods or materials being held for sale. *See also* **stock** (meanings 1 and 2).

stock market *see* **stock exchange**.

stockout the condition of having no supplies of a particular kind of goods or materials.

stockpile *verb* to gather **stockpiles** of (goods or materials). *The nations of the world are stockpiling weapons at an alarming rate.*

stockpile *noun* a large amount of a certain kind of goods or materials that is kept together for possible future use.

stocks *see* **stock** (noun).

stocktaking the act or **process** of checking the actual amount of goods which one is holding for sale. *We have a stocktaking every year. See also* **inventory**.

stock-turn (*or* **stock turnover**) (1) the total value of goods sold during a certain period, e.g. a year, divided by the average value of goods held during the year. For example, if the total cost of goods sold in a year came to £40,000 and the average value of goods being held unsold was £10,000, then the stock turnover would be 4:1. (2) *also*

stock-turn rate the total amount of a certain type of goods or materials available for sale over a period of time divided by the average amount available for sale at any one time. Thus if a business had 100,000 units available for sale over the year but only an average of 1000 units on any one day, then the stock turnover would be 100:1.

stop to give written instructions to one's bank that (a cheque which one has signed) should not in fact be paid.

stoppage (1) a situation where work has stopped because of **strike** action. *Bad relations between management and workers have caused frequent stoppages.* (2) the act of keeping back some money from a worker's pay e.g. because he owes money which has been given to him in advance of his wages.

storage (1) the act of **storing** goods or materials; the space for storing them. *They put their furniture in storage while they were away last summer.* (2) the amount of money paid for goods or materials to be stored. *One of our biggest expenses last year was storage for goods that we could not sell.*

storage device a part of a **computer** (often a **disk** or tape) on which information can be put in, kept and taken out again when it is needed.

store *noun* (1) a place where goods and materials can be kept. *Get some more paint from the store.* (2) a shop: *grocery store.* (3) a shop where many kinds of goods are sold. *There is a very large store in the main street where you can buy almost anything. See also* **department store**. (4) a supply of goods or materials that has been built up for future use. *We've built up a nice store of vegetables from our garden that will keep us supplied for most of the winter.* (5) the state of being kept for future use: *We have plenty of materials in store.* (6) (**computers**) = **storage device**.

store *verb* (1) to keep for future use: *to store materials; to store information.* (2)

to put in a **store** (meaning 1). *It will cost quite a lot to store all these materials.* (3) (**computers**) to put (information) into a **storage device**. *Store these data immediately.*

stores requisition a written request for goods held in a **store** (meaning 1).

storyboard a series of drawings which show the different parts of a film or television advertisement in the order in which they will appear.

straight-line method of depreciation (**accounting**) a method of allowing for the **depreciation** cost of a **fixed asset** which is worth less as it gets older, by which the worth of the asset is lowered by the same fixed amount each year; the amount is arrived at by dividing the cost of the asset by the **estimated** number of years that it will be able to be used.

strategic planning *see* **corporate planning**.

strategy a plan for reaching certain **targets** over a period of time. *See also* **tactics**.

stratification (**market research**) a method used to make sure that the various groups making up the **target** group are properly represented in every **sample**.

stratified sampling: random sampling from a **population** (**target** group) that has been divided into various groups (e.g. according to age, sex, **income**). Each group is then properly represented in each **sample**. *See also* **quota sampling**.

stream: on stream especially of large units such as factories, large **computers** etc., in operation, in production. *Our new North Sea oil wells will be coming on stream later this year.*

stress interview a type of **interview** where the people being interviewed for selection are questioned in an unfriendly way, so as to find out how well they can deal with this kind of difficult situation.

strike *noun* (1) the act of **striking** (meaning 1). *We have had several strikes in the factory this year.* (2) a situation where employees have refused to work: *to be on strike.* (3) the act of finding coal, oil, or similar **minerals**. *We have been prospecting in this area for months, and we expect to make a strike soon.*

strike *verb* (1) to refuse to do one's work, usually because one feels that one is not being paid enough or because of one's working conditions. *The workers want a pay rise, and are threatening to strike.* (2) to find supplies of (a **mineral**, e.g. coal or oil) underground. *They claim to have struck oil.*

strike a bargain to agree on a price that suits the buyer and seller; to come to an agreement that suits both sides. *Let's strike a bargain: we'll display your goods, if you display ours.*

strikebreaker a person who continues to work when others are on **strike** or in some other way causes the strike to have less effect.

striker a person who is on **strike**.

structural unemployment lack of jobs because of large-scale changes in the way that society or the **economy** is organised. *There is a great deal of structural unemployment today because more and more manual and clerical jobs can be done by machines.*

subassembly a number of pieces of machinery which are joined together to form a part of a larger machine.

subcontract *verb* to make an agreement with someone else that they will do part of some job that one has agreed to do. For example, a builder may subcontract some of his work to another craftsman, such as an electrician.

subcontract *noun* an agreement to **subcontract**.

subcontractor a person who agrees to do parts of jobs that someone else has got a **contract** for. *Plumbers and electricians are very often subcontractors for builders.*

subject to contract words included in a written agreement which mean that the agreement will not be binding on either **party** until a proper legal **contract** has been signed.

sub judice (*Latin, meaning* under a judge) being considered by a judge or court. *This case is still sub judice, so the newspapers are not being allowed to comment on it.*

sub-lease to **lease** (property) from a person who has already leased it from someone else.

sublet to rent out to a person (a property or part of a property which one is already renting from someone else). *I am renting that house from Mr Smith, but I am not staying there myself as I have sublet it to Mr Jones.*

subliminal advertising a type of advertising where a message is put over to the audience in a way that they are not consciously aware of, e.g. by flashing up the message very quickly on a cinema screen. *Subliminal advertising is illegal in many countries.*

submit (1) to give in (to someone or something more powerful). (2) to give (something) to a person, e.g. for a decision: *to submit a claim ; to submit a plan to the authorities.*

subordinate *adjective* lower ; less important: *a subordinate position.*

subordinate *noun* a person who is in a lower position in an organisation. *A manager should always treat his subordinates with respect.*

subpoena *noun* a **document** put out by a court which orders a person to appear before that court (perhaps to be a witness or to answer charges etc.).

subpoena *verb* to give a **subpoena** to (a person).

subrogation a **process** by which an **insurance company** that has paid a **claim** to an insured person can make its losses smaller by taking over the insured's rights, against a **third party** who is responsible for the damage (i.e. people who might have been to blame for the accident etc. having happened in the first place).

subroutine a part of a **computer program** which carries out a specific repetitive task. When this has been carried out by the **computer** it automatically returns to the next instruction on the main **program**.

subscribe (1) **subscribe to** to promise to pay money to some organisation, usually regularly, very often used for a newspaper or magazine. *Do you subscribe to that journal?* (2) to sign one's name at the end of (a legal **document**, e.g. a **contract**, a will). (3) to sign the **memorandum** of a **proposed** new **registered company**. (4) **subscribe for** to ask for **shares** in a new company: *to subscribe for 500 shares. See also* **subscription**.

subscribed capital an amount of **authorised capital** in a new company that has been issued and paid for in cash.

subscriber a person who **subscribes** to something.

subscription (1) the amount that one pays for something over a certain period: *a subscription to a newspaper/a club/a private charity. The annual subscription to my golf club has been doubled.* (2) the act of signing a legal **document**. (3) a request to buy **shares** in a new company. *See also* **subscribe**.

subsidiary (*or* **subsidiary company**) a type of company where more than half the **shares** are owned by another company or where another company can control who will be on the **board of directors**; the controlling company is called the **holding company** or the **parent company**.

subsidise to help by giving a **subsidy** to.

subsidy (1) money given by the government to keep the price of some goods lower than it would otherwise be. *In some countries, there are government subsidies for rice, bread and other basic foods.* (2) money given by the government to businesses, e.g. to keep down unemployment, or to help the business over a difficult time in its affairs. *Sometimes the government gives subsidies to key industries.* (3) any kind of **financial** help.

subsist to manage to stay alive. *The people in this area subsist on a diet of rice and fish.*

subsistence (1) the way in which one manages to stay alive: *to live at subsistence level*, i.e. to have only enough to live on, and no more. (2) (*also* **subsistence allowance**) the amount of money a person is paid to cover certain basic needs while he is away from home on business, e.g. food and the cost of a place to stay. *The company will pay you £20 a day subsistence.*

substantial fairly large in size, value or importance. *There has been a substantial increase in our sales.*

substitute *verb* to put (a thing or person) in place of another.

substitute *noun* a thing or person **substituted**.

successor a person who or thing which follows another, especially a person in an organisation. *I'd like you to meet my successor as marketing manager.*

sue to bring a **claim** against (a person) in a court of law. *He was sued for not paying his debts.* See also **damages**.

suggestion scheme a **process** by which any employee in an organisation with ideas for making it more efficient or profitable can make his or her ideas known to the management, usually in return for a reward of some kind.

sum insured the greatest amount that an **insurance company** will have to pay to a person who is insured with the company for any particular **claim**. *The sum insured for your house is £70,000 : you can claim up to that amount but not any more than that.*

summary a short account of something, giving only the most important points: *a summary of the report.*

Summer Time the practice in some countries of putting clocks forward one hour in the summer months.

summons an official **document** which orders a person to appear before a court, either for trial or to give evidence.

sundries various, usually small things taken together. *The estimate should leave an allowance for sundries.*

sunk cost (1) (*US*) an amount of money already spent on a business **project**, which cannot easily be recovered if the project is **cancelled**. (2) an amount of money spent on buying a **fixed asset**.

superannuate (1) to give (a person) a **pension** because he will no longer be able to work (usually because of age or ill-health). (2) to get rid of (a person or thing) because he/it is out-of-date or no long necessary.

superannuation (1) a **pension** that is paid to a person who is no longer able to work (usually because of age or ill-health). (2) an amount of money that may be taken away each month from a worker's salary to pay for the pension he will get when he is no longer able to work. (3) the act of **superannuating**; a situation where a person or thing has been **superannuated**.

superintend to be in charge of; to see that (something) is done properly. *I superintend all the work that is done in this section.*

superintendent (1) a person who is in charge of something, who sees that something is done properly. (2) in UK police, a person in the rank above inspector. (3) in US police, a person who is in charge of a police station.

superior *adjective* (1) better (than someone or something else); of higher quality. *Our tests show that this product is superior to all the others.* (2) of very high quality: *a superior brand of whisky.* (3) showing that one thinks oneself better than other people.

superior *noun* a person who is in a higher position in an organisation. *It's not a good idea to annoy your superiors.*

supermarket a large **self-service store** which sells a wide variety of goods, but especially those in constant demand, e.g. food, drink, and household goods. *See also* **hypermarket, superstore.**

superstore a very large store, selling food and other goods, between a **supermarket** and a **hypermarket** in size.

supervise to watch to make sure that (something) is done properly or that nothing wrong or bad happens. *Would you supervise the work on the new project?; to supervise an examination; to supervise children at play.*

supervision the act of **supervising**. *In that factory they are very worried about security: you will be under supervision the whole time,* i.e. you will be watched.

supervisor (1) a person who **supervises**, e.g. one in charge of a group of workers etc. (2) in a university, a lecturer who checks on a student's work.

supplement *noun* (1) something which is added to complete something else or to give more information about it. *A supplement which brings this report up-to-date will be appearing next week.* (2) a separate section of a newspaper or magazine. *This journal has a business supplement that now appears with every issue.* (3) = **supplementary payment.**

supplement *verb* to provide something extra that is needed. *The workforce will be supplemented with extra men until the job is finished.*

supplementary extra; provided to complete something or make up for something that is missing: **supplementary payment,** i.e. extra payment.

supplementary benefit (*UK*) an amount of money paid weekly by the government to various groups of people whose **income** is below a certain minimum level.

supply *noun* (1) the act of giving something that is needed or asked for. (2) (**economics**) the availability of goods or materials. *The world supply of oil is a matter of great concern to world leaders.* (3) *in plural* **supplies** food and/or **equipment** needed for a certain purpose. *Charity organisations are sending food supplies to the famine area.* (4) *in plural* **supplies** goods needed by a company to run its business but not part of what it sells or produces: *office supplies,* i.e. paper, pens, notebooks etc.

supply *verb* to give (something that is needed or asked for). *Will you be able to supply spare parts for this machine?*

supply curve a type of **graph** which shows in diagram form the information given in a **supply schedule.** *See also* **demand curve.**

supply schedule a list showing how much of its **product** a company is willing to sell at various prices; usually the higher the price, the greater the number of items supplied.

support buying a situation where a government buys its own currency on the **foreign exchange market** in order to keep the value of the currency from falling.

surcharge *noun* (1) an extra payment or tax that has to be paid. *We normally deliver goods in 48 hours, but you can have them delivered more quickly on payment of a surcharge.* (2) an extra amount that can be printed on a postage stamp to make it worth more.

surcharge verb (1) to make (a person) pay something extra. *You will be surcharged for any luggage above the allowed limit.* (2) to increase the value of (a postage stamp) by printing a new value across it.

surety (1) see **guarantor**. (2) money or something of value given as a **guarantee** that something will not be lost or damaged, or that a person will act as he has promised to do.

surplus a quantity or amount of something that is more than is needed. *The EEC always has a surplus of food.*

surrender value (also **cash surrender value**) the amount of money which an **insurance company** is willing to give a person if he wants to give up his **life assurance policy**; usually the amount increases as the policy gets closer to its **maturity date**.

survey noun (1) a general description of a subject. *A survey of economic trends in the last ten years has just been published.* (2) a measurement of an area of land. *They have just completed a survey of the northern section of the county.* (3) (*UK*) an examination of a house to see if there is anything wrong with it: *to pay for a survey to be done.* (4) an organisation which is concerned with **surveying** (meaning 3) an area or a country: *the Ordnance Survey.* (5) a study of what people want or think which uses **sampling** methods. (6) a careful examination of something in order to be able to make a report on it: *a survey of working conditions in factories.*

survey verb (1) to look over (something); to examine. *From this hill, you can survey the whole city.* (2) to deal with (a subject) generally. *In his talk, the chairman surveyed the company's performance in the past year.* (3) to measure (an area) carefully paying special attention to heights and distances, so that a map or plan can be made of it. (4) to examine (something) carefully so as to be able to report on its

condition: *to survey a ship*; *to survey something to see the extent of damage incurred. You should always have a house surveyed before you buy it.*

surveyor a person whose job it is to **survey** land, buildings etc.

suspend (1) to stop for a time. *Police have suspended their inquiries until they have more evidence to go on.* (2) to stop (a person) from doing his job for a time. *He has been accused of stealing company funds, and has been suspended from his duties until after his trial. See also* **suspension**.

  suspend payment to stop paying out any more money, as when certain businesses discover that they are in danger of going **bankrupt**, and so do not pay any of their debts until they are sure that they can pay all of them. *See also* **suspension**.

  suspend trading to stop carrying out one's business for a time or for good, depending on whether business problems can be solved. *See also* **suspension**.

suspense account a type of **account** for things which cannot be put into the proper account for various reasons, e.g. not enough details are known about the **transaction**, as the transaction is not complete.

suspension (1) the state of being stopped for a time, or until certain decisions are taken: *suspension of payments*; *suspension of trading.* (2) the act of stopping a person from doing his job; the condition of being stopped from doing one's job. *His suspension lasted three weeks, and during that time the police examined the charges against him. See also* **suspend**.

sweated labour work done for very low pay. *These goods are cheap because they have been produced by sweated labour.*

switchboard a board where telephone lines can be connected, e.g. in a telephone exchange, office or hotel; the people who operate a switchboard.

switch selling a method of selling goods, now illegal in UK, by which possible customers' attention is attracted by an offer of goods at an attractive price: but the salesman's aim is actually to persuade them to buy something else which is not nearly such good value.

SWOT analysis a method of judging how well a business or organisation is doing by examining its strengths (S), weaknesses (W), the business opportunities (O) it has, and any threats (T) or dangers that there might be to its success.

sympathetic strike a **strike** by a group of employees, not against their own employers, but because they want to show their support for another group of workers who are having a **dispute** with their employers; the two groups of workers may be in different factories etc., or perhaps even in different industries. *They say that the miners are going to have a sympathetic strike in support of the nurses' pay claim.*

syndicate *verb* (1) to publish in several newspapers or magazines on a regular basis. *His articles on business trends are syndicated in newspapers all over the world.* (2) to form a **syndicate**; to manage something by means of a **syndicate**.

syndicate *noun* (1) a group of businessmen who are working together for one **project** or to reach a certain business aim, with each member of the group working for his own profit, although he needs the help of the other members of the group to get it. For example, a group of **underwriters** who come together to **insure** a large risk, or a group of companies which come together to work on a large government **project**. (2) = **cartel**.

syndicated market research a situation where the cost of carrying out **market research** is shared by a number of companies, which also, of course, share the results of the research, e.g. **consumer panel** and **retail audit** studies.

synergy a **process** by which taking two or more related actions achieves results which are greater than what might be expected from the effects of each separate action on its own, e.g. two companies deciding to use the same sales representatives; often described as $2 + 2 = 5$.

system (1) a number of different things making one complete whole: *a computer system; the economic system.* (2) the way things have been or can be arranged to work; a method. *He is proposing a new system of transport for the city. We shall have to change our present system of working – it's useless.*

systematic following a **system** (meaning 2); well-organised. *The plan was easy to understand because everything was laid out in a very systematic way.*

systems analysis an area of knowledge concerned mainly with the way in which the advantages of a **computer** can be used by an organisation in the most effective way taking into account the needs of the organisation, the weak points of the present method of working etc.

systems analyst a person whose job it is to deal with **systems analysis**.

systems selling a **process** by which a number of different **products** which can be made to work together are sold together, and not separately, e.g. a video camera, videotape recorder and television set could be sold as one video unit.

T

tab (*short for* **tabulator**) a key on a typewriter or **computer keyboard** which allows **columns** to be spaced automatically.

table *verb* to bring (something) before a meeting for discussion or for a decision. *I intend to table a motion tonight concerning the need to increase our membership fees.*

tabloid a type of newspaper with a small page size (i.e. about 30 × 40 cm (12 × 16 inches)), and usually presenting news in a sensational way so as to attract the largest possible readership.

tabulate to set out (information) in the form of a table. *Details of our current trading position are tabulated at the end of the report.*

tabulator *see* **tab**.

tachograph an instrument which records the speed and distance travelled by a **vehicle**.

tactics detailed ideas for reaching certain limited aims, which may be part of a larger **strategy**. *We should discuss now what our tactics are going to be at tonight's board meeting.*

takeaway of food, which can be taken away and eaten elsewhere; of a shop etc., selling such food.

take-home pay the amount of money which is actually paid to an employee after the money he owes for **income tax**, **superannuation** etc. has been taken away. *I earn £1000 a month, but my take-home pay is only £750 a month.*

take over (1) to gain control over. *His business is expanding fast : he took over three other companies last year.* (2) **take over from** to be responsible for duties previously done by someone else. *Watch what I do carefully : you'll be taking over from me soon.*

takeover the act of taking control of an organisation. *The bakery's sales have been better since the takeover by a grocery chain.*

takeover bid an attempt by a company to get control of another by offering to buy the **shares** of the other company at a price that might be attractive to its present **shareholders**.

take stock (1) of a shop, store etc. to check all the goods on the shelves and make sure nothing has been lost or stolen. *We take stock on Sundays, when the shop is closed. See also* **stock-taking**. (2) to examine or think about (something) carefully so that a decision can be made. *We're taking stock of the situation : it may be we'll have to close down the business.*

takings the amount of money that has been taken in exchange for goods or **services**. *Every night the shopkeeper would carefully count the day's takings.*

talk shop to talk· about business matters with other people in the same business, especially in the situation where such matters might not normally be discussed. *This is supposed to be a party – you shouldn't be talking shop!*

tally *verb* of figures etc., to be the same, to correspond. *My totals don't tally with yours.*

tally *noun* a record of something; something on which this is kept. *It is always better to keep a tally of your expenses.*

tangible asset a physical thing of value belonging to a person or company, e.g. a house, furniture, machinery etc. *See also* **intangible asset**.

tape recorder a machine which can record and play back sounds, e.g. music.

tare (*or* **tare weight**) (1) the weight of box, wrapping or similar container (taken away from the total weight of goods sent). (2) the weight of a vehicle when it is empty of goods and passengers.

target (1) something aimed at; something one wants to reach. *Our target is to sell twice as much of our product as last year. We just failed to achieve our target.* (2) a person or thing that is the object of the bad, remarks or feelings of others. *Because of the company's poor performance, the chairman has been the target of much angry criticism.*

target audience a group of people that advertising material is specially aimed at. *If you want a reach your target audience, you have to find out what newspapers and magazines they read.*

target market the market to which a company plans to sell, e.g. the student market, the overseas market.

tariff (1) a **levy** or tax that has to be paid on goods **imported** into a country. (2) a scale of prices charged for **services**, e.g. in a hotel. *If you look at the tariff, you'll be able to check the cost.* (3) (*UK*) the rate of payment for certain services. *The electricity board has a special tariff for customers using large amounts of electricity.*

tariff barrier the point at which a tax has to be paid when **importing** or **exporting** goods.

task a particular piece of work to be done. *I've made a list of the various tasks you'll have to perform in the course of your duties.*

task force a small group of workers and/or managers who have been brought together to deal with a certain problem or to reach a certain aim.

task method of budgeting (*especially advertising*) a method of working out how much a **process** is going to cost by **analysing** in detail how it is to be done.

tax *noun* an amount of money which people or organisations have to pay to the government to pay for its expenses, e.g. raised on what people earn, what they buy or what they own.

tax *verb* (1) to make (people or organisations) pay money to the government: *to tax earnings/profits etc.* (2) to make heavy demands on. *Finding the money for these new developments is going to tax all our resources.*

taxable on which tax must be paid: *taxable income,* i.e. the part of what a person earns that he has to pay tax on.

tax allowance an amount of **tax relief**. *You can claim a tax allowance on certain kinds of business expense.*

taxation (1) the act of **taxing** (meaning 1). (2) the amount of money paid in taxation. *A large proportion of my income goes in taxation.*

tax avoidance legal methods used in order not to pay more tax than one has to. *See also* **tax evasion**.

tax credit an amount of tax on the **dividend** of a **share** already paid by the company and therefore not paid by the **shareholder**. *See also* **tax voucher**.

tax evasion illegal methods used in order not to pay tax one really ought to pay. *See also* **tax avoidance**.

tax exemption a situation where taxes do not have to be paid by an organisation because of the special kind of work that organisation does. *Churches and charitable organisations are usually given tax exemption.*

tax haven (*or* **tax shelter**) a country which encourages companies to have their **headquarters** in it, and rich people to come and live in it, by having very low taxes and perhaps other benefits.

tax rebate an amount of money which one gets back after having paid one's taxes, e.g. because one's **income** has dropped, or because one was charged too much tax in the first place.

tax relief the amount of money that can be taken away from the total of **taxable income**, because it has been spent in a special way, e.g. in UK there is tax relief on **mortgages** (house-loans) and certain kinds of personal **insurance**.

tax shelter *see* **tax haven**.

tax voucher a **document** sent by a company to a **shareholder** showing how much has been held back by the company for the payment of taxes on **dividends**: the document should be kept by the shareholder as proof that the necessary tax has been paid. *See also* **dividend warrant, tax credit**.

tax year a period of twelve months over which **income** is worked out for tax purposes. *See also* **fiscal year**.

technical (1) connected with a special area of knowledge, especially practical subjects, such as engineering. *He has great technical knowledge of car engines.* (2) difficult because of needing special knowledge. *I can't understand this book on motor mechanics: it is too technical for me.*

technician a person who has a practical skill and knowledge, especially in connection with machines and machinery. *The factory employs several technicians to service the machinery. He works as a technician in the hospital laboratory.*

technique (1) a special way of doing something which needs practical skill and knowledge. *We shall train you in the business techniques you will need for this job.* (2) a special ability. *He has this technique of persuading customers that his advice is the best available.*

technological of **technology**. *Children will have to be educated so that they can deal with the technological change that is bound to come.*

technology the area of knowledge that deals with applying the discoveries and inventions of science to industry and commerce. *It is technology that turns scientific inventions into profit!*

telephone answering service a method by which messages sent by telephone can be recorded when no one is there to answer them; they can thus be answered later.

telephone selling a method of selling goods in which contact with possible customers is by telephone only.

teletext general name for information etc. displayed on a television screen under such **viewdata systems** as **Ceefax**, **Oracle**, **Prestel**.

telex a machine which works like a telephone except that the messages sent or received are printed out. This means that the person who is to get the message does not have to be there at the time the message is sent, but can pick it up from the telex machine at any time: *to send a message by telex.*

telex *verb* to send (a message) by **telex**.

teller (*also* **cashier**) a person who works in a bank and whose main job is to pay out and receive money.

temp a person employed to work in an office on a **temporary** basis, usually doing typing and secretarial work. *See also* **temporary staff service**.

temporary lasting for only a short time. *He has a temporary post as a telephone engineer. Compare with* **permanent**.

temporary staff service an organisation that supplies **temporary** staff (especially for office duties), usually to cover holiday periods, illness etc., in return for a **fee**. *See also* **temp**.

tenant person who has the use of property that belongs to someone else in return for paying a certain amount of money (rent), usually every week or every month. *See also* **lease**.

tender *noun* (1) an offer to supply goods or **services** for a certain amount of money. *The city council are inviting tenders for the building of the new school.* (2) something that can be used in exchange when buying and selling; currency. *See also* **legal tender**.

tender *verb* (1) (*formal*) to give; to offer. *If the company ignores my advice, I shall tender my resignation.* (2) **tender for** to offer to supply goods or **services** for a particular amount of money. *We are going to tender for the contract to build the new hospital.*

tenure (1) being in possession of property. *The property is yours if you agree to three conditions of tenure.* (2) being in possession of a particular job. *Tenure of this post is for four years.* (3) a situation where one is secure in one's job, after a period where one's **contract** has to be renewed from time to time. *Jack has finally got tenure in his job at the University.*

term (1) a word or phrase used to name something: *technical terms.* (2) a certain period of time, e.g. that during which a **lease** continues, during which an **insurance** lasts, for which a **bill of exchange** is drawn. *The term of this bill is one month from today.* (3) *in plural* **terms** the conditions, e.g. of an agreement. *If you want to buy our goods you will have to accept our terms.*

term days *see* **quarter days**.

terminal (1) a (building in) an airport; a large bus or railway station: *an airport terminal. See also* **air terminal**. (2) any **device** by which **data** may be put into or got from a **computer**. *There are several terminals linked to this computer, and there is at least one on each floor of the building.*

term insurance a type of **insurance** by which money will be paid out if the insured person dies within a certain period of time. *He took our term insurance for 25 years.*

term loan (*especially US*) a situation where money is lent to a person by a bank for a certain period of time, and has to be repaid to the bank by **instalments** over that period: *a ten-year term loan of $40,000.*

terms of trade the way of working out how well a country is doing in its trade with other countries by which a certain range of **import** prices is divided by another range of **export** prices, and the result multiplied by 100. If the figure is more than 100%, then the terms of trade are good (favourable) since import prices are lower than export prices; if less than

100%, the terms of trade are thought to be bad (unfavourable). *See also* **balance of trade**.

territorial waters the amount of the sea around a country over which the country **claims** a certain kind of legal control. *No foreign ships will be allowed to fish within our territorial waters.*

testimonial (1) a statement as to the good qualities of a person or **product**. *He showed us several testimonials to his hard work and good character. They published many testimonials from satisfied customers.* (2) a public occasion when a person is honoured for what he has done.

test marketing a less expensive method of finding out how attractive to customers a new **product** is likely to be, by which the product is **launched** only in one carefully-chosen area, and this **sample** is taken to show how popular it will be all over the country.

theory (1) a way of thinking about something, a number of ideas which make up a plan or **system**. (2) the ideas behind something (rather than its being put into practice). *That's all right in theory but can it really be done?*

theory X (**management training**) the idea that human beings are naturally lazy and that a manager's job is to order or force people to work.

theory Y (**management training**) the idea that human beings are naturally active and that a manager's job is to take advantage of this by showing members that it is in their own interests to help to reach the aims of the organisation.

think tank a group of experts who are paid by a company or government to try to solve a certain problem, or a certain kind of problem.

third-party insurance a kind of **insurance** which covers not the insured person himself but anyone who may be affected by his actions under certain conditions. A common example is with car insurance, where the driver is forced by law to insure for anyone who may suffer injury or damage because of his actions as a driver.

Third World the less-developed countries of the world, especially those of Africa, Asia and Latin America.

three-shift system a method of keeping a factory, shop etc. continuously working, by getting workers to work in one of three **shifts** of 8 hours each, so covering the 24 hours of the day.

threshold agreement a method of making sure that employees' wages keep up with the **cost of living**. The employer agrees that if prices go up by more than a certain amount (as measured by the **retail price index**), then he will increase his workers' wages by a certain amount.

through bill of lading a type of **bill of lading** used when the **cargo** has to be handed on from one **carrier** to another.

throughput the largest amount that can be produced or handled. *This machine has a throughput of 500 items per hour. Our computer can handle a throughput of 100 enquiries every 10 minutes.*

thruster a manager who is very active in doing business and in looking for new business. *See also* **sleeper** (meaning 1).

till (1) a container used in a shop in which money is put in and taken out as **purchases** are paid for. (2) *also* **cash register** a container as in meaning 1, which also adds up and usually **records** how much is put into it each time it is used.

time and motion study a form of **work study** in which a worker's movements are carefully watched to see if they can be done more quickly or efficiently.

time bill a type of **bill of exchange** which is to be paid on a certain date.

time card a card which records the exact time that an employee starts and finishes work when he/she puts it into a **time clock**.

time clock a machine into which an employee can put his **time-card**.

time deposit (*US*) *see* **deposit account**.

time rate a method of paying workers by the amount of time they have worked, rather than by how much they have produced (usually so much per hour, or per day). *See also* **piece rate**, **time work**.

time scale the amount of time that a certain piece of work will take. *The time scale for this project will be in order of five or six years.*

time-sharing (**computers**) a system by which users at different **terminals** can use a computer at the same time.

time-sheet a piece of paper on which a worker records the hours he/she works.

time work work for which payment is made by the amount of time that is taken to do it. *See also* **piece work**, **time rate**.

time zone an area of the world in which the same time is used. *The earth is divided into 24 time zones.*

tip *see* **gratuity**.

TIR carnet *see* **transport internationale routier**.

title (1) a name of a book, article, film etc. *He has written some excellent books on marketing : I'll just give you a note of the titles.* (2) a legal right of ownership. *As soon as the contract is signed, the title to the land passes to you.*

title deeds a **document** which shows that a person is the owner of a property. *Before you buy any property from him, insist on seeing the title deeds.*

token (1) a small piece of plastic etc. used instead of a coin in certain circumstances, e.g. in certain machines. (2) a piece of paper which can be exchanged for goods, e.g. *in a shop: a book token.* See also **gift voucher**. (3) a sign or symbol. *Please accept this small gift as a token of our gratitude.*

token strike a very short **strike** (which may be followed by a longer one) to show how strong feeling is on some question.

toll an amount of money that has to be paid for the use of certain roads and bridges, and also other means of transport. *The Forth Road Bridge is a toll bridge.*

ton a measure of weight equal to 2240 pounds (**long ton**, *UK*) or 2000 pounds (**short ton**, *US*). See also **metric ton(ne)**.

tonnage (1) the measure of the amount of **cargo** that can be carried by a ship. (2) the measure of the weight of the cargo of a ship.

tonne *see* **metric tonne**.

total loss something that is **insured** which has been completely destroyed or so badly damaged that it cannot be repaired. *After the accident, my car was written off as a total loss.*

tout *verb* (1) to try to sell (e.g. tickets) at a higher price than they are really worth. (2) to try to get business in a pushing way. (3) to try to get information about racehorses for betting purposes.

tout *noun* a person who **touts**.

track record the past successes and failures of a person or an organisation. *Before you hire him, check to see what his track record is like.*

trade *noun* (1) the business of buying and selling goods and **services**. *Trade between Europe and the third world is increasing. He is in the book trade,* i.e. the business of buying and selling books. (2) an occupation; a kind of work (especially skilled work). *You*

should learn a trade: it might make it easier to get a job later.

trade *verb* to buy and sell goods and **services**. *We are not allowed to trade on Sundays. See also* **trade-in, trade-off**.

trade association an organisation set up by businesses within a certain trade to protect and develop it in various ways. *Compare with* **employers' association**.

trade barrier any kind of tax or **duty** which makes the buying and selling of goods and **services** between countries more difficult.

trade counter a counter in a **warehouse** etc. where goods are sold to **retailers**.

trade cycle (*or* **business cycle**) a period of time during which business moves from a time of good profits and high employment (**boom**) to a time of low profits and high unemployment (**slump**), and then back to boom conditions again. *See also* **boom; depression; recession; slump**.

trade deficit *see* **trade gap**.

Trade Descriptions Act (*UK*) an act of parliament which makes it illegal to describe goods in any way which is false or could be misleading to the public.

trade discount a lowering of the amount charged for goods by a manufacturer or **wholesaler** to one of his customers (who is also in business).

trade fair (*or* **trade exhibition**) an exhibition where manufacturers and others who are in the same area of business come together to display their goods and to see what others have to offer.

trade gap (*or* **trade deficit**) the amount by which a country's **visible imports** are more than its **visible exports** leading to an unfavourable **balance of trade**.

trade-in the act of **trading in**. *If you decide to buy this refrigerator we will accept your old one as a trade-in.*

trade in to offer (something one has, e.g. a car, television set) as part payment for something else of the same kind. *I am trading in my old car for a new one.*

trademark (*also* **trade name**) the name or special design put on goods made by a particular manufacturer to show that they have been made by that manufacturer, and not by someone else. This name or design can be protected by law and may not then be copied by others. *If you want to check whether the goods are genuine you should look carefully at the trademark. See also* **brand**.

trade mission a group of businessmen who make a short visit to another country to try and develop **trade** (meaning 1) between the two countries.

trade name (1) the name under which a company does business. (2) = **trademark**.

trade-off an exchange of one thing for another, especially as part of a deal. *Also used as a verb* **trade off**.

trade press magazines and newspapers which are aimed at those who are in a certain area of business, keeping them informed of new developments in that area.

trade price the amount of money paid by a **retailer** to a **wholesaler** or manufacturer for goods which is going to sell to the public.

trade promotion the act or **process** of persuading **wholesalers** and/or **retailers** to keep a certain kind of goods in **stock**.

trade reference a **document** needed by a person who is asked to supply goods and **services** on **credit** to a business for the first time, which will show that the business has paid its debts to another **supplier** and is therefore a good risk.

trade secret a particular part of the **process** of making a **product** which is known only to the manufacturers and to no one else.

trade union (*or* **trades union**) a group of workers who have formed themselves into an organisation which can **negotiate** with employers about wages and conditions of service.

trade union dues (*also* **trade union contributions**) the amount of money which a person who belongs to a **trade union** has to pay to the union.

trade unionist a person who belongs to a **trade union**.

trade union recognition an agreement by the management of a company to **negotiate** with a certain **trade union** or group of trade unions.

trading account a **document** giving the main facts relating to the **gross profit** (or loss) of a company; the amount of profit or loss is carried over to the **profit and loss account**.

trading certificate a **document** given out by the **Registrar of Companies** which allows a company legally to start doing business.

trading down a **process** by which a business tries to attract customers by selling cheaper goods, hoping to increase profits or sales by selling more goods. *See also* **trading up**.

trading estate an area where there are a number of factories, usually built at government expense. They may be offered at lower than usual rents for a time in order to attract business to that area.

trading stamps special stamps which are given away with certain goods, or by a certain **retailer**: the stamps can be saved and later exchanged for cash or a range of goods.

trading up the **process** by which a business tries to increase profits by selling a more expensive kind of goods. *See also* **trading down**.

train to prepare (a person) to be able to do something (or to do something better) by teaching, and giving useful experience; to prepare oneself to do something by learning and experience. *All our personnel are trained for two years before they take up their duties.*

trainee *noun, adjective* (a person who is) being trained in some skill: *a trainee manager. Our factory takes on trainees directly from school.*

training the **process** of being taught to do something, or of improving one's skills in something: *management training.*

training manual a book or **document** which describes how people should be taught if they are to learn certain skills.

training programme a list of things which have to be done, and how they have to be done, when a particular group of students have to be taught certain skills.

transact to do, carry out (a piece of business).

transaction (1) a piece of business that has been done. *Over a thousand transactions were recorded on the Stock Exchange today*, i.e. over a thousand deals where shares were bought or sold. (2) *in plural* **transactions** published records of a society, meeting etc.

transaction costs legal and other **fees** which have to be paid when a business deal is done. *The transaction costs incurred in buying or selling property can be quite high.*

transfer *noun* (1) act or **process** of **transferring** or being transferred: *the transfer of money/passengers, etc.* (2) a person or thing transferred, e.g. a design, a football player. *The Rovers new transfer is playing for them today.*

transfer *verb* (1) to move from one place to another. *He has been trans-*

ferred from Glasgow to the main office in London. At Rome, you will have to transfer to another plane. I'd like to transfer some money from my deposit account to my current account, please.* (2) to change the legal ownership of (something). *I have transferred these shares to my son.* (3) to copy (a design, photograph etc.) from one surface to another.

transfer pricing a **process** in a company by which goods and services **transferred** from one section or division of the company to another are charged against the receiving section etc. for **cost control** within the company.

tranship to load (goods) from one ship etc. onto another. *This cargo will have to be transhipped at New York.*

transhipment (1) the act or **process** of **transhipping**. (2) **cargo** that has been transhipped.

transmission (1) the act of **transmitting**. (2) something that is transmitted: *a radio transmission.* (3) part of a motor-car which carries power from the engine to the wheels.

transmit (1) to send or pass on from one person or place to another. *Doctors are investigating how the disease was transmitted.* (2) to send by radio; to broadcast. *We are able to transmit messages to our ships at any time.*

transnational of more than one country; having branches or interests in more than one country: *a transnational business group. See also* **multi-national company**.

Transport International Routier (**carnet**) (*or* **TIR carnet**) a **document** which allows a **sealed** container to be transported by road through different countries with very little or no payment of **customs duty** until the country where the container's contents have to be unloaded.

traveller's cheque a special type of cheque which is easily changed for cash in foreign banks (often also in hotels and shops); the person using it will also be **compensated** for their value if they are lost or stolen.

treasurer a person who looks after the money belonging to a club, society etc.: *honorary treasurer*, i.e. one who is not paid for his services.

treasury (1) a place where large amounts of money and other valuables are kept. (2) (*often* **the Treasury**) a government department which is in charge of the **finances** of a country.

treasury bill (*UK*) a type of **bill of exchange** which is offered by the government at a **discount** (i.e. for less than the value of the bill), does not give any **interest**, and is repaid within a short time (usually three months); these bills are **tendered** for by **discount houses**.

treaty (1) a formal agreement between two countries: *a peace treaty*. (2) any kind of formal agreement: *for sale by private treaty*, i.e. privately between the buyer and seller, not by **auction**.

trend *noun* a tendency to go or develop in a certain way or direction. *The trend in retailing these days is away from small shops and more towards supermarkets.*

trend *verb* to go or develop in a certain way or direction. *House-prices are trending upwards again.*

trial balance a method of checking the correctness of **accounts**, by listing all the **debit balances** in one **column** and all the **credit balances** in another, and adding them up to see if they agree: this will show up some kinds of mistake (e.g. adding incorrectly) but not others (e.g. some **transactions** completely missed out).

trial order the act of asking for a small amount of some goods to check, e.g. on their quality, or on how they will sell, before ordering the full amount. *I'll make a trial order of 500 units, and we'll see how they go.*

tricks of the trade (*informal*) things one learns to do as part of one's job. *As an assistant manager, I learnt most of the tricks of the trade by watching my boss.*

trust *noun* (1) belief in the good qualities of a person or thing; confidence. *Don't put your trust in him: he's very unreliable.* (2) a situation where others have belief in one's good qualities, or that one will do things properly: *a position of trust.* (3) property or money which is managed by others for someone or something. *He set up a trust for the education of poor children.* (3) (*US*) a group of companies which have combined to have an unfair position of strength in a certain area of business; a **monopoly**. *See also* **investment trust**.

trust *verb* to have confidence or belief in (e.g. a person's good qualities or abilities). *You can trust him to do an excellent job.*

trustee a person who has the responsibility of managing money or property on behalf of others.

trustee savings bank (*UK*) originally a form of **savings bank guaranteed** by the government, now a **commercial bank**.

turnkey contract a type of agreement in which a person pays someone else to look after the setting up of a large **project**; when the project is set up, the person paying expects to be able simply to 'turn the key' to get everything working smoothly.

turnover (1) the total amount of goods or **services** sold over a certain time, usually expressed either in terms of value or sometimes of units sold. *This company has a turnover of £300,000,000 a year.* (2) the rate at which new goods have to be bought in to replace those that have been sold. *Turnover of sports equipment goods always increases sharply in the summer as you would expect.* (3) the rate at which workers leave an organisation and are replaced by others. *Since unemployment has increased, the turnover of staff has got less.*

turnover tax a type of tax which is charged on **products** at each stage of the **process** from manufacture to **retailer**; no stage is excused from paying the tax. *See also* **value added tax**.

two-bin system a method of **stock control** by which the goods in **stock** are kept in two separate containers; when one container is empty, it means that it is time for fresh supplies to be ordered.

typing pool a group of typists who do typing for a number of people in a company.

U

uberrimae fidei (*Latin, meaning* of the greatest good faith) of a **contract**, for it to be **valid**, all the facts related to it must be given.

ultimate consumer the person who actually uses or has the benefit of goods that are bought, e.g. a wife may buy things in a shop, not for her own use, but for her husband or children, who become the ultimate consumers.

ultimo (*or* **ult**) (*Latin*) sometimes used in correspondence, last month.

ultra vires (*Latin, meaning* beyond one's powers) (*law*) beyond what a person or company is lawfully allowed to do. *As far as this committee is concerned, that matter is ultra vires, and will have to be dealt with by someone else.*

umpire a person who is called in to give a decision on a **dispute** when the **arbitrators** who have been appointed cannot agree.

UN *see* **United Nations**.

unanimous in complete agreement, with everyone agreeing: *a unanimous decision.*

uncalled capital an amount of money which a company has been allowed to raise as part of its **authorised capital**, which has been issued but not yet fully paid. *See also* **paid-up capital**; **unissued capital**.

UNCDF *see* **United Nations Capital Development Fund**.

unconstitutional not allowed by the laws or **regulations** of an organisation or a country. *It is unconstitutional for the President to interfere with judges' verdicts in court.*

unconstitutional strike a situation where workers refuse to work because of a **dispute** with the management in a way which goes against some agreement or **agreed procedure** (e.g. a no-strike **policy**). It may or may not be an **official strike**. *See also* **unofficial strike**.

uncontrollable cost a cost which has to be met by a company but which is outside its control, e.g. one caused by changes in government **policy**, changes in the **exchange rate** etc.

uncontrollable factors the environment in which a company operates over which it has little or no control, e.g. political or social changes.

UNCTAD *see* **United Nations Conference on Trade and Development**.

undercapitalised of a company, not having enough **capital** to support the kinds of things that have to be done.

underdeveloped country *see* **developing country**, **Third World**.

under-employment (1) a situation where a person does not have enough work to do, e.g. if the work is too easy for him, or if there is not enough work available. (2) a situation of less than **full employment**.

undermanning a situation where there are not enough workers to do a job that has to be done, or not enough to do it properly. *See also* **overmanning**.

undermentioned mentioned later (in a letter etc.). *We shall be glad to discuss the undermentioned factors with you if necessary.*

undersell to sell goods more cheaply than others. *He stayed in business only by underselling his competitors.*

understaffed *see* **staff** (verb).

undertake to agree to do (something).

undertaking something **undertaken**. *This undertaking may prove to be too much for our resources.*

underwrite (1) to agree to buy any **shares** that are left unsold when there is a new **share issue**. (2) (**insurance**) to agree to meet the costs of (all or part of a risk). (3) to **guarantee** to cover (the costs of a **project**) if it should fail.

underwriter (1) a person working for an **insurance company** who advises it on what risks to accept and what **premiums** to charge. (2) a member of an **insurance** group (e.g. **Lloyds**) who agrees to meet the costs of all or part of a risk. (3) a person who, for a **commission**, agrees to buy up any **shares** left unsold from a new **share issue**.

underwriting manager (1) = **underwriter** (meaning 1). (2) a person who arranges **insurance** on behalf of an **underwriter** (meaning 2).

undischarged bankrupt a person who has been unable to pay his business **creditors** and who has not been legally released from the results of his **bankruptcy**.

undistributed profits *see* **retained earnings**.

UNDP *see* **United Nations Development Programme**.

undue influence a legal reason for a person not being bound by a **contract** he has signed: he can claim that he was persuaded to sign it under the strong influence of someone else, e.g. a parent.

unearned income money which is not got from one's employment but from other **sources**, such as **investment**; sometimes this kind of **income** is more highly taxed.

uneconomic not profitable; costing too much to be worthwhile. *Some railway routes have been closed down because they are uneconomic to run.*

unemployed not having work, not able to find work.

unemployment (1) the state of not having employment. *Unemployment has been shown to have bad psychological effects.* (2) the number of people who cannot find work: *an area of high unemployment.*

unemployment benefit money that a person is paid by the government while he is **unemployed**.

unfair dismissal (*or* **wrongful dismissal**) the act of taking a person away from his or her job or being taken away from one's job for a bad or unimportant reason. *The lady broadcaster is suing her employers for unfair dismissal: they said she was not attractive enough.*

unfavourable balance of trade *see* **balance of trade**.

unilateral on the part of one person, group or organisation only (where more than one are involved). *The union made a unilateral decision to break off the negotiations.*

union *see* **trade union**.

union shop a place of work where all the workers must belong to a **trade union**; new workers who are not union-members may be taken on but they must join a union when they start work.

unique selling proposition (*or* **USP**) some attractive quality in a **product** which is not shared by any other competing product.

unissued capital part of the **authorised capital** of a company which has not yet been given out in the form of **shares** to the **shareholders**.

unit cost (**accounting**) a cost used in the working out of the costs of goods; it is reached by dividing the total cost of the goods by the number of units of the goods in **stock**. *The company produced 500 articles. The total cost was £5000. Therefore the unit cost was 5000 ÷ 500 = £10.*

United Nations (*or* **UN**) a union of independent states formed in 1945 for the development of friendly relations between states and for international cooperation. Membership: 157 countries. Headquarters: New York. Official languages: Arabic, Chinese, English, French, Russian, Spanish.

United Nations Capital Development Fund (*or* **UNCDF**) a fund formed by the **United Nations** in 1966 to help **developing countries** by means of **grants** and loans of money. Headquarters: New York.

United Nations Conference on Trade and Development (*or* **UNCTAD**) a **United Nations** organisation formed in 1964 to help to speed up the **economic** growth of **less-developed countries** by helping their trade. Headquarters: Gevena. Membership: 162 countries. Official languages: as United Nations.

United Nations Development Programme (*or* **UNDP**) a programme formed by the **United Nations** in 1965 to speed up the social and **economic** growth of **less-developed countries** by giving help on industrial matters. Headquarters: New York.

unit-holder a person who has **invested** in a **unit trust**.

unit price a statement of how much something costs according to each unit of measurement, e.g. so much per kilo, so much per ounce etc.; thus things can be more easily compared to find out whether they are good value.

unit trust (*UK*) an organisation which gives people the opportunity to **invest** in **shares** in a way that is supposed to have less risk in that the investors (**unit-holders**) buy units,

and their money is then invested by the unit trust in a range of shares: the value of the units can rise or fall according to how the shares do.

universe *see* **population** (meaning 2).

unlimited liability a situation where each member of a company is legally responsible for his share of the total debts of the company.

unlisted company (*or* **unquoted company**) a company of which the **shares** are not among those listed by the **stock exchange**.

unload (1) to take away a load or **cargo** from. *The ship's cargo will be unloaded before midnight.* (2) to get rid of. *When he realised what a bad state the company was in, he tried to unload as many of his shares as possible.*

unofficial strike a **strike** when workers do not have the support of their own **trade union**.

unsecured creditor a person who is owed money, but does not have as **security** something of value to the person who owes him money (the **debtor**); if the debtor goes **bankrupt** then he will be paid only after **secured creditors** etc. have received their share.

unskilled work work for which little training or skill is required.

unsocial hours time of working when most other people are able to relax, e.g. evening work, weekend work. *People in bars and restaurants often have to work unsocial hours.*

unsolicited goods goods which are sent to a possible customer who has not asked for them, in the hope that he/she will agree to buy them: in UK he/she is not legally required to return them.

upgrade (1) to make (a job or the person doing it) more important or better rewarded, without changing the job itself much. *See also* **promote** (meaning 3), **downgrade**. (2) to improve (a **product**) without making basic changes in its **design**. *This* model of our car has now been upgraded in various ways: for example, a radio is now fitted as standard.

upmarket of **products** which are expensive, and more likely to be bought by better-off people. *This is a very upmarket perfume, and it's terribly expensive.*

upset price (*US and Scottish*) the lowest price that will be accepted by the seller at an **auction** or the sale of property. *He has put his house on the market at an upset price of £50,000. See also* **reserve price**.

USP *see* **unique selling proposition**.

usury the act or **process** of lending money at an **interest rate** that is too high or illegally high. *The interest rates he charges amount to usury.*

utility (1) usefulness. *This machine may not look all that good, but you cannot deny its utility.* (2) *see* **public utility**.

V

vacancy the state of being **vacant**; a post which is vacant. *There are vacancies for typists in our office.*

vacant empty; of a job or building, not having anyone in it: *situations vacant*: i.e. advertisements in a newspaper etc. for jobs which are available.

vacation (1) (*UK*) the part of the year when the law courts or the universities are closed. (2) (*US*) a holiday.

valid (1) having some basis of truth; supported by evidence. *He made many valid points in his speech.* (2) following the necessary rules and laws, legally correct and acceptable: *a valid passport*, i.e. one which is not out-of-date etc.; *a valid contract*.

validate (1) to check and show that (something) is what it claims to be or is legally correct: *to validate a document.* (2) to make (something) legal or official.

validity the state of being **valid**. *You had better check the validity of this document in overseas countries before you go abroad.*

valuation the act or **process** of **valuing** (meaning 1); the price arrived at in this way: *to get a valuation for one's house/a work of art etc.*

value *noun* (1) how much something is worth (which may be different from its price). *We decided to buy the car because it seemed such good value (for money)*, i.e. it seemed to be worth as much as, or more than, its price. (2) how much something means to a person. *This brooch is of sentimental value only*, i.e. it is not worth much money, but it is valuable to me for other reasons.

value *verb* (1) to give an expert opinion on how much (something) is, or might be, worth. *That is a very fine painting: you should get it valued.* (2) to hold (something or someone) at a certain worth. *She is a very good secretary: I value her services highly.*

value added the difference between what a business gets from selling its **products** and the amount paid for **supplies** and materials.

value added tax (*or* **VAT**) a type of tax, commonly used in Europe, which is charged on the difference between what a person pays for goods or **services** and what he/she sells them for. For example, a **retailer** will pay VAT on goods that he buys (input tax) and charge his customers VAT on the goods when he/she sells them (output tax), and he/she will then pay to the government at certain fixed times the difference between all the input tax he/she has paid and all the output tax he/she has collected. *See also* **turnover tax**, **zero-rated**.

value analysis a method of checking that the design, material and manufacture of a **product** are as **economic** as possible; each separate stage of the whole **process** is carefully examined to make sure that money is not being wasted.

valuer a person who **values** (meaning 1).

value received words used on a **bill of exchange** to show that money or goods to the value of the bill have been received from the **drawer** of the bill.

variable cost a situation where the amount it costs to produce something increases according to how much more is produced, and gets less according to how much less is produced. *See also* **fixed cost**, **semi-variable cost**.

variance (1) the difference between what something actually costs and its **standard cost** (*see under* **standard costing**). (2) the state of one thing being different from another; disagreement: *to be at variance with*, i.e. not to agree with, or to be different from.

variety reduction a method of lessening costs, e.g. of a **product**, by bringing about fewer differences in design, materials and manufacture. *See also* **standardisation**.

VAT *see* **value added tax**.

VDU *see* **visual display unit**.

vehicle something which can be used as a means of transport, especially one with wheels, e.g. a car, bus, lorry.

vending machine a machine which gives out e.g. drinks, sweets, cigarettes, stamps when money is put into the machine.

vendor (*especially law*) a person who sells something.

venture *noun* a business enterprise that carries a certain amount of risk. *I wonder if his new venture will succeed?*

venture *verb* to do something which carries danger or risk; to risk (something). *He has ventured all his capital in the new business.*

venture capital *see* **risk capital**.

verify to make sure that (something) is true or correct; to check.

vertical integration the joining of companies so that more of the various stages that a **product** goes through come under the same organisation, from the **raw materials** at one end to the **retailing** of the **product** at the other: if a cloth manufacturer bought over a woolfarm, or bought a chain of tailor's shops, both would be examples of verticle integration. *See also* **backward integration**, **forward integration**, **horizontal integration**.

very important person *see* **VIP**.

vested interest (1) a right to property which is legally **valid**. (2) a special interest in some matter, because it will cause personal loss or gain. *He should not judge this case, because he has a vested interest in it.* (3) a person or organisation, especially a powerful or wealthy one, which has such a personal interest in something. *There are many vested interests in this scandal which would like to prevent the truth becoming known.*

vet to examine; to check up on. *This post involves material security: all candidates for it will be carefully vetted.*

video *adjective* connected with television; broadcast using television pictures; connected with **videotapes** or **video(tape) recorders**.

video *noun* = **videotape** or **video(tape) recorder**.

videotape a tape which **records** a film and can be shown on a special television set.

video(tape) recorder (*or* **VTR**) a type of **tape-recorder** for **videotapes**; it can also **record** and play back television programmes by means of **videotapes**.

viewdata a **system** by which information can be called up and shown on one's television screen, using either television transmissions or the telephone line. In some cases goods and **services** displayed can be ordered by the user and paid for by

credit card: in UK, a well-known service along these lines is **Prestel**, run by British Telecom. *See also* **Ceefax**, **Oracle**.

VIP (*or* **very important person**) (*informal*) a person who is important enough to have special arrangements made for him/her: *the VIP lounge in an airport; to give someone the VIP treatment*, i.e. to treat someone with great respect.

visa an official stamp which is put on a passport to allow its owner to enter or leave a country: *an entry visa*.

visible exports/imports goods and materials **exported** from or **imported** into a country as opposed to other **services** which can earn or cost foreign currency such as banking or **insurance**. *See also* **invisible exports/imports**.

visiting card *see* **business card**.

visual *adjective* connected with seeing; able to be seen: *to use visual aids in teaching*, i.e. blackboard, photographs etc.

visual *noun* a picture or drawing, which, e.g. a **representative** could use to give information about the **product** he is trying to sell.

visual display unit (*or* **VDU**) a type of television screen on which information from a **computer** is shown.

vital statistics important information about the population of a country, e.g. how many are born and die each year, how many get married and divorced and so on.

vocation one's chosen trade or profession; what one does, or would like to do, for a living.

vocational guidance an area of knowledge which deals with advising people (especially young people) on the best kind of job for them to do, and the kind of training they will need to do that job. *See also* **occupational guidance**.

vocational training a kind of training that a person needs to do a certain job, especially a skilled or semi-skilled job.

void (1) of a **contract**, **insurance policy** etc.; not having any legal force. *This contract has not been witnessed and it is therefore null and void.* (2) empty; not occupied by anyone. *No one has been appointed to his post meantime: it had been left void.*

voidable contract a type of **contract** in which one of the people who have signed it can avoid meeting its terms because of a fault in the contract, e.g. an error, but the contract itself is still legal until the fault is declared.

volume discount the amount by which the price of each unit of a **product** becomes less if a large enough number of the units is bought. *See also* **quantity discount**.

volume of sales *see* **sales volume**.

voluntary controls rules and **regulations** worked out by an organisation for its own members with the aim of making government action unnecessary: *voluntary controls in advertising*.

voluntary group a group of **retailers** who sell the same kind of goods, who come together to buy these goods through one **wholesale** business (usually to cut costs).

voluntary liquidation the **process** by which a company decides to stop operating; the directors would then have to make a **declaration of solvency**.

voluntary redundancy the act of agreeing to lose one's job, in a situation where an organisation has too many workers; usually there is some kind of payment to persuade workers to agree to go.

voting right the right of a **shareholder** to vote at the shareholders' meetings of a company, as stated in the **Articles of Association** of the company.

voucher (1) a **document** which shows that a certain amount of money was paid; a document which gives details of any financial **transaction**. (2) (*UK*) a document given out instead of money which may be later used to **claim** goods or **services**. *See also* **gift voucher**; **luncheon voucher**.

VTR *see* **video tape recorder**.

W

wage (*often plural* **wages**) an amount that is paid to a person regularly (usually weekly) for work done. *He earns a wage of £150 a week. He collects his wages every Friday. See also* **salary**.

wage differential the difference in the amount paid to workers at different levels within the same kind of work, or to different kinds of workers within the same organisation. *If we let wage differentials get too small, workers may lose their ambition to be promoted.*

wage freeze forbidding any increase in wages, usually as an attempt by the government to control **inflation**.

wage-price spiral a situation where an increase in wages causes an increase in prices, which in turn makes workers ask for higher wages, resulting in still higher prices and so on.

wage rate the amount of money that is paid to workers, expressed as so much per unit of time (hour, day etc.: **time rate**) or so much per unit of goods produced (**piece rate**). *His wage rate was fixed at £8 per hour.*

wages *see* **wage**.

wages policy (*or* **wage policy**) (1) the way in which an industry, company or factory acts in relation to wages, e.g. **systems** of payment, wage **differentials**. (2) the national **criteria** which affect the outcome of wages bargaining.

wage worker a person who is paid weekly. *Compare with* **salaried**.

waiting time (1) the time when a worker is there and ready to work but cannot do so because of some reason beyond his control, e.g. if a machine has broken down. (2) the time that those providing certain **services** may charge for because their **clients** keep them waiting. *If you are not ready in time for a taxi, you may have to pay for his waiting time.*

warehouse a large building for keeping goods in, e.g. for safekeeping, or until they can be moved into a shop for sale. *While we were abroad, we had our furniture stored in a warehouse. We need more supplies of tinned food from the warehouse.*

warehouse company (*or* **warehouseman**) a business that stores goods for others for a **fee**.

warrant *noun* (1) a **document** that gives a person the legal right to something, or to do something: *a search warrant* (which gives the police the right to search someone's house); *a travel warrant* (which gives a person the right to travel at someone else's expense); *a share warrant* (which states that a person has the right to a certain number of **shares** in a company). (2) a **document** which states that a person is the legal owner of goods which have been left with a **warehouse**; ownership can be given to someone else by giving him/her the warrant.

warrant *verb* (1) to give the right to do something; to give a good reason for. *I don't think the possible profits in that business warrant the amount of capital he has invested.* (2) to **guarantee**. *This company warrants all the cars that it sells.*

warranty (1) a **guarantee** of goods bought, with arrangements to fix anything that goes wrong within a certain period of time. *All our used cars have a 12 month warranty.* (2) a promise made in a **contract** which is not, however a main part of the contract: even if the promise is not kept, the contract is not held to be broken, but a **claim** for damages may be made against the person who has not kept his/her promise. (3) a statement made by a person that all the information he/she has given is correct, e.g. one who has taken out an **insurance policy**; a false statement means that the policy is **void**.

wastage *see* **natural wastage**.

wasting asset a type of **fixed asset** which is gradually used up as the business goes on, e.g. in the coal-mining business the coal itself would be a wasting asset.

waybill a **document** which is made out by the person responsible for moving goods from one place to another, giving details about the goods and the conditions under which they are being moved.

WDV *see* **written-down value**.

wealth tax a type of tax which may be paid on property and other forms of wealth belonging to a person, when the total value of the wealth is greater than a certain amount.

wear and tear *see* **fair wear and tear**.

welch (*or* **welsh**) to fail to pay a debt (especially a **gambling** debt); to fail to do something one has promised to do.

welfare (1) of a person, being in a good state. *He is very anxious about their welfare.* (2) helping people in need, e.g. to see that they have enough food, clothes, medical care etc.

welfare state a country which provides for the education and health of its citizens, and security against the effect of **unemployment**, sickness, old age etc.; a society which is organised along these lines. *Our population is getting older, so the expenses of running the welfare state increases all the time.*

wharf (*plural* **wharfs** *or* **wharves**) a platform built into the water where ships can load and unload.

wheeler-dealer (*informal*) a businessman who uses every chance to make bargains which will benefit

himself personally. *Be careful if you have to do business with him: he is something of a wheeler-dealer, they say.*

white-collar worker a person who does not work with his/her hands, especially someone who works in an office. *See also* **blue-collar worker**.

white goods (1) large machines used in the household (especially the kitchen) such as refrigerators, dish washers and washing machines. (2) household linen such as sheets, tablecloths etc.

whole-life insurance a type of **insurance** where the amount of money that a person is insured for is paid only on his death, and there is no other payment. *See also* **endowment**.

wholesale *adjective* (1) connected with **wholesale** (noun). *He started up with a wholesale business; later on he bought some shops. See also* **retail**. (2) on a very large scale. *The fire caused wholesale destruction of property.*

wholesale *adverb* (1) in quantity from or by a **wholesaler**: *to get goods wholesale. See also* **wholesale** (noun); **retail** (adverb). (2) in very large quantities. *They are cleaning the whole area, and knocking the old houses down wholesale.*

wholesale *noun* the sale of goods in large quantities to shopkeepers and traders who then sell them to the public. *See also* **retail** (noun).

wholesale *verb* to sell (goods) **wholesale**. *They wholesale fruit and vegetables. See also* **wholesale** (noun), **retail** (verb).

wholesale-price index a method of showing how the prices of **wholesale** goods are going up or down by taking the average price of a range of the wholesale goods in one particular year (when the average will be said to equal 100), and then comparing that with prices in later years. Thus if the price of wholesale goods goes up, the **index** could become (for example) 108, 112 etc.

wholesaler a person who gets goods in large quantities from manufacturers etc., and sells them in quantity to shopkeepers and traders.

wildcat strike a type of **strike** which is started, often suddenly, by the workers without the approval of their **trade union** and without following **agreed procedures**.

wind: wind up (1) to close down (a company). *See also* **liquidation**. (2) to bring (a meeting etc.) to an end.

winding-up *see* **liquidation**.

window dressing (1) a **display** of goods in a window so as to attract the attention of possible customers. (2) trying to make something look better than it really is. *Don't be misled by their attractive offices: they are just window-dressing for a very inefficient business.*

W.I.P. *see* **work in progress**.

withdraw (1) to take out or away (usually something which one has already put in): *to withdraw money from a bank. I am going to withdraw my name from the list of applicants for the job.* (2) to take back; to **cancel**. *I will withdraw the remarks I made about the chairman: they are not true.*

withdrawal the act of **withdrawing**.

without recourse (or French **sans recours**) words written on **bills of exchange** etc., meaning that the person holding the bill etc. cannot come back to the person who has **endorsed** it for payment even if the bill is not **honoured**.

with-profits endowment assurance a type of **insurance** where the insured person gets a **guaranteed** amount of money after a certain period of time, and in addition a share of the profits which the **assurance company** has made over that period.

word processor a machine with a **keyboard** and usually a **visual display unit** for printing, **storing** and retrieving text.

worker(s') director a person who is supposed to represent the workers' interests on the **board of directors** of a company or similar organisation.

workers' control a **system** of running an organisation by which all the important decisions are made by the workers themselves, or their **representatives**.

work group a small number of people who work together, perhaps on a particular **project**.

work-in a situation where workers stay in a factory etc. that is to be closed down and continue to work on as before. *The workers are furious about the closing down of the factory: they are going to stage a work-in. See also* **sit-down strike**, **sit-in**.

working capital (*also* **circulating capital**) the difference between the **current assets** of a company and its **current liabilities**; this is the amount of money which the company can use to carry on with its business.

working conditions the physical things which affect people as they are working, e.g. the amount of heat and light, how safe the machines they work with are.

working week the normal number of hours worked in a week; above this amount, **overtime** may have to be paid. *Our working week is 35 hours, from Monday to Friday.*

work-in-progress (or **W.I.P.**; *US* **work-in-process**) (1) **products** which are being manufactured but not yet completed. (2) the value of such incomplete products.

work measurement the act of finding out how long it will take to do a certain piece of work. *See also* **work study**.

workmen's compensation the amount of money which an employer has to pay to a worker who is injured in doing his/her duties, when it is not the worker's fault.

work permit a **document** given to a foreigner allowing him/her to work in a country for a certain time.

works council a type of committee within an organisation which has **representatives** of the management and other workers; it discusses matters affecting the organisation, especially as these relate to the interests of the workers.

work-sharing the act or **process** of making more employment available, e.g. by having less **overtime**, or by allowing two people to do a job as **part-time workers**, instead of having only one worker do it.

work study (1) an area of knowledge which deals with the best and quickest ways of doing work, by carefully **analysing** how the work is done. (2) the act of **analysing** work in this way. *See also* **motion study**, **time and motion study**.

work-to-rule *noun* a kind of action which workers can take against their employers if they do not want actually to **strike**: the workers obey every rule that exists affecting their work, which means that the work is done very slowly, and production suffers.

work to rule *verb* to work in this way.

World Bank *see* **International Bank for Reconstruction and Development**.

wraps: under wraps (*informal*) hidden, out of sight. *We're keeping the new model of our car under wraps until the motor show.*

writ a **document** put out by a court which states that a person named on it must do something, or stop doing something, as decided by the court: *to issue a writ against someone.*

write down (**accounting**) to record the value of (a **wasting asset**) at a certain lower level than the previous year.

write off *verb* (1) (**accounting**) to record (something) as having no **cash value**, e.g. a piece of machinery that cannot be repaired or a debt that cannot be paid back; the **book value** may be set off as a loss against any profits. (2) to lower gradually the book value of (a **wasting asset**) over a period of time. *This new machine will be written off over a period of ten years.*

write-off *noun* (1) something that has been **written off**. (2) act of **writing off** something. (3) the **book value** of something that has been written off. (4) something so badly damaged that it cannot be repaired. *After the accident, my car was a write-off.*

write up (1) (**accounting**) to state that (some **asset**) is worth more than it actually is. (2) to write a description of (something) so as to bring it to public notice. *He has written up an account of the chairman's farewell party for the local press.*

writing-down allowance the amount of money that may be set against profits for tax purposes because of **depreciation** of **wasting assets**.

written-down value (*or* **WDV**) (**accounting**) the amount an **asset** is worth after **depreciation** has been allowed for.

wrongful dismissal *see* **unfair dismissal**.

X

xerography a method of making copies of a **document**, chart etc. *See also* **photocopy**.

xerox *noun* (**trademark**) a method of **photocopying**; a copy made by this method.

xerox *verb* (**trademark**) to make a copy by **xerox**.

Y

year book a book which is published every year dealing with a certain area of knowledge, business etc., which gives up-to-date information on that area: *the Gardener's Year Book.*

year's purchase a method of stating how much a business or property is worth according to the number of years it will take for the buyer to get back the money he/she has paid. For example, if a property costs £70,000 and the profit from it comes to £10,000 per year, then the price is 7 years' purchase of the profits.

yield (1) the amount of money which a person receives from **stocks** and **shares**, either as a percentage of the original price paid, or as a percentage of their current value. (2) what is produced from something else, e.g. land, a mine. *This land will give a good yield of crops.*

York–Antwerp rules (**marine insurance**) a set of rules to guide those concerned with **claims** arising from **financial** loss at sea.

Z

z chart a **graph** which shows production or sales in 3 ways: (1) the totals for each week or month; (2) the total for the week or month added to the previous one; (3) the average totals.

zero-rated with reference to **value added tax**, certain goods and **services** are within the **VAT system** but are rated at 0%.

zip code *US* = **postcode**.

Appendices

Appendix 1   Profit and loss accounts

J Black & Company PLC
(Manufacturers)
Profit and Loss Account
for year ended 31 December 1984

	£	£
Sales		
Less:		3,206,900
Manufacturing Costs:		
Materials	1,260,000	
Direct labour	1,001,700	
Production overheads	258,300	
Total production costs:		2,520,000
Gross profit		686,900
Less expenses:		
Management salaries	20,000	
Sales salaries	13,500	
Salesmen's commission	5,010	
Market research	10,000	
Agents' commission	62,910	
Salesmen's expenses	22,600	
Transport and warehousing	100,080	
Advertising etc	94,500	
Sales promotion	12,000	
General administration	25,700	
Sundry items	3,600	
Financing, audit fee, etc	11,500	
Depreciation	22,000	
Total expense		403,400
Profit before tax		£283,500

Jones & Company Ltd

(Retailers)
Profit and Loss Account
for Year ended 31 December 1984

	£	£	£
Gross sales			540,000
Less: Returns			40,000
Net sales			500,000
Cost of goods sold:			
Stock at beginning		80,000	
Plus Purchases		290,000	
Cost of goods available for sale		370,000	
Less: Stock at end		70,000	
Cost of goods sold			300,000
Gross margin (gross profit)			200,000
Expenses			
Selling expenses			
Sales salaries	60,000		
Advertising expense	20,000		
Delivery expense	20,000		
Total Selling Expense		100,000	
Administration Expense			
Office salaries	30,000		
Office supplies	10,000		
Miscellaneous expenses	5,000		
Total Administration Expense		45,000	
General expense			
Rent and rates	15,000		
Total General Expense		15,000	
Total expenses			160,000
Profit before tax			£40,000

Appendix 2   Balance sheet

White and Company PLC
Balance Sheet as at 31 December 1984

	£	£
Fixed assets		
Land & Buildings at Cost	60,000	
Less: Depreciation	1,000	
		59,000
Plant & Machinery at Cost	40,000	
Less: Depreciation	4,000	
		36,000
Vehicles at Cost	5,000	
Less: Depreciation	1,250	
		3,750
Total fixed assets		£98,750
Current assets		
Raw Materials	25,000	
Work in Progress	12,500	
Finished Goods	10,000	
Debtors	50,000	
Cash	45,000	
Total current assets	142,500	
Less: **Current liabilities**		
Creditors	45,000	
Expenses due	2,500	
Taxation	20,000	
Dividends payable	3,000	
Total current liabilities	70,500	
Working capital		72,000
Net capital employed		170,750
Less: LOAN CAPITAL (7% Debentures secured on Fixed Assets)		50,000
Net worth of company		£120,750

The above **NET WORTH** has been financed as follows:

	£	
Subscribed Capital		
100,000 Ordinary Shares of £1 each	100,000	
Reserves		
General Reserve	20,000	
Profit and Loss Account	750	
Total shareholders' interest		£120,750

Appendix 3   Break-even chart

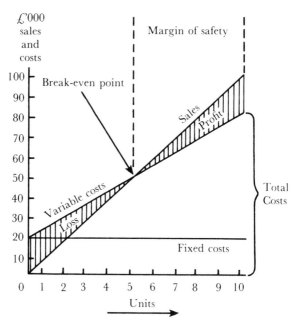

In this example:

Selling Price of Machine:	£10,000 each
Planned Unit Sales:	10 machines
Planned Total Sales:	10 × £10,000 = £100,000
Variable Cost per Unit:	£6,000
Total Fixed Costs:	£20,000
Break-Even Point (Volume)	5 Units
Margin of Safety	5 to 10 Units

A *break-even chart* reveals the level of sales at which all costs are covered. Sales beyond the break-even point will result in a profit, while sales below it will result in a loss. The chart is commonly used in relation to a single project or product.

Appendix 4 Master budget

Computer manufacturers PLC

MASTER BUDGET
For the year ending 31 December 1984

			Computers		£'000 Total
			Type A £	Type B £	£
1	**Sales**	£'000	2000	1660	3660
	Manufacturing Costs:				
	Direct Labour		500	500	1000
	Direct Material		600	700	1300
	Factory Overheads		100	200	300
	Add Opening Stock		30	30	60
	Less Closing Stock				
2	**Cost of goods sold**		£1230	£1430	£2660
3	Gross Profit (1 less item 2)		770	230	1000
4	Selling and Distribution Costs		70	100	170
5	Administration Costs		400	100	500
6	Net Profit (3 less items 4 & 5)		£300	£30	£330
7	Fixed Assets		2200	200	2400
8	**Net** Current Assets		800	200	1000
9	**Capital employed**		£3000	£400	£3400
10	**Return on capital employed**		10%	7.5%	9.7%
11	**Liquidity ratio**		2:1	0.9:1	1:1

		£'000
12	**Profit appropriations**	
	Transfer to General Reserve	50
	Transfer to Asset Replacement Reserve	50
	Taxation	100
14	**Total appropriations**	250
15	**Profit and loss balance** (13 less item 14)	£80

Appendix 5   Circulating capital

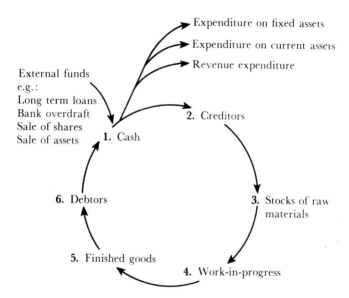

External funds
e.g.:
Long term loans
Bank overdraft
Sale of shares
Sale of assets

Expenditure on fixed assets

Expenditure on current assets

Revenue expenditure

1. Cash

2. Creditors

3. Stocks of raw materials

4. Work-in-progress

5. Finished goods

6. Debtors

Appendix 6　Costs in a company

Reference to: total fixed costs, total variable costs, total costs, marginal cost, average fixed cost, average variable cost, average cost per unit, direct materials, direct labour.

Fixed costs in a company are such costs as rent, rates, managers' salaries and any other item of expense which is not directly linked to the quantity of products produced.

Variable costs are costs which vary because they are directly linked to the number of products produced. These include costs such as direct materials, direct labour, packaging etc.

The following table shows how total fixed costs, total variable costs, total costs, marginal cost, average fixed cost, average variable cost and average cost per unit can be worked out.

(1)	(2)	(3)	(4)	(5)	(6)	(7)	(8)
Quantity produced	Total fixed costs	Total variable costs	Total costs	Marginal cost	Average fixed cost	Average variable cost	Average cost per unit
			(2) + (3)		(2) ÷ (1)	(3) ÷ (1)	(4) ÷ (1)
0	£200		£200	—	—		
1	£200	£60	£260	£60	£200	£60	£260
2	£200	£120	£320	£60	£100	£60	£160
3	£200	£180	£380	£60	£66.66	£60	£126.66
4	£200	£220	£420	£40	£50	*£55	£105

Note: Variable costs per unit may fall because of experience in the production of the product, resulting in less scrap, more efficient use of machines, men and materials etc.

Appendix 7   Channels of distribution

Example: The Grocery Trade

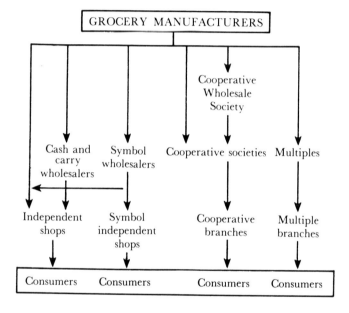

Appendix 8   UK business examining bodies

UK examining bodies for business-related subjects include the following:

Association of Business Executives
Association of Certified Accountants
Association of International Accountants
British Computer Society
Business Education Council
Chartered Institute of Public Finance and Accountancy
Chartered Insurance Institute
City and Guilds of London Institute
Communication Advertising and Marketing Education Foundation
Council for National Academic Awards
Council of the Stock Exchange
Faculty of Teachers in Commerce Ltd.
Institute of Administrative Accountants
Institute of Administrative Management
Institute of Bankers
Institute of Chartered Accountants in England and Wales
Institute of Chartered Accountants in Scotland
Institute of Chartered Secretaries and Administrators
Institute of Cost and Management Accountants
Institute of Internal Auditors – UK
Institute of Management Services
Institute of Marketing
Institute of Personnel Management
Institute of Supervisory Management
Institute of Taxation
Institution of Industrial Managers
London Chamber of Commerce and Industry
Management and Marketing Sales Association Examination Board
Market Research Society
National Computing Centre
National Examinations Board for Supervisory Studies
Pitman Examinations Institute
Royal Society of Arts Examinations Board
Scottish Business Education Council (SCOTBEC)
Society of Company and Commercial Accountants Ltd.

Appendix 9   Computer hardware

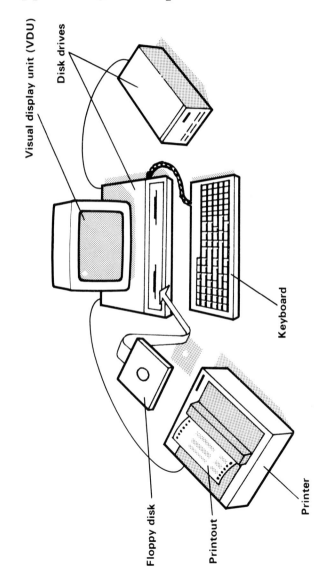

Appendix 10　Currencies of the world

Note: Franc CFA = Franc de la Communautée Financière Africaine

Country	Unit of currency
Afghanistan	Afghani
Albania	Lek
Algeria	Algerian dinar
Angola	Kwanza
Antigua	East Caribbean dollar
Argentina	Argentinian peso
Australia	Australian dollar
Austria	Schilling
Bahamas, The	Bahamas dollar
Bahrain	Bahrain dinar
Bangladesh	Taka
Barbados	East Caribbean dollar
Belgium	Belgian franc
Belize	Belizean dollar
Benin	Franc CFA
Bermuda	Bermudan dollar
Bolivia	Bolivian peso
Botswana	Pula
Brazil	Cruzeiro
Brunei	Brunei dollar
Bulgaria	Lev
Burma	Kyat
Burundi	Burundi franc
Cambodia	Riel
Cameroon	Franc CFA
Canada	Canadian dollar
Cape Verde Islands	Escudo caboverdianos
Cayman Islands	Cayman Islands dollar
Central African Republic	Franc CFA
Chad	Franc CFA
Chile	New peso
China, Peoples Republic of	Yuan or renminbi

Country	Unit of currency
Colombia	Colombian peso
Congo (Brazzaville)	Franc CFA
Costa Rica	Colon
Cuba	Cuban peso
Cyprus	Cyprus pound
Czechoslovakia	Koruna
Denmark	Danish krone
Dominica	East Caribbean dollar
Dominican Republic	Dominican peso
Ecuador	Sucre
Egypt	Egyptian pound
El Salvador	El Salvador colon
Equatorial Guinea	Ekuele
Ethiopia	Ethiopian dollar
Falkland Islands	Falkland pound
Faroe Island	Krone
Fiji	Fijian dollar
Finland	Markka or Finnmark
France	French franc
Gabon	Franc CFA
Gambia	Dalasi
German Democratic Republic	Ostmark or DDR-Mark
Germany, Federal Republic	Deutsche Mark
Ghana	Cedi
Gibraltar	Gibraltar pound
Greece	Drachma
Greenland	Danish Krone
Grenada	East Caribbean dollar
Guadeloupe	French franc
Guatemala	Quetzal
Guinea	Syli
Guyana	Guyanese dollar
Haiti	Gourde
Honduras	Lempira
Hong Kong	Hong Kong dollar
Hungary	Forint
Iceland	Icelandic krona
India	Indian rupee
Indonesia	Rupiah

Country	Unit of currency
Iran	Rial
Iraq	Iraqi dinar
Ireland	Irish pound
Israel	Shekel
Italy	Italian lira
Ivory Coast	Franc CFA
Jamaica	Jamaican dollar
Japan	Yen
Jordan	Jordanian dinar
Kenya	Kenya shilling
Korea, Democratic People's Republic of North Korea	Won
Korea, Republic of South	Won
Kuwait	Kuwait dinar
Laos	Kip
Lebanon	Lebanese pound
Lesotho	South African rand
Liberia	Liberian dollar (also US dollar)
Libya	Libyan dinar
Liechtenstein	Swiss franc
Luxembourg	Luxembourg franc
Macau	Pataca
Madeira	Portugese escudo
Malagasy Republic	Franc Malgache
Malawi	Kwacha
Malaysia	Malaysian dollar
Maldive Islands	Rupee
Mali	Mali franc
Malta	Maltese pound
Mauritania	Ouguiya
Mauritius	Mauritian rupee
Mexico	Mexican peso
Monaco	French franc
Mongolia	Tugrik
Montserrat	East Caribbean dollar
Morocco	Dirham
Mozambique	Metical
Nepal	Nepali rupee
Netherlands	Netherlands guilder

Country	Unit of currency
Netherlands Antilles	Antilles guilder
New Zealand	New Zealand dollar
Nicaragua	Cordoba
Niger	Franc CFA
Nigeria	Naira
Norway	Norwegian krone
Oman	Omani ryal
Pakistan	Pakistan rupee
Panama	Balboa
Papua New Guinea	Kina
Paraguay	Guarani
Peru	Sol
Philippines	Philippine peso
Poland	Zloty
Portugal	Portugese escudo
Puerto Rico	US dollar
Qatar	Qatar riyal
Reunion	Franc CFA
Romania	Leu
Rwanda	Rwanda franc
St Lucia	East Caribbean dollar
St Vincent	East Caribbean dollar
Saudi Arabia	Saudi Arabian riyal
Senegal	Franc CFA
Seychelles	Seychelles rupee
Sierra Leone	Leone
Singapore	Singapore dollar
Somalia	Somali shilling
South Africa, Republic of	South African rand
South West Africa (Namibia)	South African rand
Spain	Spanish peseta
Sri Lanka	Sri Lanka rupee
Sudan	Sudanese pound
Surinam	Surinam guilder
Swaziland	Lilageni
Sweden	Swedish krona
Switzerland	Swiss franc
Syria	Syrian pound

Country	Unit of currency
Taiwan	New Taiwan dollar
Tanzania	Tanzanian shilling
Thailand	Baht
Togo	Franc CFA
Tonga	Paanga
Trinidad and Tobago	Trinidad and Tobago dollar
Tunisia	Tunisian dinar
Turkey	Turkish lira
Uganda	Ugandan shilling
United Arab Emirates	Dirham
United Kingdom (UK)	Pound sterling
United States of America (USA)	US dollar
Upper Volta	Franc CFA
Uruguay	Uruguayan new peso
USSR	Rouble
Venezuela	Bolivar
Vietnam	Dong
Virgin Islands	US dollar
Western Samoa	Tala
Yemen Arab Republic	Yemeni riyal
Yemen, People's Democratic Republic of	Southern Yemen dinar
Yugoslavia	Yugoslav dinar
Zaire	Zaire
Zambia	Kwacha
Zimbabwe	Zimbabwe dollar